THE POLITICS OF SUFFERING

PUBLIC CULTURES OF THE MIDDLE EAST AND NORTH AFRICA

Paul A. Silverstein, Susan Slyomovics, and Ted Swedenburg, *editors*

THE POLITICS
OF SUFFERING

Syria's Palestinian Refugee Camps

Nell Gabiam

Indiana University Press

Bloomington and Indianapolis

This book is a publication of

Indiana University Press
Office of Scholarly Publishing
Herman B Wells Library 350
1320 East 10th Street
Bloomington, Indiana 47405 USA

iupress.indiana.edu

Library of Congress Cataloging-in-Publication Data

Names: Gabiam, Nell, author.
Title: The politics of suffering : Syria's Palestinian refugee camps /
    Nell Gabiam.
Description: Bloomington : Indiana University Press, [2016] | Series:
    Public cultures of the Middle East and North Africa | Includes
    bibliographical references and index.
Identifiers: LCCN 2015050921 | ISBN 9780253021281 (cloth : alk.
    paper) | ISBN 9780253021403 (pbk. : alk. paper) | ISBN
    9780253021526 (ebook)
Subjects: LCSH: Refugees, Palestinian Arab—Syria. | Refugee
    camps—Syria.
Classification: LCC HV640.5.P36 G33 2016 | DDC
    362.87089/927405691—dc23 LC record available at http://lccn.loc
    .gov/2015050921

1 2 3 4 5   21 20 19 18 17 16

To my mother, Mary Jo Gabiam

Contents

Acknowledgments

Writing this book would not have been possible without the support of the Palestinian refugees of Ein el Tal, Neirab, and Yarmouk who opened their homes and lives to me between spring 2004 and spring 2006 and, under much more tragic circumstances, during spring and summer 2015. I am immensely grateful for the kindness and generosity they showed me and for the trust that they gave me. Syrian friends and acquaintances contributed to the generally warm and friendly atmosphere I encountered while doing fieldwork. I am also grateful to the United Nations Relief and Works Agency for Palestine Refugees (UNRWA) for allowing me to engage in participant observation during the Neirab Rehabilitation Project and to the UNRWA staff that I interviewed. The views expressed by UNRWA staff during interviews do not necessarily represent the official views of UNRWA as an agency.

The research that is at the origin of this book started roughly ten years ago while I was a graduate student in anthropology at the University of California, Berkeley. In the anthropology department, I am grateful to Donald Moore and Laura Nader, who provided crucial guidance and support from the very beginning and helped shape me as a scholar, and to Stefania Pandolfo for her useful feedback on an earlier incarnation of the book. Nezar AlSayyad, in the College of Environmental Design, has been a sympathetic and helpful reader and listener. I also benefited from the support of faculty outside UC Berkeley. I am particularly indebted to Dawn Chatty at the University of Oxford's Refugee Studies Centre and to Ghada Talhami at Lake Forest College in Illinois, both of whom read and commented on earlier versions of the book. I am grateful for the encouragement and support I have received from my colleagues in the departments of anthropology and political science at Iowa State University, which has been my academic home for the last five years. The support of friends and colleagues helped sustain me during the grueling process of writing and attempting to turn what began as my doctoral dissertation into a book. I would especially like to thank Anaheed Al-Hardan, Salomé Aguilera-Skvirsky, Diana Allan, Leila Hilal, Ali Bangi, Christina Gish Hill, Alan Mikhail, Saida Hodžić, Derrick Spires, Lisa Calvente, Monica Martinez, Rosemary Sayigh, Ted Swedenburg, Lex Takkenberg, Alex Tuckness, Maximilian Viatori, David Vine, and Brett Williams.

Research for this book was made possible by a Fulbright (DDRA) grant, a Social Science Research Council-Mellon Mays research grant, a UC Berkeley Normative Time grant, and an Iowa State University Professional Development grant. A University of Chicago Provost Postdoctoral Fellowship (2009–2011) provided me with the time to write an initial draft. A Woodrow Wilson Career Enhancement fellowship (2014–2015) gave me the opportunity to take a sabbatical and focus on completing the final draft. My sabbatical year was spent at Georgetown University's Center for Contemporary Arab Studies. I am grateful for the warm and welcoming environment and for many fruitful exchanges with the center's faculty, students, and staff.

My gratitude extends to Indiana University Press and to the two anonymous reviewers for their incredibly helpful and constructive feedback. My thanks also go to Rebecca Tolen for her guidance and feedback and to the editorial and production team for the care and attention they gave the manuscript. I am grateful to Paul Silverstein, Susan Slyomovics, and Ted Swedenburg for welcoming the book into Indiana University Press's series on Public Cultures of the Middle East and North Africa.

As a scholar, I was introduced to the Middle East and to the Palestinian refugee issue through an undergraduate anthropology class I took at Columbia University with Avram Bornstein on "Peoples and Cultures of the Middle East and North Africa." It is through Bornstein's class that I discovered my ignorance with regard to the world and, especially, with regard to the Palestinian question. I am grateful to him for inspiring me to want to learn more about the world I live in.

Finally, I wish to thank my biggest source of support and inspiration, my mother Mary Jo Gabiam. My mother spent seven years in Kuwait and a summer in Gaza as an elementary and middle-school teacher. It is through her that I discovered the Middle East as a real place and with her that I traveled to Syria for the first time, in 1999. Many of the early books I read on the Middle East and on the Palestinian question were plucked from her bookshelf. She read and commented on countless drafts of this book and has been a loyal companion on this long journey. It is to her that I dedicate the book.

Note on Transliteration

For Arabic words and phrases that appear in this book, I followed the transliteration guide of the *International Journal of Middle East Studies*. I made an exception with regard to the Arabic names of individuals, in that I privileged the phonetic pronunciation in order to make them more accessible to an English-speaking audience. I also simplified the transliteration of well-known Arabic terms that are routinely used in English (for example, *intifada* or *Al Jazeera*) using their common spelling in English-speaking contexts.

THE POLITICS OF SUFFERING

Introduction

In December 2005, as we sat in the living room of his family's house in the Palestinian refugee camp of Neirab in Syria, Younes, a young Palestinian university student in his early twenties, reflected on the controversial Neirab Rehabilitation Project that was taking place in the camp. Sponsored by the United Nations Relief and Works Agency for Palestine Refugees (known as UNRWA), the project sought, among other goals, to relocate families living in Neirab's World War II–era barracks to brand-new UNRWA-built houses in the neighboring Palestinian refugee camp of Ein el Tal. Speaking about the families who had already made the move from the Neirab barracks to the new houses in Ein el Tal, Younes referred to them as having "gone from a life of death (*ḥayāt al-mawt*) to real life, from living in coffins to living in nice houses" (field notes, December 23, 2005). But Younes could not leave it at that. To live in comfortable houses, he quickly added, was one of the refugees' rights as human beings, a right that should be clearly separated from their right of return to their homes in what is now the state of Israel. Living in good conditions, Younes explained, "should not mean the disappearance of the right of return" (field notes, December 23, 2005). Younes's comments illustrate refugees' fears that supporting camp improvements will be understood as acknowledging that refugees might stay in their host state permanently, thus undermining their claim to return. They allude to suffering as emblematic of the Palestinian refugee condition and as legitimating Palestinian insistence on the right of return.

One of the most potent symbols of Palestinian suffering and of Palestinians' commitment to the right of return to their former homes is the refugee camp, which serves not only as a reminder of the suffering that Palestinians have experienced since their forced displacement during the 1948 Arab–Israeli war but also as a sign that its inhabitants' stay is to be temporary (Al Husseini 2011; Farah 1997, 1999; Feldman 2008b; Khalili 2007; Peteet 2005; Ramadan 2010). Despite their important symbolic role in keeping alive Palestinian political claims linked to the past, refugee camps are not frozen in time: they are dynamic spaces that have undergone much change since their establishment in the aftermath of the 1948 war. A dominant perspective among Palestinian refugees is that improving the infrastructural and socioeconomic fabric of the camps threatens both their identity as refugees and their claims of return to their Palestinian homeland. Such a perspective is encouraged by the fact that, historically, infrastructural and socioeconomic development were used by the United Nations as well as Israel as a means of integrating refugees within their surroundings as an alternative to return (Schiff 1995; Weizman 2007; Hazboun 1996).

UNRWA is the agency that has been charged with ensuring the welfare of the refugees since 1949. In the last decade, it has initiated internal reforms that aim to shift the agency's main role from provider of humanitarian relief to promoter of development in its areas of operation. These reforms are themselves part of a broader shift in global humanitarian assistance to refugees whereby socioeconomic development is increasingly proposed as a mode of assistance in protracted refugee situations. In Syria, UNRWA's attempt at reform took shape as the Neirab Rehabilitation Project, which targeted Neirab and Ein el Tal, two small and isolated camps outside the city of Aleppo in the north of the country.

In 2004, the Neirab Rehabilitation Project gained the distinction of becoming UNRWA's pilot project for testing the feasibility of large-scale development in Palestinian refugee camps. More specifically, it became a testing ground for the agency's attempt to institutionalize a camp improvement program, based on an urban development approach, across its fields of operation. Thus, the lessons learned from the Neirab Rehabilitation Project at that time served as the basis for UNRWA's 2006 establishment of its Infrastructure and Camp Improvement Program, which has been used in camps in Lebanon, Jordan, Gaza, and the West Bank.

To determine what is at stake in the Neirab Rehabilitation Project in relation to the goals of urban development, I introduce a third camp where I also conducted research: Yarmouk, in the Syrian capital of Damascus. By several accounts, Yarmouk had successfully integrated into Damascus and yet had maintained its identity as a camp (Kodmani-Darwish 1997; Tiltnes 2007). It sometimes came up as the backdrop against which Palestinian refugees debated the merits of the Neirab Rehabilitation Project. Yarmouk also helps us to think about the question "What is it that makes a place a camp in the twenty-first century?"

In prewar Syria, Yarmouk stood for the promise of what could be achieved through development in Neirab and Ein el Tal. It simultaneously stood for what could be lost as a result of development in Neirab and Ein el Tal. From a humanitarian perspective, Yarmouk could be hailed as a success story of refugees who overcame exile and dispossession and turned their camp into a thriving community. At the same time, it embodied the blurring of the boundaries between the camp and the city. This blurring threatened to erase the camp's ability to testify to Palestinian suffering brought about by forced displacement and to affirm the temporariness of its inhabitants' stay. Neither suffering nor temporariness was readily palpable in Yarmouk's symmetrically laid out modern apartment buildings, its large roads, or its bustling commercial areas.

Of course, as I write these lines Yarmouk tells a different story, one that is more familiar to those who study and read about Palestinian refugees. As a result of the war in Syria, Yarmouk was almost completely depopulated in the aftermath of Syrian government shelling in December 2012 in response to its having been infiltrated by Syrian rebels. It also suffered significant destruction. Reports of starvation among the few remaining inhabitants made headlines in the summer and fall of 2013 (Al Jazeera 2013; UNRWA 2013a). In May 2013, Ein el Tal, one of the camps targeted by the Neirab Rehabilitation project and a major focus of my fieldwork, suffered a fate somewhat similar to that of Yarmouk: its entire population was ordered to leave by Syrian rebels who occupied it and declared it a military zone.

One cannot fully grasp the implications of the current war in Syria for Palestinian refugees without having a clear understanding of the refugees' sociopolitical status in Syria before the war. Drawing on my prewar ethnographic research, this book captures a crucial historical moment through its account of life in three Palestinian refugee camps. These sites are now inaccessible to researchers and will remain so for some time, but the insights afforded by my research into camp life, the Palestinian experience, and the shift in UNRWA's approach to aid, along with what this shift says about wider changes in humanitarianism globally, extend beyond the immediate context of prewar Syria.

In fact, the notion that development, as opposed to minimal relief assistance, should be part of the international response to refugee crises has been gaining traction in the past twenty years in the Office of the United Nations High Commissioner for Refugees (UNHCR), which is the main organization that assists refugees worldwide (UNHCR 2003).[1] The unfolding Syrian refugee crisis has placed renewed emphasis on development as a form of refugee assistance. This renewed emphasis has important policy implications in terms of global refugee assistance. The unprecedented number of Syrian refugees (estimated to be nearly 4.2 million as of October 2015), the expectation among the international community of a drawn-out Syrian war, and the pressures that the crisis is exerting on the resources of Middle Eastern host countries have led the United Nations to devise a Regional Refugee and Resilience Plan for 2015–2016 (UNHCR and UNDP 2015).[2] Known as the 3RP and sponsored by the United Nations Development Programme (UNDP) and UNHCR, the plan is presented as a "paradigm shift in the response to the [Syrian] crisis by combining humanitarian and development capacities, innovations, and resources" (UNHCR and UNDP 2015:6). UNRWA, given its experience as a humanitarian agency that now vocally promotes development in refugee camps, was a major participant in the discussions that led to the establishment of the 3RP (interview with UNRWA employees at the agency's Amman headquarter, March 23, 2015).

An UNRWA employee involved in the coordination of the response to the Syria crisis summarized why UNRWA is at the forefront of global discussions about lessening the divide between humanitarian and development aid when addressing refugee crises:

> I think, at least in terms of the Syria crisis, there's the realization that humanitarian funding doesn't stretch and that the crisis is stretching . . . this has led to all sorts of conversations about tapping into development funding and that there has to be a spectrum. We can't just do this or do that. . . . So I think there's recognition that we can no longer afford to be compartmentalized and the funding shouldn't be compartmentalized either. . . . So [the realization is basically that] we need development funding in Syria today. And now people are kind of looking around and saying Ok–who can do development? And UNRWA is quite well placed. (Interview, March 22, 2015)

Contrary to what one might assume, then, UNRWA's experimentation with large-scale, sustainable development in the last ten years has not been an ill-fated, fleeting adventure. Rather, it is symptomatic of profound and ongoing global shifts in humanitarian assistance to refugees: as protracted refugee situations become the norm rather than the exception, emergency humanitarian aid and development assistance are becoming intertwined in ways that compel us to rethink the meaning of refugeehood as well as the meaning of the refugee camp in the twenty-first century.

From Humanitarianism to Development

No single definition of the term *humanitarianism* exists, and humanitarianism's boundaries have historically been fluid (Calhoun 2008; Feldman 2007a). In the 1990s, with the end of the Cold War and the apparent increase in intrastate conflict, humanitarianism went through significant transformations, and the issue of where to draw its boundaries became the subject of intense debate (Barnett and Weiss 2008; Calhoun 2008; Chandler 2001; Kennedy 2004; Rieff 2002; Terry 2002). Since the late 1980s, the International Committee of the Red Cross (ICRC) definition of humanitarianism–predicated on "the impartial, independent, and neutral provision of relief to those in immediate need because of conflict and natural disasters"–has ceased to be the industry standard (Barnett and Weiss 2008:5). Humanitarianism can now be understood to include an entire range of activities, including development, human rights, democracy promotion, gender equality, peace building, and even military intervention (Barnett and Weiss 2008; Calhoun 2008; Chandler 2001). Still, aid agencies distinguish humanitarian aid from development aid. Humanitarian aid tends to be associated with the attempt to alleviate suffering and save lives in an "emergency" situation that typically emanates from natural or man-made disasters or organized violence (Calhoun 2008; Fearon 2008). Development aid is generally associated with improving the normal state of affairs (Fearon 2008).

Development defined as "improving the normal state of affairs" is not entirely new to UNRWA. Established in 1949, the agency made its initial purpose not just to provide emergency relief assistance but also to promote large-scale socioeconomic development in its areas of operation. However, for reasons that will be explained in greater depth in chapter 2, by the late 1950s it had given up the development aspect of its mandate but has since then engaged in targeted interventions such as education and small loan programs that fall under the definition of development. What is new today, however, is UNRWA's comprehensive embrace of development as the main ideology through which it frames its assistance to Palestinian refugees. The key concepts that informed the agency's development approach during the implementation of the Neirab Rehabilitation Project were "sustainability," "capacity building," and (refugee) "self-reliance."

UNRWA's shift must be understood partly as the result of a severe funding crisis that the agency was facing at the turn of the twenty-first century. To address this crisis, it organized a conference in June 2004 in partnership with the Swiss Agency for Development and Cooperation (SDC) (UNRWA 2004). Held in Geneva, the conference featured sixty-seven countries and thirty-four intergovernmental organizations. Shortly afterward, in 2005, UNRWA finalized a "Medium Term Plan" that had been the subject of review and discussion at the conference. It presented the plan as an effort "to restore the living conditions of Palestine refugees to acceptable international standards and set them on the road to self reliance and sustainable human development" (UNRWA 2005a:2).

A second factor accounting for UNRWA's recent reforms is the broader global policy shift that is taking place in refugee assistance, especially when it comes to protracted exile. UNRWA's purported transition toward a more developmental approach in Palestinian refugee camps follows a broader reform process in the UN. Since the 1990s, UNHCR has taken steps to incorporate development in its policy on durable solutions for refugees (UNHCR 2003).

A third factor responsible for UNRWA's recent reform process is the Oslo peace process or, rather, the post-Oslo climate. An obstacle that had stood in the way of UNRWA engagement in large-scale socioeconomic or infrastructural projects in Palestinian refugee camps was opposition (to varying degrees) from Arab host states. Officially, the main host states–Jordan, Lebanon, and Syria–consider the camps as temporary spaces housing refugees until they are able to exercise their right of return to their Palestinian homes. The advent and subsequent failure of Oslo seems to have ushered in a shift among the host states, which appear to be more flexible regarding attempts to comprehensively improve camp conditions (Al Husseini and Bocco 2009; Oesch 2014). It must be noted that these shared policies toward large-scale improvement projects in Palestinian refugee camps have not translated into identical policies on the legal status of refugees. In the 1950s, the Jordanian government extended Jordanian citizenship to its

Palestinian population and the Syrian government extended most Syrian citizenship rights to its Palestinian population without officially granting them citizenship. Lebanon differs drastically from Jordan and Syria in that its refugees are denied citizenship and face severe restrictions with regard to access to health care, employment, and property ownership (Suleiman 2010).

A final factor that helped lay the ground for UNRWA's current reform process is an apparent shift in refugee attitudes concerning attempts to drastically change the living conditions or features of their camps (Al-Hamarneh 2002; Misselwitz 2009; Al Husseini 2011, 2010). Indeed, host states have not been alone in opposing drastic changes to the fabric of the camps; the refugees themselves have historically been concerned that the camps maintain an aura of temporariness as a means of asserting refugees' commitment to the right of return and as a form of resistance to what they see as attempts to resolve the refugee issue through economic rather than political measures. With the failure of the Oslo peace process–a sign that there was no imminent durable solution to the Israeli–Palestinian conflict–it became more acceptable in refugee circles to broach the idea of comprehensive and long-term improvements (Misselwitz 2009).

This emerging shift among Palestinian refugees cannot be told as the linear story of a progressive change in attitude. This story has been, and continues to be, rife with tensions and contradictions. As noted by Muna Budeiri (2014), compared with outside actors, including UNRWA, Palestinian refugees are mostly responsible for the progressive urbanization and modernization of their camps. Additionally, it is not unusual for Palestinian refugees to criticize what they see as UNRWA's lack of concern for the harsh living conditions in some camps. For instance, over the course of my fieldwork I routinely heard refugees in Neirab and Ein el Tal, the sites of the Neirab Rehabilitation Project, complain of UNRWA complacency in the face of their hardships. These complaints were occurring at the very same time that UNRWA was facing significant resistance in the camps with regard to implementation of the project.

Indeed, there were two major rumors circulating in both Neirab and Ein el Tal at the time of my fieldwork in 2005: the first argued that the project was a deftly articulated plan by UNRWA and its Western donors to promote the permanent settlement of Palestinians in Syria and to do away with the right of return; the second argued that the real aim of the project, which drew on an understanding of development as self-reliance, was the progressive dismantlement of UNRWA and consequently the disappearance of the Palestinian refugee issue. At the same time that these rumors were making the rounds and jeopardizing UNRWA's credibility, it became evident that in Ein el Tal, some resistance to the project was (paradoxically) due to anger over what refugees saw as UNRWA's failure to fulfill previous promises to improve camp conditions.[3]

The complex and contradictory ways in which Palestinians react to camp improvements bring to light that "many of the things that development promises–whether it is electricity, roads, formal education, and biomedical healthcare or greater prosperity and consumption–are, in fact, highly desired by vast numbers of people in the nominally developing world" (Ferguson 1999; Smith and Johnson-Hanks 2015:436). However, Palestinian refugees' complicated engagement with the discourse of development must also be read within a specifically Palestinian context. It is my contention that the complex and contradictory ways in which Palestinian refugees view improving camp conditions are indicative of two seemingly opposed currents that, while not necessarily tied to a deliberate plan on the part of a particular actor, have different political implications for the refugees. This is especially the case when it comes to the right of return. I refer to these two seemingly clashing currents as the "politics of suffering" and the "politics of citizenship."

The Politics of Suffering versus the Politics of Citizenship

The tension between what I call "the politics of suffering" and "the politics of citizenship" is captured by the picture on the book cover. I took the picture in the barracks area of Neirab Camp in October 2010, before the Syrian uprisings started. My guess is that when looking at the picture most people would assume that the partial ruin is a reference to the refugee camp while the apartment building signals a world beyond it. The picture, however, depicts an almost completed modern apartment building standing in a spot previously occupied by a barrack and behind it, a partially destroyed barrack, awaiting transformation into a modern apartment building. The picture gives an insight into the promise of development. It also gives an insight into the implications of a blurring of the distinction between the camp and the city. Once the barracks became slated for destruction, a move that had initially found consensus among all project stakeholders, it became clear to many in Neirab that the destruction of the barracks meant the silencing of an important witness to the suffering they had endured as refugees and, therefore, an important ally in their quest for justice.

Palestinian refugees in Ein el Tal and Neirab usually described their suffering using the term *mu'ānā*, a noun that comes from the Arabic root *ānā*, meaning "to incur," "to suffer (from)," or "to endure." It can also mean "to be anxious" or "to be preoccupied" or "to take pain (in doing something)." Refugees usually talked about *mu'ānā* to point out the hardships of their everyday lives, often connecting it to the events that resulted in their forced exile: had they not been historically exiled and dispossessed, they would not be facing their current hardships.[4] For the refugees of Ein el Tal and Neirab, suffering took on political meanings that were sometimes at odds with formal, state-centered understandings of social equality and progress.

The Neirab Rehabilitation Project aimed to put an end to suffering understood as dilapidated housing and an unhealthy physical environment, overcrowding, low income, lack of employment, and a general lack of socioeconomic opportunities. It did not address suffering as a consequence of political subjugation or injustice. It did not capture suffering as it was expressed to me by Anwar Fanous, a Palestinian official working for the General Authority for Palestinian Arab Refugees (GAPAR), Syria's government body that oversees the country's Palestinian population and maintains a strong presence in the camps.[5] At the time, Fanous was GAPAR's representative for the Aleppo area. He was from Neirab Camp, where he lived in the barracks with his wife and four children. According to a high UNRWA official closely involved with the Neirab Rehabilitation Project, Fanous was the one who first brought the harsh living conditions of the barracks to UNRWA's attention and insisted that something be done about them.

I often saw Fanous, a smallish man with an intense gaze and a severe demeanor, at project meetings, but had never dared to approach him. I was aware that he knew of me because I needed permission from GAPAR to be in the camps of Neirab and Ein el Tal. I waited until a few days before my departure from northern Syria to finally ask him for an interview. To my surprise, he accepted. During the interview, I was struck by a particular moment when this man–who never smiled, never acknowledged my presence at public events, and had the power to banish me from Neirab and Ein el Tal at the slightest faux pas–suddenly tried to convey how he felt knowing that anybody from any part of the world could visit his homeland while he could not. This caused 'azza 'alā al-qalb, "sorrow to the heart," he explained repeatedly as he put his hand on his chest–an expression not only of emotional pain but also of the sense of injustice at not being able to set foot in his homeland.

In addition to expressing their suffering as emotional pain resulting from the injustice of living in forced exile, Palestinian refugees also saw it as a political tool. Suffering took on the form of stoicism, something that needed to be endured to maintain the memory of exile and actualize the narrative of return.[6] Stoicism dignified Palestinian suffering understood as part of a larger struggle for liberation and return. Those who earned a camp community's respect were those who had struggled for Palestinian freedom through their political activism, especially those who had shed blood for the cause. Most were those who lived in humble conditions in the camp, not those who had achieved the dream of modernization, who lived in villas and were economically prosperous, who met the international indicators of well-being that are important to UNRWA. Anthropologist Rosemary Sayigh notes that when Palestinians embraced resistance and armed struggle in Lebanon in the late 1960s, the notion of struggle was closely tied to a "special capacity for suffering" (1979:166). UNRWA's development discourse is invested in bestowing dignity in the form of "capacity building," "self-reliance," and economic prosperity but not in the form conferred by suffering that is viewed strategically, as sacrifice in the name of a larger political struggle.

There is now a solid body of literature exploring the relationship between suffering and political agency (Allen 2009; Asad 2003; Benbassa 2010; Brown 1995; Fassin 2002, 2012; Fassin and Rechtman 2009; Petryna 2002; Ticktin 2006, 2012). To fully understand Palestinian refugees' engagement with the Neirab Rehabilitation Project, one has to understand suffering both as a passive state that one strives to overcome and as agentive–that is, suffering itself as a kind of action (Asad 2003). Agentive suffering, understood as a political tool or as having political effects, falls within the scope of what I term the *politics of suffering*. I use this term to describe the ways in which suffering becomes a means–whether deliberately or not–of attaining political legitimacy and rights. For Palestinians in Neirab and Ein el Tal, ongoing suffering testified to the original injustice of the *Nakba*, which is the term used by Palestinian refugees to describe the dismemberment of Palestinian society and the forced displacement and exile of more than half of the members of this society in the aftermath of the 1948 Arab–Israeli war; it acted as a conduit for neither forgetting the traumatic past nor the claims of redress linked to that past; and it included bodily and material sacrifice in the name of the Palestinian Political struggle.

UNRWA's focus on eradicating poverty and suffering is framed by a state-centric approach expressed especially in the prominent role played by the Syrian government in project implementation and in the agency's use of an urban development approach. While the Syrian government legally recognizes that Palestinian refugees on its soil have most of the social rights associated with citizenship, this does not mean that the refugees are always able to access or make the most of these rights in practice, and poverty remains an issue in the camps. In UNRWA's vision, the goal of development is, on the one hand, to incorporate individuals as much as possible in the institutional framework of the state and, on the other hand, to pursue progress by enabling individuals to attain the social privileges associated with citizenship, if not citizenship itself. Conceived in this manner, development is part of a politics of citizenship. A framing of Palestinian victimhood as one in which Palestinians are marginalized from the rights, privileges, and opportunities that accrue to citizens of an independent state because they are not fully integrated in this state does not take into account the issue of return to one's place of residence before exile. Return becomes irrelevant. What is important is the acquisition of substantive citizenship rights, if not citizenship altogether, and the home that counts is not where one has historical or emotional links–the home that counts is where one has the possibility of becoming a full citizen.

Palestinian refugees in Neirab and Ein el Tal did not reject development outright, nor did they reject many of the material outcomes promised by the Neirab Rehabilitation Project. What was at stake for them was the need to articulate a vision of progress and improvement that did not ignore their history or seem to compromise their political claims. As noted by Laleh Khalili (2007), the last few decades have seen the emergence of a global human rights and humanitarian discourse that addresses the suffering of victims of injustice "in such a way that suffering and tragedy are made immanent to their being, sometimes to the exclusion of their political struggle for justice" (Khalili 2007:35). UNRWA-sponsored development is based on an understanding of suffering that is not really able to accommodate Palestinian political claims. UNRWA's imbrication in the Western-dominated order that created it and that is mostly responsible for funding it, as well as its historical mandate as a humanitarian agency, have curtailed its ability and willingness to address or sometimes even acknowledge the political concerns of the refugees it assists.

However, rather than simply point out the shortcomings (and achievements) of UNRWA's approach to development in Palestinian refugee camps, this book explores efforts, both Palestinian refugees' and others', to come up with a vocabulary and set of practices that transcend the apparent dichotomy between the politics of suffering and the politics of citizenship.

Fieldwork in Syria

My first encounter with a Palestinian refugee camp in Syria was Yarmouk in the summer of 2002, when I was still a graduate student and had traveled to Damascus to study Arabic. I followed a fellow student, an aspiring journalist, who wanted to visit the camp. I was struck by how seamlessly Yarmouk blended into the surrounding city. Without the giant arch featuring a portrait of former President Hafiz al-Asad that signals the entrance, it would have been impossible for a newcomer to know that she was crossing a boundary of sorts. With symmetrically arranged apartment buildings, Yarmouk had the appearance of a typical working/middle-class Syrian neighborhood. It was also a popular commercial area, attracting Syrians from other parts of Damascus. I became interested in examining what it meant for Palestinians living in Yarmouk to be refugees, given the extent of their socioeconomic and physical integration into its surroundings. Thus, when I began my fieldwork in spring 2004, I was based in Damascus and remained there for one year.

In addition to spending a significant amount of time in Yarmouk interviewing Palestinians of various generations and backgrounds, I followed the activities of the Yarmouk Youth Center, one of the camp's many active grassroots organizations.[7] I also worked as a volunteer at the UNRWA field office in Damascus. I wanted to examine the relationship between the agency and the refugees it has been assisting for over six decades.

In the second year of my volunteer work with UNRWA, I had the opportunity to participate in the Neirab Rehabilitation Project, which was taking place in the north of the country, outside Aleppo, Syria's second largest city. One of the project assistants had become ill and had taken a leave of absence, so the project manager was looking for some extra help. The director of UNRWA in Syria at the time was very receptive to the idea of having an anthropologist participate in one of the agency's projects.[8] UNRWA was in the midst of reassessing its relationship with Palestinian refugees, and the director felt that an anthropologist's skills would be useful to this effort. For this reason, I spent a large part of 2005 in Aleppo and its surroundings working as a Neirab Rehabilitation Project volunteer.

While working on the project, I was not allowed by Syrian authorities to live in either Ein el Tal or Neirab, so I commuted from Aleppo. Palestinian refugee camps are generally under heavy scrutiny by Syrian authorities, and foreigners are usually discouraged from visiting or spending time in them unless in an official capacity.[9] It was not unusual for foreign researchers to live in Yarmouk, which was harder for Syrian authorities to police given its level of integration into Damascus. However, it would have been almost impossible for a foreign anthropologist to settle in or even have regular access to a smaller and more isolated camp like Ein el Tal or Neirab. Through my relationship with UNRWA, I had special permission to come and go, except for spending the night in Ein el Tal or Neirab or both depending on where the project needed me. Overall, I ended up spending most of my time in Ein el Tal, where the project office was located and where phase 1 of the project was still being implemented when I arrived.

With regard to the limitations I faced in conducting research in Syria (or the lack thereof), perhaps a few words need to be said about my own identity and positionality in relation to my object of study: I am the daughter of a Black Togolese father and a White American mother and I was raised in Togo. Most people in Syria, whether Syrian or Palestinian, did not immediately identify me as someone from the West. They usually guessed that I was East or North African or South Asian. I found out over the course of my fieldwork that I could sometimes "pass" for Palestinian. When I went shopping in Aleppo's commercial district with my friend Muna from Neirab, she introduced me to vendors and store owners as her "cousin," fearing that they would raise their prices if they found out I was American. These merchants usually accepted my undercover identity until they started a conversation with me in Arabic, forcing me to reveal my accent.

It is hard to know the extent to which the identities I was associated with, coupled with my not being readily recognizable as Western or American, affected my fieldwork or my rapport with the Syrians and Palestinians I encountered.

I usually introduced myself to people as an American, although anyone who got to know me very quickly knew my entire background. I purposefully chose to emphasize my American identity when meeting people for the first time because I felt that if I did not disclose this information, and these people found out later, they might become suspicious. My fieldwork coincided with a period during which the US government was particularly unpopular in Syria and American foreign policy was a sensitive issue. When I arrived in April 2004, the atmosphere was tense: about a year before, the United States had invaded Iraq, a deeply unpopular action with both Syrians and Palestinians. To make matters worse, the US government, which at the time was still confident in its invasion of Iraq, was hinting that Syria might be next. Additionally, a few weeks before my arrival, angry Palestinian protesters from Yarmouk had marched to the American embassy in Damascus, scaled the walls, and taken down the US flag in the aftermath of Israel's assassination of Sheikh Ahmad Yasin, Hamas's spiritual leader. After the protest, the embassy issued a security briefing urging Americans in Syria to avoid Palestinian areas. As a result of the prevailing atmosphere, I was forbidden–not by Syrian authorities but by the Fulbright office in Damascus–from living in Yarmouk.[10] The head of the Fulbright office at the time considered the area too dangerous for me as an American researcher.

I decided it was preferable for people to find out my American identity sooner rather than later, and overall I did not find this disclosure to be a significant hindrance. I made one exception, however, and that was with cabdrivers, to whom I introduced myself as being from Africa (*min afrīqia*). I had noticed that when I identified myself as an American to Syrian cabbies, most of whom are rumored to be government informants, I was inevitably bombarded with questions during the entire trip. When I identified as an African, I stirred no curiosity and could enjoy a peaceful ride. I did once elicit the pity of a cabdriver who refused to let me pay my fare once he found out I was from Africa.

While working as an UNRWA volunteer on the Neirab Rehabilitation Project from the spring of 2005 to the spring of 2006, I assisted as an Arabic-to-English translator during informal meetings with Palestinian refugees in Ein el Tal and Neirab, and served as a note taker during UNRWA-organized community meetings and focus group discussions (these involved groups of Palestinian men, women, boys, and girls). In the fall of 2005, I participated in an UNRWA-sponsored study of living conditions in Neirab's barracks which consisted of a questionnaire and formal interviews with twenty-four families. Aside from the participant observation I engaged in through my UNRWA activities in the Damascus and Aleppo areas, I conducted about thirty formal interviews with Palestinians of varying ages, occupations, and genders living in Ein el Tal, Neirab, and Yarmouk.[11] I also conducted about a dozen formal interviews with UNRWA staff (both foreign and Palestinian) directly involved in the Neirab Rehabilitation

Project and interviewed the project's two main Syrian government representatives (who were themselves Palestinian refugees). I carried out brief follow-up research in the summer of 2009 and the fall of 2010 in Ein el Tal and Neirab. In 2015, as part of an effort to document what had happened to Ein el Tal, Neirab, and Yarmouk and their inhabitants as a result of the war in Syria, I carried out additional research in several Middle Eastern countries and in Europe. In the spring of 2015, I spent one month interviewing UNRWA employees at the agency's headquarters in Amman, Jordan as well as Palestinians from Ein el Tal, Neirab, and Yarmouk living in Lebanon, Turkey, and the United Arab Emirates.[12] Most of these had fled the war in Syria, and six of them were Palestinians I had known during my 2004–2006 fieldwork. In the summer of 2015, I spent a month interviewing Palestinians from Ein el Tal, Neirab, and Yarmouk who had fled to Europe and sought asylum in France and Sweden.[13] Four of them were Palestinians I had known during my 2004–2006 fieldwork.

Like other anthropologists who have written about development, I was both an investigator and a participant in the Neirab Rehabilitation Project (Bornstein 2005; Li 2007; Mosse 2005). As David Mosse argues, it is almost impossible to sustain long-term participant observation in a development agency without making a practical contribution to its functioning (2005). However, he also states that "the impression that development agencies (donors, field agencies or others) always feel they have something to hide, or that confidentiality and proprietary claims over knowledge inevitably characterize the relationship between agencies and their contracted consultants or researchers [here citing Panayiotopoulos 2002] is wrong" (2005:12).

UNRWA employees were generally comfortable with having an anthropologist in their midst. With regard to my participation in the Neirab Rehabilitation Project, UNRWA's director in Syria (at the time) was not just accommodating; he was excited about having an anthropologist on board. He was especially interested in my involvement because UNRWA was in the process of reforming its operations and part of this process was to critically evaluate the agency's role in Palestinian refugee camps.

The "independent" team set up by UNRWA to lead the Neirab Rehabilitation Project was also receptive to my presence. Because of UNRWA's insistence that the project be a participatory one in which the agency and community members would interact as partners, project leaders felt that an anthropologist's perspective would be useful in making sure that local realities, opinions, and sentiments were taken into account in planning and implementation. A critical evaluation of the project had actually been incorporated into the project design, and consultants had been hired for this job. In such a context, I did not have to go undercover to try to assess the relationship between UNRWA and Palestinian refugees. I was one more person who could help the agency determine what it was doing right and what it was doing wrong in terms of its assistance to the refugees.

I realized over the course of my fieldwork that Palestinian refugees generally value the opportunity to tell their stories to foreigners as a way to balance out Western bias against them. Some Palestinians saw their relationship with UNRWA as a means through which they could meet and interact with foreigners and share their experiences with them in the hope that these experiences would reach a larger (usually Western) public. I therefore did not have much trouble meeting Palestinians in Neirab and Ein el Tal who were willing to talk. It also helped that, in addition to the handful of foreign volunteers assisting UNRWA, the agency had recruited local volunteers from the camps to help with the Neirab Rehabilitation Project. I was thus part of a larger group of volunteers, a majority of whom were Palestinian. The Palestinian volunteers, whom I got to know through my work with UNRWA, played a crucial role in my gaining acceptance and trust in Neirab and Ein el Tal.

It is impossible for me to completely separate my role as an anthropologist from my role as an UNRWA volunteer and participant in the Neirab Rehabilitation Project. I cannot pretend, as I write this analysis, to have been an outsider peering at the stage where development was supposed to be taking place and taking notes from a distance. "Development" was my primary field site and the focus of my participant observation as an anthropologist. Conducting participant observation at this site, as an anthropologist whose services were deemed valuable by UNRWA, allowed me to interact with the different actors who, in the name of improving the lives of Palestinians refugees, had converged on Neirab and Ein el Tal. It allowed me to investigate the logics and justifications behind the actions not only of the Palestinian refugees who were the target of development (see Fassin 2012) but also of UNRWA officials, Syrian government employees, and the project's initial donors: the American, Canadian, and Swiss governments. I was able to meet and interact with representatives of these governments during their visits to the camps to evaluate progress. I was also able to attend UNRWA-organized meetings held in the camps that featured donor representatives.

This book explores the intersection of humanitarianism, development, and citizenship in the Palestinian refugee camp. It focuses on the shift from a relief-centered discourse to a development-centered discourse on the part of UNRWA and on the ways in which Palestinian refugees engaged with this shift in discourse. By drawing on examples from Ein el Tal, Neirab, and Yarmouk, I show that Palestinian refugee camps are not static spaces to be acted on; they are themselves productive of particular ideologies–ideologies not necessarily synchronic with the discourse of development being promoted by UNRWA and its underlying assumptions about citizenship.

Chapter 1 focuses on the relationship between Palestinian refugees and the Syrian government, a major participant in the Neirab Rehabilitation Project. Understanding Syro–Palestinian relations requires an examination of Syria's

Ottoman past, the European colonization of the Middle East, and the pan-Arabism that characterized the Middle East from the late nineteenth to the mid-twentieth century. I show how this larger historical context came to inform the rhetoric of Syrian government representatives, who were themselves Palestinians, to justify Syrian participation in the Neirab Rehabilitation Project and to galvanize refugee support for it.

In chapter 2, I examine UNRWA and the role it has played over the past six decades in Palestinian refugee communities in Middle Eastern host countries. I analyze the contradictions and tensions that characterize UNRWA's overall relationship with Palestinian refugees living in camps which stem from the fact that UNRWA is a humanitarian organization that has become the primary means of addressing an essentially political problem. I show that the key to understanding the ambivalent relationship between UNRWA and the refugees is recognizing that the agency is not monolithic or neatly bounded. It is a hybrid resulting from the overlap of the Western-dominated political order that oversaw its creation and the very Palestinian refugees it was created to assist.

In chapter 3, I analyze conflicting interpretations of the Neirab Rehabilitation Project. UNRWA framed development through a neoliberal narrative that focused on overcoming material hardship and emphasized self-reliance and individual empowerment through capacity building. Such a framing elided empowerment understood as the result of a collective political struggle focused on the right of return, which has traction in Palestinian refugee camps. While some refugees in Neirab and Ein el Tal resisted UNRWA's neoliberal narrative, others embraced it, albeit as a process whose end point was political–that is, one that could actually facilitate return. According to this narrative, poverty is debilitating and needs to be overcome so that Palestinian refugees can focus more on their political goals. Another argument put forth by this narrative is that the acquisition of globally recognized and marketable skills will facilitate successful resettlement in the Palestinian homeland once return becomes a possibility.

Chapter 4 examines the significance of the built environment to Palestinian refugee identity. Virtually all of those involved in the Neirab Rehabilitation Project agreed that something had to be done about Neirab's crumbling World War II–era barracks, which had initially served as shelter for allied troops and their horses. At the same time, a significant number of the camp's inhabitants saw the barracks as a "witness" to their traumatic experience of forced displacement and dispossession and thus as an ally in seeking redress. I show that, while these contradictory feelings were never really resolved, what was ultimately important for the inhabitants of Neirab was not that the landscape of the camp remain unchanged but that the camp continue to exist as a space of difference that emphasizes its inhabitants' specific Palestinian identity, history, and political claims.

In chapter 5, I focus on Yarmouk, which before the war in Syria had been touted by some as an example of successful refugee integration into a host country. Despite this integration, Yarmouk did not lose its identity as a Palestinian refugee camp. Using it as an example, I reflect on what was at stake in Neirab's and Ein el Tal's continued existence as camps despite the changes effected by development. I argue that the Palestinian refugee camp is not just a physical architectural space but a mental, affective, and embodied one as well.

In the conclusion, I focus on expressions of Palestinian refugee identity that transcend the tension between the politics of suffering and the politics of citizenship. These examples force us to rethink the role of the camp as a space of particular relevance to Palestinian refugee identity and rights as well as some of the dominant assumptions that underlie the concept of citizenship.

By the time Syria descended into full-fledged war in July 2012, the Neirab Rehabilitation Project was close to completion. In the epilogue, I discuss how the war has affected Palestinian refugees. I focus more specifically on the repercussions that it has had on the three camps that are the focus of this book: Ein el Tal, Neirab, and Yarmouk.

1 Informal Citizens

Palestinian Refugees in Syria

In May of 2011, while in the United States, I decided to call Muna, with whom I had established a friendship during my fieldwork in Neirab and Ein el Tal. While I had called Muna periodically since returning to the United States, this time I was a little hesitant. The tide of uprisings across the Arab world, which had started in Tunisia in December 2010, had recently reached Syria and the Syrian government was blaming "foreign instigators" for the unrest it was facing. I was worried that, as an American, calling acquaintances in Syria during this tense time might make these acquaintances nervous or even put them at risk of special scrutiny (assuming that government officials were listening in on calls, something that was not unheard of).

I decided in the end that Muna was a good enough friend that she would understand I was just calling as I usually did to say hi. However, once I reached her, she was the one who unexpectedly brought up the unrest in the region. Not the unrest involving Syrians but that involving Palestinians, including herself. She asked me if I had heard that Palestinian refugees in various parts of the Middle East had marched to the Israeli border a few weeks earlier, on May 15, to demand that Israel acknowledge their right of return. She proudly announced to me that she, as well as many others in Neirab Camp, had participated in the march. I told her that I had indeed seen pictures of the protesters on the Al Jazeera news network. "Al Jazeera" had an unanticipated effect: "Kaẕāb! Kaẕāb! [liars! liars!]," she responded, raising her voice. "Don't watch Al Jazeera; they're all liars," she continued, urging me to watch Al Manar, the Hizbullah-controlled satellite TV station instead.

I was well aware that Al Jazeera had been running news stories emphasizing the brutality of the Syrian government crackdown on protesters, while I suspected that Al Manar was airing stories that were much more sympathetic to and defensive of the Syrian regime. Indeed, it is no secret that Hizbullah is a longtime ally of the Syrian government. It has now officially entered the Syrian conflict, fighting on the side of the government against anti-Asad rebels. Choosing to be careful and not pursue a potentially sensitive conversation over the phone, I did not ask Muna to explain herself. At the end of our phone call, I was left with two possible interpretations. On the one hand, it was possible that Muna was expressing genuine support for the Syrian government; after all, the government has generally been welcoming and protective toward Palestinian refugees living on Syrian territory. In this sense, it is not surprising that the refugees would feel anxious about the current instability and the prospect of regime change. On the other hand, it was possible that Muna's reaction to my mention of Al Jazeera, which had been airing news footage and stories that painted the Syrian government in a negative light, was a protective mechanism in case Syrian authorities were eavesdropping on our conversation.

Since the beginning of the Syrian war, Palestinians, as a collective, have managed to avoid being fully associated with one side or the other of the conflict. However, my conversation with Muna brings up the fact that there are real implications, should the violence continue to escalate, with regard to Palestinian refugees being seen as supporting either the Asad regime or the rebels. My conversation with Muna also brings up an interesting aspect of the relationship between Palestinian refugees and the Syrian government: Muna, as a Palestinian, could celebrate her participation in an event that was connected to the recent uprisings against various authoritarian regimes in the Arab world while implicitly expressing support for the Syrian government, which was a target of these uprisings. Because the political activism of the refugees is generally directed against Israel, which is also a Syrian foe, the refugees occupy an ambiguous position in Syria's political landscape. Given their lack of formal citizenship, they can be seen as particularly vulnerable to any sort of government backlash against presumed anti-government rhetoric or activity, but the fact that their political activism is generally directed against Israel gives them a greater amount of political organization and expression than their Syrian counterparts have.

This ambiguity defies dominant assumptions about citizenship, assumptions that are grounded in a nation-state-centered understanding of citizenship and rights. While they are not citizens in the formal sense of the term, Palestinians in Syria not only have access to the overwhelming majority of social rights enjoyed by Syrian citizens but are also integrated into the country's national imaginary through Syrian government rhetoric. This rhetoric not only considers Palestinians to be a part of Syria's historical national imaginary but also sees Syrians and Palestinians as united through their struggle against a common enemy–usually identified as Israel but sometimes extending to Israel's unequivocal ally, the United States, and Western imperialism more broadly. I begin my analysis of the Syro-Palestinian relationship by examining the relatively warm welcome that was extended by the Syrian government and people to Palestinian refugees, who were not seen as foreigners having crossed borders when they began arriving en masse as a result of the 1948 Arab–Israeli war.

A Warm Welcome in Syria

Of the roughly seven hundred and fifty thousand Palestinians who fled their homes or were expelled from them by Israeli forces during the 1948 Arab–Israeli war, approximately ninety to one hundred thousand sought refuge in Syria (Kodmani-Darwish 1997; Takkenberg 1998). Probably because of their urban origins, the first refugees settled in and around Damascus. At the time of my fieldwork, 70 percent of all Palestinians in Syria lived in the Damascus area (Kodmani-Darwish 1997), most of them in Yarmouk Camp. The rest, many of whom came from small northern Palestinian villages, were scattered in other camps or towns across the Syrian landscape.

By 2013, the number of registered Palestinian refugees had grown to 499,181.[1] According to official UNRWA surveys taken before the Syrian war, only one-third lived in camps. This information is misleading, however, if one takes into account both official camps, which were specifically set up by UNRWA as humanitarian spaces, and unofficial camps, which were set up by the Syrian government to accommodate Palestinians who did not initially move to UNRWA-administered camps. Before the current war, Syria counted nine official and three unofficial camps.[2] Among the latter are Ein el Tal and Yarmouk, two of the three refugee camps featured in this book. While in practice UNRWA does not distinguish between official and unofficial camps and provides services to both, it does not include the latter in its surveys of Palestinian camp populations. If unofficial camps are taken into account, it can be argued that the majority (more than two-thirds) of Palestinian refugees in Syria lived in camps before the current war.[3]

The hospitality of the Syrian government and people is often mentioned in interviews with first-generation refugees such as Abu Hosam, a major figure in UNRWA's Neirab Rehabilitation Project. At the time of my fieldwork, Abu Hosam held the title of Neirab Project liaison officer, which meant that he was the main intermediary between the project team and the Neirab community. A retired UNRWA English teacher and a respected member of Neirab's first generation of refugees, he is a striking and imposing figure who appears to be in his late sixties or early seventies and who is always dressed in a suit and tie. He once told me, while showing me a picture of himself as a young English teacher in Algeria in the 1970s, that his Algerian peers often compared his looks to French movie star Alain Delon.

I met Abu Hosam one morning in early June 2005 in his UNRWA office in Neirab. The walls of the office were graced with pictures and statistics about the Neirab Rehabilitation Project. This was the first place for any member of the Neirab community to come to ask questions, make suggestions, or articulate grievances. During my interview with him, Abu Hosam emphasized the hospitality that fleeing Palestinian refugees received from Syrians: "We were warmly welcomed in Syria and we were treated well. Some kind Syrian people distributed food, clothing, money, and so on. They were very kind" (interview, June 1, 2005).

The issue of Syrian hospitality arose during a Palestinian oral history project I was a part of in Yarmouk Camp in Damascus. One of the interviewees, who was in his eighties and lived in Yarmouk, emphasized the cordial manner in which he was received after abandoning his defeated Syrian-led Arab army unit in northern Palestine and fleeing to Syria in 1948. He referred to Syrians as "deep-rooted people" and added: "They don't have racism and everyone knows that Palestine, Syria, Jordan, and Lebanon are one country. Colonization separated them" (interview, June 2005). While these comments are somewhat idealistic, it is historically accurate that present-day Syria, Israel/Palestine, Jordan, and Lebanon once constituted Bilād al-Sham, or Greater Syria, an area under the control of the Ottoman Empire:

> While it was almost never politically united, this vast area—bounded by the Taurus mountains to the north, the Mediterranean to the west, the Euphrates to the east, and the Arabian desert to the south—was in the minds of its inhabitants a whole, homogeneous in culture, threaded with economic ties and was called for centuries Bilad al-Sham. Each of the main cities of the region had its own character and jealous particularity, and its constellation of leading families, but there was a sense in which Jerusalem and Jaffa, Sidon, Beirut and Tripoli, Damascus, Homs and Hama, Latakia, Aleppo and Alexandretta were all kin, and of all these Damascus was acknowledged to be the most important. (Seale 1988:14)

During World War I, allied forces, in anticipation of the defeat of the Ottoman Empire, which had taken the side of the central powers, were involved in two agreements that drastically altered the geopolitical landscape of Bilād al-Sham: The Sykes-Picot Agreement of 1916 and the Balfour Declaration of 1917. After the war and as a result of the Sykes-Picot agreement, signed by the British and the French, Palestine came under British control; the rest of Bilād al-Sham came under French control.[4] The Balfour Declaration led to the establishment of a Jewish state in Palestine, to which the British had laid claim. The inhabitants of Bilād al-Sham had made clear their opposition to the various amputations and political restructurings imposed on their territory and had voiced their desire to be independent and undivided (Seale 1988). In 1919, a political party called the Syrian National Congress rejected the Sykes-Picot agreement and the Balfour Declaration "and demanded sovereign status for Syria-Palestine," a demand that was greeted with overwhelming support by the inhabitants of the region (Seale 1988). Thus, Syrians and Palestinians historically share the national imaginary of Bilād al-Sham and the struggle to prevent its fragmentation, a fact that helps explain the relatively warm welcome the majority of Palestinian refugees received as they streamed into Syria during the period of 1947–1949.

Another development that helps explain the refugees' friendly reception is the emergence of pan-Arab Ba'thist ideology.[5] Brought to prominence by a trio of schoolmasters, Zaki Al-Arsuzi (an Alawite), Michel Aflaq (an orthodox

Christian), and Salah al-Din Bitar (a Sunni Muslim), ba'thism emerged as a political force in 1940. Michel Aflaq, who would become the head of the Ba'th Party, founded in 1947, argued that Arabs belonged to a single nation and were members of "an ancient race with many glorious achievements to its credit" (Seale 1988:30). However, because this nation had fallen into backwardness and had capitulated to foreign control, Aflaq sought to "rouse the Arabs from what he considered a living death"(Seale 1988:30). He summarized his plan of action in the slogan "Unity, Freedom, Socialism," with freedom primarily conceived as "freedom from foreign domination whether military, political or cultural" (Seale 1988:31). Thus, the Ba'thist ideology preached the reunification of the "Arab nation" and advocated eliminating obstacles impeding its progress toward a brighter future. Part of this mission was to eradicate the artificial borders imposed by Western imperialism (Hinnebusch 2001). When Syria came under Ba'thist rule in 1963, it was perceived by adherents as a country at the vanguard of Arab unity and Arab liberation struggles across the Middle East. Palestine, especially as it used to constitute the southern part of Bilād al-Sham, easily fit into the Ba'thist political imaginary and its goal of Arab reunification. Palestinian refugees in Syria, as victims of Western imperialism, were for their part "disproportionately attracted to the Ba'th," and many became members (Hinnebusch 2001:31).

At the same time, too much emphasis should not be placed on the role of Ba'thist pan-Arab ideology, especially in various Syrian governments' approach toward Palestinians. As mentioned previously, the Ba'th Party came to power only in 1963. By 1949, Syrian authorities had already taken steps to provide relief and employment for Palestinian refugees (Brand 1988). More important, in 1956 the Syrian government, led by Shukri al-Kuwatli, took a major step with Law No. 260, which guaranteed refugees access to public education, employment, and health care (Brand 1988). Law No 260 remains the backbone of the refugees' legal entitlements in Syria.

A fourth factor behind Syria's welcoming of Palestinian refugees is that the refugees have never constituted more than 3 to 4 percent of the country's population, unlike in Jordan and Lebanon, where they represent about 30 and 10 percent of the respective populations (Al Husseini and Bocco 2009). Contrary to Jordan and Lebanon, Syria generally did not see its refugees as a threat to Syrian employment or natural resources (Al Husseini and Bocco 2009; Kodmani-Darwish 1997; Takkenberg 1998). It also holds the distinction of being the only Arab country to have integrated Palestinian refugees into its army with the establishment of the Palestine Liberation Army (*jaysh taḥrīr filasṭīn*) in 1964 (Brand 1988). A 1988 study by anthropologist Laurie Brand argues that "the right to work and join labor unions, equal access to government services, including education, and the duty to serve in the army have combined with strong popular Arab nationalist sentiment in Syria to allow for a greater degree of socioeconomic and, in some cases, political integration than in any other Arab state but Jordan" (1988:624).

During my fieldwork, I noticed that relations between Palestinians and Syrians were generally cordial, and I never observed any acts of discrimination toward refugees by Syrian individuals. When I worked as an UNRWA volunteer, I was always amazed that I could not distinguish the few Syrian employees from their Palestinian counterparts. There was nothing in their dress, appearance, mannerisms, or interactions that gave me clues. I would only find out a particular employee was Syrian after being told. The one exception was a Christian Syrian employee who always wore a gold necklace with a sparkling cross around her neck. I rightly guessed she was Syrian, as I had never encountered a Christian Palestinian during my time in Syria (while there is a significant Christian Palestinian minority, the Palestinians who live in Syria are overwhelmingly Sunni Muslim). When I strolled around Damascus or Aleppo with Palestinian friends, Syrians often detected a Palestinian accent and asked the speaker if he or she was Palestinian, but otherwise there was nothing noteworthy about the interaction. It was also not unusual for my Palestinian friends and acquaintances to have close Syrian friends.

At the same time, there are some negative stereotypes of Palestinians among Syrians. For instance, some Syrian friends mentioned that Palestinians are commonly viewed as "untrustworthy" and as "troublemakers." Some also seem to resent the fact that Palestinians are entitled to public-sector jobs and accuse them of taking jobs away from Syrians who need them. I heard this from Shereen, the daughter of my first Syrian landlord in Damascus (where I lived during my first year of fieldwork). Much later, a Syrian acquaintance who had learned that I was going to be working in Neirab Camp told me to be careful. He had met some Palestinians from Neirab during his military service and, he said, they were particularly hot-headed.[6] Earlier work by anthropologist Laurie Brand supports some of these sentiments. She notes that Syro-Palestinian relations deteriorated in 1982–1983 because of Syria's fallout with the Palestinian political faction Fatah over the civil war in Lebanon (Brand 1988). She also notes that around this time Syria witnessed a serious decline in its economy. According to Brand, "This combination led some Syrians for the first time to accuse Palestinians of having taken Syrian jobs" (1988:635).

The General Authority for Palestinian Arab Refugees (GAPAR)

The main institution serving as a link between the Syrian government and the Palestinian refugees is the General Authority for Palestinian Arab Refugees (GAPAR). On January 25, 1949, the Syrian government created the Palestine Arab

Refugee Institution (PARI), whose role was to "attend to the affairs of our Palestinian brothers, organize aid to them, attend to their needs, provide them with
appropriate employment, and suggest measures with regard to their self-determination now and in the future" (GAPAR 2002:10, translation by author). In 1974,
PARI became known as GAPAR and was considered part of the Syrian Ministry
of the Interior. It now functions under the umbrella of the Syrian Ministry of
Employment and Social Affairs but enjoys a certain amount of independence and
operates very much as a government ministry in itself although it does not have
that title. GAPAR's administrative board is made up of a director, representatives
from the foreign affairs, defense, and employment and social affairs ministries,
a representative from the Ba'th Party, and two representatives from the Palestinian refugee community (GAPAR 2002). GAPAR's director is himself a Palestinian
refugee, as are the majority of the agency's employees.

In the introduction to GAPAR's 2002 manual, the Palestinian director, who is
also a member of the Syrian Ba'th party, gives thanks:

> Syria, the steadfast Arab fortress which nursed the children of our Palestin-
> ian people who came to it fleeing from the Zionist massacres and terrorism
> that extended all over Palestine; Syria which shared its daily bread and school
> benches and industrial tools with the children of Palestine within a unique
> brotherly relationship; this relationship that was strengthened through strug-
> gle after the March 8 revolution of 1963 [the Syrian Ba'th revolution] which was
> led by our great party, the Arab Socialist Ba'th party, which took root and grew
> after the creation of the noble reform movement which was led by our ever-
> lasting leader, President Hafiz al-Asad. . . . From [these events] came a unique
> relationship of struggle that seeks to support the Palestinian people and its
> Intifada struggle against the Israeli occupation to reclaim usurped rights,
> starting with the right of return. From this unique relationship [emerged] the
> prevailing slogan that was coined by the everlasting leader [Hafiz al-Asad]:
> Palestine before the Golan. (GAPAR 2002:1; author's translation)

The Syrian government early on took measures that would contribute to the
socioeconomic welfare of its Palestinian refugees. These measures culminated in
the adoption of Law No. 260 in 1956, which recognizes Palestinians who reside in
Syria "as Syrians with regard to the stipulations of the law and executive regulations relating to the rights of employment, commercial activity, and education
all the while retaining their original nationality" (GAPAR 2002:26, translation and
emphasis by author). GAPAR's official manual detailing the status of Palestinian
refugees in Syria explains that Law 260 is based on two principles:

1. Palestinians must be treated exactly like Syrians.
2. The Syrian government opposes the resettlement of Palestinians [in Syria]
   "in any shape or form and under any circumstance" (2002:27).

In practice, "exactly like Syrians" translates to the following rights and obligations:

- A *laissez-passer* issued by the government permitting travel outside the country (though not having the same status as a citizen's passport for the purpose of visas for travel to other countries).[7]
- Access to government education, health, and other social services on the same terms as Syrian citizens.
- Access to employment and self-employment on the same terms as Syrian citizens.
- The right to purchase property for an individual's own use (except arable land).
- The obligation of men to undertake a two-year military service in the Palestine Liberation Army.
- The right of association with political, cultural, and social parties as Syrian citizens but not including the right to vote in Syrian elections.
- The right to hold public office by appointment.

Palestinians in prewar Syria seemed to be content with this state of affairs, which gave them citizenship rights without formal citizenship, and which they had never, as a collective, demanded.

The place occupied by Palestinian refugees in Syria's sociopolitical landscape defies assumptions about citizenship and belonging in the twenty-first century. There have been other accounts of belonging and citizenship that question an overemphasis on formal citizenship in terms of rights and opportunities (Gupta 2012; Holston 2008; Vora 2013). For instance, anthropologist Neha Vora (2013), whose work focuses on the middle-class Indian diaspora in the United Arab Emirates, argues that Indians, although barred from citizenship in the Emirati nation-state regardless of how long they have been in the country, are integral to the country's functioning and its economy. At the same time, and similarly to Palestinians in prewar Syria, Indians in the United Arab Emirates have not shown any interest in acquiring formal Emirati citizenship, even though they have in many ways integrated the country's social fabric. For Vora, by virtue of existing outside official Emirati notions of citizenship and yet being central to the way Emirati citizenship is lived and understood, these Indians defy the norms associated with liberal democratic models of citizenship: they are *impossible citizens* who, through their participation in Dubai's neoliberal economy, are able to take part in activities associated with Emirati citizenship without having access to (or for that matter seeking) formal Emirati citizenship.

Despite the similarities with Indians in the United Arab Emirates, Palestinian refugees in Syria are not *impossible citizens*: their relationship with the host state is not based on the foreigner-citizen dichotomy that prevents Indians from demanding or acquiring Emirati citizenship. Rather, the refugees are *informal citizens.* They might not be officially recognized as Syrian nationals in the restricted nation-state-based understanding of nationality, but they are not completely external to Syrian identity as understood through the historical prism of Greater Syria. It is because Syria and Palestine are part of the historical unit of Greater Syria, which Syria continued to claim after independence from the French, that Syrian authorities did not consider Palestinian refugees as foreigners having crossed borders (Kodmani-Darwish 1997).

Despite the relatively positive picture just painted, it is important not to idealize the conditions of Syria's Palestinian refugees. Palestinians who fled to Syria as a result of crises following the 1948 war, such as the civil war in Lebanon, have not been systematically accorded legal rights (Brand 1988). Additionally, as the current war shows, the lack of any formal citizenship (unlike members of the Indian diaspora in Dubai, who have access to at least some Indian citizenship rights) has had serious consequence for Palestinians' ability to seek protection in times of crisis. The current war aside, the lack of formal citizenship, which means that refugees carry a Syrian *laissez-passer* rather than a passport, hinders the ability to travel outside the country. Additionally, although Palestinians in Syria have generally been treated favorably, especially when compared with their treatment in other host countries, some of them have found themselves "victims of occasional political purges of the Syrian government" (Baroud 2014). A prominent example is the violent crackdown on those who were members of *Fatah*, the Arafat-led political faction, following the 1983 fallout between then President Hafez al-Asad and Palestinian leader Yasser Arafat (Baroud 2014; Bitari 2013; Brand 1988; Talhami 2001).

Finally, while most Palestinian refugees have a status similar to that of Syrian citizens, which includes access to public health care, education, and employment, they have not, as a collective, been shielded from poverty or social hardship. According to the Norwegian Fafo Institute for Labor Research, "The poorest and most underprivileged Palestinians are predominantly found in rural settings where they tend to share living conditions with Syrian nationals living in similar surroundings (comparable access to educational institutions, medical facilities and job opportunities)" (Tiltnes 2007:8). Many of these Palestinians could be found in Neirab and Ein el Tal before the Syrian war, which is one of the major reasons that these camps became the target of the Neirab Rehabilitation Project. In the next section, I take a closer look at living conditions in these two camps.

The Sites of the Neirab Rehabilitation Project

Neirab Camp

Most of the Palestinian refugees who made their way to Syria were from the towns of Akka, Haifa, and Safad and surrounding villages in the northern part of historic Palestine (which is now within the state of Israel). While the majority settled in and around Damascus, some ended up in the north, around Aleppo. These refugees had first fled to Lebanon, where some stayed. Some who reached Syria did so unintentionally. According to refugee accounts, a number of Palestinians who had fled in 1948 to the Lebanese city of Tyre (Ṣur in Arabic) were rounded up by authorities and put on a train normally used to transport animals that took off in the direction of Syria. Those who experienced this voyage bitterly recount the fateful ride that would determine their new abode. They remember having to stand for hours surrounded by animal stench and dirt, watching some die of hunger, thirst, or exhaustion along the way.[8] According to some accounts, cars were disconnected from the train near various cities along the route as a means of distributing refugees across Lebanese and Syrian territory (UNRWA 2003:8). It was through this process that Neirab Camp came into being.

During my interview with Abu Hosam, the project liaison officer to the Neirab Rehabilitation Project, he recounted (in English) the long journey that brought him from the village of Jish in Palestine to Syria, where he became one of the first Palestinian occupants of the Neirab barracks:

> I was nine years old when the catastrophe fell upon us. It was a November day when two or three [Israeli] air fighters raided our village before sunset. After that, the people left their houses to neighboring fields in order to avoid bombs. After sunset some artillery began against the houses and villages. We spent that night in the fields and we thought–especially my mother thought–that our leaving was only temporary so she didn't take anything of the furniture or blankets except for one blanket to cover us. (Interview, June 1, 2005)

Abu Hosam and other villagers eventually sought refuge in a cave in a nearby valley, where they stayed until the following morning. When they received news that Jish had capitulated to Israeli forces, they decided to continue their flight, arriving in Yarun, a village in southern Lebanon. Abu Hosam recalled that his group of refugees was not warmly received: "They said to us, 'You destroyed your country and now you want to destroy ours'" (interview, June 1, 2014). The group continued their journey, which took them to Tyre:

> When we arrived [in] the city of Tyre, the Lebanese authorities there prepared [a large cargo] train. We boarded the train and we began our long journey knowing nothing about our destination. The train began to stop in some cities. It stopped in Beirut. Some families got off; we don't know how. Others in Homs in Syria, in Hama (also in Syria), we don't know how. Until we arrived in Aleppo city at the main station. There, a large pickup truck stopped in front of each wagon [train car] and we boarded these trucks to Neirab Camp. (Interview, June 1, 2005)

Named after the nearby Syrian village of Neirab, Neirab Camp is located 13 kilometers (8 miles) east of the northern Syrian city of Aleppo. At its center are the barracks, which in 1948 were long rectangular, zinc-covered buildings left over from World War II, when they served as shelters for allied troops and stables for horses. The ninety-four barracks remaining became shelters to approximately thirty-five hundred newly arrived Palestinian refugees. Each barrack was partitioned with flour sacks into one-family units (UNRWA 2003; Al-Hafiz 2006). During our interview, Abu Hosam recalled with a chuckle instances of people rolling over into a neighboring section at night while they were sleeping. Funny occurrences aside, the barracks were "draughty and squalid to the extreme," and newly arrived refugees were exposed to freezing winters and insect and rodent infestations (Azzam 2005; UNRWA 2003, 2007:7; Al-Hafiz 2006).

Abu Hosam also recalled that for many years the first Palestinian inhabitants of Neirab Camp used public toilets and baths (women bathed inside the barracks using large basins). In the 1960s, UNRWA replaced the partitions with concrete walls and built corridors to separate each barrack into two halves, each consisting of a row of rooms with doors opening to the outside. It also built wooden ceilings under the zinc roofs to stem the effect of extreme winter and summer temperatures. By the seventies, refugees themselves had started making changes in their housing. Those who had the means moved out of the barracks and built new accommodations for themselves on surrounding land donated by the Syrian government. There were no strict criteria as to how the space was to be subdivided, so people appropriated whatever space they could afford to build on.

Most of those who stayed in the barracks enlarged their one-room dwellings by appropriating the space between the rows of barracks for tiny kitchens and bathrooms. If the bathroom space was too small, some people bathed in the kitchen area, using the kitchen drains to evacuate the water (a situation that continued to exist at the time of my fieldwork). Finally, a few of the more affluent inhabitants bought additional rooms in the barracks from people who were moving out, enabling them to enlarge their dwellings and sometimes even build an additional story.[9]

As of 2005, there were seventy-two barracks remaining that housed some six thousand refugees out of a total camp population of approximately seventeen thousand (UNRWA 2003).[10] Demographic increase and finite space had resulted in a cramped camp with a maze of narrow alleys and very little public or private space. Neirab officially has an area of 148,000 square meters, with the barracks area having the highest density–89 persons per 1,000 square meters (or 89,000 persons per square kilometer) before the war. By way of comparison, the population density in Mumbai, considered one of the most densely populated city in the world, is 29,850 persons per square kilometer.[11] The density of the rest of the camp was roughly 38 persons per 1,000 square meters (or 38,000 persons per square kilometer) (UNRWA 2003; also see Chakaki 2006). It must be pointed out, however, that the limits of Neirab have expanded in a social sense, with wealthier

Palestinians buying land and building houses in part of the area immediately surrounding the official limits of the camp.

Much of the area surrounding Neirab's official boundaries is considered agricultural by the Syrian government, and according to Syrian law it is illegal to build on it. Thus, over the years the camp has remained physically isolated from other communities. For the purposes of the Neirab Rehabilitation Project, UNRWA went beyond the official boundaries, considering Palestinians living in the immediate vicinity of Neirab as a part of the camp. I do so as well in this book.

Despite space constraints, Neirab was bustling with activity at the time of my fieldwork. Close to the barracks was the marketplace, where camp inhabitants bought their daily supplies of meat, fruits, and vegetables. The main street, which runs through the market, as well the streets that border the camp's official limits, were lined with stores selling everything from pharmaceutical products to shoes and jewelry. Along those streets were also a few *shāwarmā* (skewered beef and chicken sandwiches), roasted chicken, and falafel stands. The walls of the camp were filled with posters and images of political parties, political activists, prisoners, and martyrs fallen for the Palestinian cause.

According to an UNRWA survey carried out in Neirab in the fall of 2005, 89 percent of Neirab's adult males were employed and about half of them had jobs involving skilled or unskilled manual work such as construction, blacksmithing, or carpentry; about 16 percent worked as teachers. Among the rest were a few taxi drivers, tailors, sanitation workers, computer technicians, office and medical workers, business owners (4 percent), and engineers (2 percent). According to the survey, 36 percent of the men in Neirab were employed by the Syrian government, 2 percent were employed by UNRWA, and 49 percent were self-employed (UNRWA and TANGO 2006).

As for the women, about 30 percent were employed, with the majority (64 percent) working as teachers (including a few university professors). Of the rest, a few worked as seamstresses (5 percent) while others worked in the medical field (6 percent) or managed food or childcare businesses in their homes (5 percent). Two percent of the working women (the same as for men) were engineers. Seventy-eight percent worked for the Syrian government, while only 6 percent worked for UNRWA. The survey found that, although the vast majority of men and a little less than a third of the women were employed, the amount of schooling received by men and women was similar. The fact that women tend to focus on child rearing and household chores once they get married and that men are considered responsible for providing for their family economically accounts for the difference in employment rates. According to the survey, the employment rate for men was somewhat deceptive because many men, especially skilled and unskilled laborers, were seasonal workers who could go long stretches of time without employment.

According to another UNRWA survey, carried out in 2006, the average monthly salary for Neirab Camp was 13,957 SP (Syrian pounds) per month, about $280/month–slightly below the Syrian average income ($300/month). Gaps in income among refugees were high and tended to align with the geographical location of camp residents. According to this survey, barracks residents had the lowest average monthly income (about $200/month). Those who fell into the lowest income category earned about $75/month (UNRWA and TANGO 2006). The average monthly income increased for camp residents living outside of the barracks and those living on private land on the outskirts of the official camp limits.

I wrote the following observations about Neirab Camp in 2008 before UNRWA began destroying the barracks. They give an idea of the camp's landscape before the changes brought about by the Neirab Rehabilitation Project:

> The lively character of Neirab Camp does not hide its weak and crumbling infrastructure and the many sanitary problems engendered by it. As one leaves the outer limits of the camp and gets closer to its center, where the barracks are located, crowdedness, tightness of space, and run-down accommodations battered by flooding, leaking, and humidity all coalesce to testify to the hardship that Palestinian refugees have traversed and continue to endure since they came to the camp in 1948. While they play an important role as a historical reminder of Palestinian forced displacement, the barracks, *al-baraksāt*, have also become for many refugees and project participants a symbol of the unacceptable in terms of what life as a refugee entails.

Figure 1.1. Neirab Camp, 1950.

Figure 1.2. Neirab Camp, circa 2005. Photograph courtesy of Thomas Ramsler.

Figure 1.3. Neirab's market street, circa 2005. Photograph courtesy of Thomas Ramsler.

Ein el Tal Camp

It could be argued that Ein el Tal, an "unofficial" camp situated about 14 kilometers (9 miles) northeast of Aleppo and housing approximately six thousand refugees, became part of the Neirab Rehabilitation Project by accident. Ein el Tal is bordered to the east and west by Syrian villages and to the north by empty, rocky terrain that the Syrian government exploits as a quarry. While a major highway connecting Ein el Tal to Aleppo passes right by the camp's southern edges, the bordering land to the south is largely vacant, making the camp a somewhat isolated place. When the Syrian government decided to donate the rocky arid land adjacent to Ein el Tal to help ease Neirab's density problem, project leaders decided that it would be unfair to have the people of Ein el Tal bear the brunt of the influx of newcomers–who were being provided with new houses–without benefiting from the upgrades being offered by the project. There were also concerns that new families might not be made welcome if they were perceived by longstanding Ein el Tal residents as enjoying better living conditions than those in the old part of the camp.

On a purely pragmatic level, the project team had to face the fact that Neirab and Ein el Tal were very different places and that while Neirab had no more space to grow it had many features that Ein el Tal lacked. To make Ein el Tal an attractive place to move to, the team promised to remedy its lack of a marketplace, the absence of public transportation all the way into the hilly camp, and the unavailability of water and electricity networks at the top of the hill, where the new houses were being built.

Also known as Mukhayyam Ḥandarāt for its proximity to the Syrian village of Ḥandarāt, Ein el Tal was established in 1962 after the Syrian government gave Palestinian refugees who had been renting homes in various parts of Aleppo the opportunity to build their own houses on land set aside for them. I became close to the family of one of the Neirab Rehabilitation Project volunteers, Ahmad Radwan. The Radwans–Ahmad, his brother, four sisters, and their parents–lived in a modest concrete house at the lower edge of Ein el Tal. The house had a veranda that opened onto a small yard with trees, bushes, flowers, and a chicken coop. This outdoor area was a comfortable place to spend time during the blistering summer days. Ahmad was a bit of a celebrity with foreign UNRWA staff, volunteers, and consultants in the early days of the project. Having graduated at the top of his class in philosophy at the University of Aleppo, he had been offered a scholarship to study at Harvard University on the condition of passing the Test of English as a Foreign Language (TOEFL) by a certain date. He ultimately was not able to satisfy those conditions.

I often visited the Radwans and joined them for lunch or dinner on numerous occasions while I worked in Ein el Tal. Regardless of the time of day, it was impossible for me to stop by their house without being fed at least a snack, even during Ramadan, when the entire family was fasting. Ahmad's father, a former UNRWA schoolteacher, was ill with leukemia and his mother worked as an accountant for a small Syrian company to support the family. Because of his sickness, Ahmad's father was always at home except for trips to the nearby mosque for daily prayers. When I came by, he was usually lying on a mat in the main living room or on the couch in the small "guest" living room, which also served as a study area for Ahmad and his siblings.

Ahmad's father had the habit of greeting each of my arrivals with a long list of grievances against UNRWA, which he felt had never taken serious interest in Ein el Tal residents and was not doing anything to help them. Among other issues, he complained about the high cost of his medical treatment, which he felt should be subsidized by UNRWA; the lack of appropriate medicine in the UNRWA clinic; the poorly functioning electricity and water services; and the fact that, in his opinion, the Neirab Rehabilitation Project was benefiting only newly arrived families from Neirab. Eventually the conversation moved to other topics.

During one of my many conversations with Ahmad's father, he recalled that when his family arrived in "Ḥandarāt" (Ein el Tal) it was simply a big barren,

Figure 1.4. Ein el Tal Camp, 2005. View from UNRWA's al-Zeeb School. Photograph by Nell Gabiam.

rocky hill with roaming foxes and wild dogs. He remembered how people carried soil from neighboring areas for planting trees and gardens and how they used stones from the rocky terrain to build their houses. Unlike Neirab, where people seemed to be sharing space in a cramped and haphazard way, houses in Ein el Tal were separated by large streets and small empty fields covered with clumps of grass often serving as pasture for residents' sheep and goats. Many of the houses had small yards.

According to a 2005 UNRWA survey, Ein el Tal had a 36 percent unemployment rate among men. As in Neirab, almost half of the employed men were involved in some type of skilled or unskilled manual labor, particularly construction, blacksmithing, and carpentry. Other jobs included teaching (7 percent), administrative work (8 percent), business ownership (8 percent), and street vending (5 percent). A little less than a third (28 percent) of the women were employed (for the same reasons as in Neirab), working as teachers (44 percent), seamstresses (8 percent), administrative workers (8 percent), medical assistants (7 percent), or hairdressers (6 percent). The 2005 survey noted that 46 percent of both male and female Ein el Tal respondents were employed by the Syrian government whereas only 1 percent worked for UNRWA (UNRWA and TANGO 2005). The average

Figure 1.5. Northern edge of Ein el Tal Camp by the quarry, 2005. Photograph by Nell Gabiam.

monthly income was reported as 11,918 SP/month (about $270/month). Families who had moved from the Neirab barracks to new houses in Ein el Tal, as a result of the Neirab Rehabilitation Project, seemed to be the worst off in terms of wage income. The monthly average earning for families in the project's new housing was a meager $90/month (UNRWA and TANGO 2005).

Ein el Tal's only clear advantages over Neirab seemed to be space and tranquility. It did not have a marketplace, and shops and food stands were few and far between; public transportation did not extend into the camp, forcing many to take a long walk uphill to get to their destination. While the streets of Neirab were bustling with people and activity from daybreak until late at night, the streets of Ein el Tal were quasi-deserted at night. The posters and graffiti that filled Neirab's walls were sparse in Ein el Tal. Neirab had the feel of a lively urbanized enclave, whereas Ein el Tal conjured the image of a sleepy hilltop village.

Project leaders became convinced that the Neirab Rehabilitation Project had to be extended to the entirety of Ein el Tal. Thus, when using the term *Neirab Rehabilitation Project*, and in line with UNRWA policy, I am referring to changes that happened in both Neirab and Ein el Tal.

Syria's Endorsement of Development in Palestinian Refugee Camps

The Neirab Rehabilitation Project was conceived on paper well before UNRWA officially decided to change its overall strategy to a focus on development rather than relief and basic services. The project later grew in scope and became an UNRWA pilot implementation of the agency's new developmental approach in Palestinian refugee camps. As mentioned in the Introduction, it was GAPAR employee and Neirab barracks resident Anwar Fanous who reportedly first brought Neirab's squalid living conditions to UNRWA's attention in the early 1990s.[12] However, GAPAR's Palestinian director at the time opposed an UNRWA proposal to rebuild the area where the barracks were located. In the late 1990s, this director's successor (also a Palestinian refugee and the current GAPAR director) became sympathetic to UNRWA's proposal and won the support of the Syrian government's upper ranks by successfully convincing them that camp improvement initiatives did not prejudice the Palestinian right of return nor were they tantamount to settlement.[13] While in the past the Syrian government had allowed UNRWA to renovate run-down camp housing on an individual basis as part of the agency's shelter rehabilitation program, it had been opposed to the kind of drastic and large-scale reconstruction and infrastructural changes UNRWA was proposing as part of the Neirab Rehabilitation Project.

When I asked GAPAR's director at the time, whom I encountered at an UNRWA-organized conference in October 2010, what had made the Syrian government change its mind about supporting the Neirab Rehabilitation Project, he responded proudly that the shift was the result of his ability to convince the upper echelons to support the project, but he did not elaborate.

Other factors account for the Syrian government's change in policy. During an interview, Anwar Fanous, GAPAR's representative for the Aleppo area, pointed to the trajectory taken by the Oslo peace process as the main reason for opposition to the Neirab Rehabilitation Project in the early 1990s. According to Fanous, it was a question of timing: UNRWA's proposal for the project coincided with the Oslo peace process, which had largely marginalized the refugee question and, related to it, the issue of refugee return. Fanous pointed to concerns in GAPAR and in the larger Palestinian refugee community that the Neirab Rehabilitation Project was connected to the Oslo strategy of marginalizing the issue of refugee return. In that sense, it was seen as part of an attempt to solve the refugees' situation economically (focusing on the improvement of their socioeconomic conditions) rather than politically (focusing on their political grievances and rights).

While GAPAR and the Syrian government as a whole eventually came to support the Neirab Rehabilitation Project, officially concluding that it did not threaten the right of return, this was not the case for all of Neirab and Ein el Tal's refugees. A speech given by GAPAR's director in December of 2005 gives some insight into the director's way of reconciling development in host countries with the goal of refugee return. The speech was delivered in Neirab as part of a joint UNRWA/GAPAR tour of all Palestinian refugee camps in Syria designed to collect feedback on UNRWA and government services in the camps. The meeting was an opportunity for representatives of the Syrian government to rally local support for the Neirab Rehabilitation Project, which had been facing some refugee resistance.

GAPAR's director pointed to the harsh conditions of Palestinian refugees living in camps in Lebanon and then to the harsh conditions encountered in the Neirab barracks. He reminded his audience of refugees from Ein el Tal and Neirab that GAPAR had turned down "20 million Euros" of foreign aid money in 1994 that would have gone into improving living conditions in Neirab. He pleaded with them: "Let's not let this new opportunity pass us by" and then asked: "Why does every improvement in our life have to be considered settlement? Would we [GAPAR] agree with the project if it were about settlement?" As for the right of return, the director said, "It is a right that is passed on from generation to generation, from father to son; no one can take it away from you." Even "the mightiest bombs . . . the harshest occupations" could do nothing to the right of return. He ended with the following assertion: "We will not be able to return without first developing ourselves so that we can be resilient [ṣamidīn]. This is how we understand [the Neirab Rehabilitation Project]. It does not compromise the right of return" (field notes, November 8, 2005).

The director of GAPAR was not only attempting to explain why the project did not threaten the right of return; he was also addressing US foreign policy as well as Israeli policy toward Palestinians. Indeed, a major source of distrust on the part of Palestinians in Neirab and Ein el Tal was the participation of the US government, a stalwart supporter of Israel, as a main project donor. It is also important to point out that the project was taking place against the backdrop of events of major political significance in the Middle East, events that pitted the Syrian and American governments against each other.

Not only did the Neirab Rehabilitation Project (as a full-fledged development project funded in part by the American government) begin roughly a year after the US invasion of Iraq in March 2003; it also started amid talk in American foreign policy circles that Syria should be the next country targeted for regime change (Hinnebusch et al. 2009). The project was also taking place against the backdrop of American accusations of Syrian responsibility in the assassination of former Lebanese Prime Minister Rafiq Hariri in February 2004 and, in its wake, intense American pressure on Syria to pull its troops out of Lebanon. Finally, it bears pointing out that the project was beginning at a time when Syria was being denounced by the Bush administration as a "state sponsor of terrorism," an accusation that pointed to Syrian support of groups such as the Lebanon-based Hizbullah as well as Hamas (the latter's outside leadership was based in Syria) (Hinnebusch et al. 2009).

It was within this larger geopolitical context that Syria and the United States became partners in a project officially seeking the amelioration of living conditions for Palestinian refugees living in camps. The United States was the biggest financial donor for phase 1 of the project, which would take place in Ein el Tal. The Syrian government, for its part, had donated land adjacent to Ein el Tal for the construction of new houses and had taken on the task of building, at its own cost, the water and electricity infrastructure for them. It was also building, again at its own cost, a sewerage network running through Ein el Tal, including the area where the new houses were being built.

Within a narrowly constructed humanitarian discourse, Syria and the United States were simply donors to a development project aiming to improve the living conditions of Palestinian refugees in Neirab and Ein el Tal. However, the larger geopolitical map reveals that the United States is a powerful international actor whose policies are usually not sympathetic to Palestinian interests. Part of the strategy used by the Palestinian director of GAPAR, as well other Syrian government representatives, to gain the trust of refugees in Neirab and Ein el Tal with regard to the Neirab Rehabilitation Project was to acknowledge the political ramifications of the refugee situation and lambast American foreign policy for being detrimental to the rights of Palestinians. Another strategy was to draw a parallel between the United States and Israel's treatment of the Palestinians and their treatment of Syria and to compare Israel's occupation of Syria's Golan Heights with its occupation of Palestinian land, thus emphasizing a common struggle between Syrians and Palestinians. At the same time, Syria was portrayed as a protector of the Palestinians, the embodiment of the rights of Arab people, and the main actor seeking to defend Palestinians against foreign aggression. All of these themes were raised by Syrian government representatives during the November 2005 joint UNRWA/GAPAR meeting with refugees in Neirab Camp.

The first official to speak at the meeting in the name of the Syrian government was Abu Raja, the representative of the Ba'th Party in Neirab who, like the GAPAR director, was a Palestinian refugee and (unlike the GAPAR director) was from Neirab. He promised the audience that Syria would struggle with the Palestinian people until the establishment of a Palestinian state with Jerusalem as its capital. "Palestinian refugees want to improve their life but don't ever want to give up on return," he added. He then went into a tirade against American foreign policy in the Middle East. In large part because of American pressure resulting from the assassination of former Lebanese Prime minister Rafiq Hariri in February of 2004, Syrian forces had had to withdraw from Lebanon in accordance with UN Resolution 1559.[14] Abu Raja asserted that "Syria has no relationship with the assassination of (Rafiq) Hariri" and argued that "those who have occupied Palestine and Iraq say this because they want to occupy Syria." He further claimed that "Syria did not go into Lebanon as an occupier." "At the same time," he continued, "Israelis have been occupying Palestine for more than 50 years and the U.S. does nothing about it. . . . Is this democracy?" He ended his welcome speech by refuting American allegations that the Syrian government sponsors terrorism, stating that "Syria is the first power that opposed the terrorists during the days of the Islamic Brotherhood" (field notes, November 8, 2005). Here he was referring to the Syrian government crackdown on the Syrian Islamic Brotherhood which, in the 1970s, began to challenge the government and its then leader Hafiz al-Asad. The standoff between the Brotherhood and the government culminated into the 1982 siege and partial destruction of the city of Hama, during which an estimated five thousand to twenty thousand people were killed (Seale 1988; Wedeen 1999).

Abu Raja was followed by GAPAR's director, who also began his speech by referring to US pressure for Syrian troops to withdraw from Lebanon. He argued that UN Resolution 1559, seeking the withdrawal, was against the Palestinian cause (*qadiyya*) and the right of return. He then argued that "the role of the international community is to apply international resolutions. Israel does not want peace. It wants to keep the Golan and Jerusalem and does not want to implement return. . . . All we ask for is return to the 1967 borders. . . . The United States is built on democracy and human rights but it won't even support this minimum. It does the opposite [of what democracy and human rights call for]." He also stated: "As Palestinians we resort to Syria first because Syria represents the rights of the Arab people. . . . Syria is Palestine. This is what we learned since we were little." He continued, saying, "We are with Syria because it is the steadfast Arab power [*al-qūwwa al-ṣāmida al-ʿarabiyya*]" and finally thanked President Bashar al-Asad for supporting the Neirab Rehabilitation Project, which "seeks to improve the lives of Palestinian refugees and defend the right of return" (field notes, November 8, 2005).

Following the speeches, several community members had questions about the project, questions that mostly expressed anxiety about who was truly behind it: Was it UNRWA, was it the donors, was it TANGO (Technical Assistance to NGOs)–the American consulting agency hired by the project team to carry out asset mappings in Ein el Tal and Neirab? The GAPAR director addressed these anxieties, understanding that they were linked to a fear that outsiders with little regard for refugees' interests were in control. He referred to the visit to Neirab by the US ambassador to Syria, which had taken place shortly after the assassination of Sheikh Ahmad Yasin, the spiritual leader of Hamas on March 22, 2004. He reminded the community that during her visit the ambassador had objected to a huge poster of Yasin on one of the walls of the camp and that refugees had refused to take it down. "This is a sign that Americans cannot silence us," he said. He also answered concerns from some refugees about the fact that the United States was UNRWA's biggest donor (which refugees viewed as a sign that the agency was vulnerable to American pressure). According to the director, the United State's prominence as a donor was a result of its not paying its dues to UNRWA for years and now having to make up for it. He added that the US government knew that if it didn't support the Palestinians, [the Palestinians] would "explode in their face" (field notes, November 8, 2005).

In light of this official government discourse identifying the plight of Syrians with that of Palestinians, it is rather interesting that during the community meeting in Neirab Abu Raja, the Palestinian Baʻth Party representative, and the Palestinian director of GAPAR reified the stereotype of Islamic/Palestinian terrorism that has gained traction (especially during the Bush administration) in American foreign policy toward both the Syrian government and the Palestinians. On the one hand, the Baʻth representative cast both Syria and the United States as victims of terrorism. By asserting that "Syria is the first power that opposed the terrorists during the days of the Islamic Brotherhood" and framing the Bush administration's "war against terror" as one in which both the Syrian government and the United States were fighting a common enemy (radical Islamists), Abu Raja collapsed the moral distinction that was being drawn at the time by the Bush administration between the two countries. For his part, the GAPAR director cast US funding of the Neirab Rehabilitation Project as implying US fear of Palestinian violence rather than US control of Palestinian destiny.

The overlap of Syrian and Palestinian identity and political destiny was not emphasized simply in Syrian government rhetoric. It was also emphasized in the socially embodied fact of Palestinians acting as Syrian government representatives. This situation raises questions about the exact boundaries of the Syrian state and where Palestinian refugees were located in relation to these boundaries.

The Limits of the (Syrian) State

In 1946 Max Weber famously defined the state as "a human community that (successfully) claims the monopoly of the legitimate use of physical force in a particular territory" (1946:78). More recently Anthony Smith defined the state as "a set of autonomous institutions, differentiated from other institutions, possessing a legitimate monopoly of coercion and extraction on a given territory" (Smith 2010:12). Others have defined the state as a site of symbolic, cultural, and imaginative production (Anderson 1983; Gupta 2012) or have urged greater attention to the affective dimensions of citizenship (Berlant 1997; Simpson 2014).

As seen earlier, the Syrian government construed Palestinians as internal to the Syrian state despite their lack of formal citizenship, by drawing on symbolic, cultural, and historical devices. Syrian authorities and their representatives asserted a mutual Syrian and Palestinian belonging to the shared geographical and cultural unit of Greater Syria and a mutual struggle to recover expropriated territory that had once been part of that unit. Syrian authorities also drew (at least rhetorically) on affective mechanisms to represent Palestinians as internal to the Syrian state project: shared outrage against the common experience of colonial amputation and Israeli expropriation of territory, and shared determination to reverse this situation.

If one thinks of the state as culturally and affectively produced, rather than simply as a set of institutions that have coercive power over a particular territory, Palestinian refugees are part of the Syrian state. Thus, they are informal citizens not simply through citizenship rights without citizenship status but also through the affective means of asserting that Palestinian refugees are a part of Syria ("Syria is Palestine"). Additionally, by engaging with refugees living in camps primarily through the prism of government officials who were themselves Palestinian refugees, sometimes from the very camps in which the Syrian government was operating, Syrian authorities were asserting a certain kind of kinship between the government and its Palestinian population.

On the one hand, the government's approach toward Palestinian refugee camps and, by extension, Palestinian refugees, can be seen as a form of resistance to dominant understandings of citizenship and, more specifically, as a form of resistance to empire and its imposed notions of nation-state-centered citizenship. In asserting that "Syria is Palestine" GAPAR's director was negating the colonial project that had led to the parceling out of the region into its current nation-state format. However, the Syrian government's approach to the Palestinian refugees must also be seen within the context of Syria as an authoritarian surveillance state and thus as a means of domination and control.

In her analysis of the authoritarian regime of former president Hafiz al-Asad, Lisa Wedeen argues that the regime's power depended on, in addition to punitive measures, a cult of personality around President Asad, who "came to embody and personify the Ba'th Party and its values" (1999:34). The Asad cult comprised symbols and rhetoric that derived their effectiveness from their disciplinary power, compelling Syrians to act as if they believed in the government's self-representation. Thus, Wedeen argues, the cult was based on compliance rather than on legitimacy. Despite Hafiz al-Asad's death in 2000, traces of his cult persist in government rhetoric (for instance, the reference in GAPAR's 2002 manual to Asad as "our everlasting leader"; see George 2003) and in the transfer of some of its elements onto the person of his son, Bashar al-Asad, who took over the presidency in 2000 after his father's death.

Wedeen argues that two elements of the Asad cult helped mitigate obvious exaggerations of Asad's persona as well as internal contradictions in the cult: family metaphors and the emotional bond that the Syrian government sought to create with the Syrian public. These elements were obviously present in GAPAR and Ba'th representatives' interactions with the Palestinian communities of Ein el Tal and Neirab. Both relied on family metaphors by referring to Syria as an elder, protective brother to Palestinians. They sought to create an emotional bond by invoking a common Syro-Palestinian struggle against foreign occupation and aggression. Such rhetorical devices served to build not just trust but also compliance with the Neirab Rehabilitation Project, in which the Syrian government was a prominent participant. Additionally, the overlap of the Syrian government and the Palestinian refugees, embodied by GAPAR's Palestinian staff as well as the government's use of Palestinians to represent the Ba'th Party and security organs in Palestinian refugee camps, enabled the government to spread its tentacles deep into the social fabric of these camps.

The climate of pervasive surveillance–the sense that one is constantly being observed, that anyone one talks to is a potential government informant–that characterizes sociopolitical life in Syria therefore extends to Palestinian refugee camps. I was to experience the reach of Syrian surveillance early on. Despite having formal permission from the Syrian Ministry of Foreign Affairs to conduct fieldwork among Palestinians, and despite having official permission from GAPAR to work as an UNRWA volunteer on the Neirab Rehabilitation Project, GAPAR and the state security apparatus were bent on controlling my movements in the camps and on limiting my interactions with refugees.

When I arrived in Aleppo in May 2005 to begin work as a volunteer, the project was in its first phase and was based in Ein el Tal Camp. UNRWA was still building new houses in Ein el Tal to which Palestinian refugees living in the Neirab barracks were supposed to be moving. Among the local Palestinian volunteers involved in this first phase was Muna, a single woman in her late thirties who would become a good friend. Muna was from Neirab, but was one of a handful of Neirab volunteers helping out with the project in Ein el Tal. A few weeks into my work in Ein el Tal, Muna invited me to attend a celebration she was having for the disabled children she worked with at the Women's Program Center (WPC) in Neirab. WPCs are community organizations established by UNRWA across Palestinian refugee camps but run more or less autonomously by the refugees (UNRWA 2015a).

Since I was working in Ein el Tal and not yet familiar with Neirab, I asked Ahmad Radwan, a project volunteer from Ein el Tal, if he would accompany me to that camp. Ahmad and I arrived on a late May afternoon and made our way toward the center. On our way, we passed UNRWA's office of Relief and Social Services and stopped by to say hi to Abu Hosam, Neirab's project liaison officer. A Syrian UNRWA employee who was also there asked Ahmad and me if we had informed "security" that we were coming. Hearing that we had not, he asked us what route we had taken into the camp. After hearing Ahmad's response, he concluded that we must have passed at least three camp security offices and that there was a good chance someone working in those offices had seen us. The UNRWA employee was especially worried about Ahmad being in trouble if he had been seen escorting me into the camp. He felt that the best course of action would be to call the camp's security office to let it know about our presence. Both the employee and Abu Hosam tried to reassure us that this was simply a routine procedure and that we had nothing to worry about, but Ahmad and I were extremely nervous; also, I felt bad for potentially getting Ahmad in trouble by asking him to accompany me to Neirab.

The message being sent to both Ahmad and me on that tense day was that I had no business being in Neirab because my duties as an UNRWA volunteer did not require me to be there at the time. After the UNRWA employee called the camp's main security office to inform it of our presence, the office in turn called GAPAR's Aleppo headquarters to inform them of the situation. A short moment later, a Syrian security representative appeared. He was none other than Raja, the son of Neirab's Ba'th Party representative, Abu Raja. Ahmad and I were allowed to proceed to the WPC and take part in the celebration, but were accompanied by Raja, who stayed on for the entire event. I later found out from Ahmad that he had not gotten into trouble as a result of the "incident," but he also explained that he had "contacts" that were high up that he could rely on in such instances.

The day before my visit to the Neirab WPC, I had spent some time on the outskirts of the camp with Wisam, another Palestinian acquaintance from Ein el Tal, who had offered to show me the camp without entering it because of uncertainty around whether or not it would be all right with GAPAR for me to be in the camp outside of my work with the Neirab Rehabilitation Project. I thought this visit had gone smoothly, but Wisam later informed me that he had been questioned by camp security after someone had informed them that he had seen us. Wisam flatly denied having accompanied me to the outskirts of Neirab and the security office dropped the matter.

As the project's focus moved to Neirab Camp in the fall of 2005, my presence there was not such a sensitive issue and GAPAR had a harder time policing my movements. For reasons that were never made clear to me, I was nevertheless initially forbidden by GAPAR to enter refugees' homes. While this decision was never explicitly reversed, over time and because of my duties, which involved conducting surveys and interviews with Neirab residents, I got away with transgressing it. However, GAPAR was intent on enforcing one major rule: UNRWA foreign employees or affiliates were forbidden from spending the night in either Neirab or Ein el Tal. I broke that rule once, staying over at my friend Muna's home at her insistence. This transgression apparently went unnoticed, but GAPAR was informed about another foreign volunteer having spent the night in the camp, which resulted in a reprimand of the project team. Anwar Fanous, GAPAR's representative for the Aleppo area, summoned one of the project assistants to his office and threatened to close down the volunteer program should he receive another report of a volunteer breaking the overnight rule.

All of these examples relate to my own experiences with Syrian security and surveillance, but the purpose of detailing them is to show the pervasive surveillance and control of everyday life in Palestinian refugee camps that reach deep into the camps as a result of the refugees' incorporation into Syrian state rhetoric and governing structures.

Syrian governance of Palestinian refugees cuts both ways. The government's extension of citizenship rights in the absence of formal citizenship is framed within a logic of Palestinian inclusion in the Syrian state project (even though Palestinians retain their "nationality of origin"). This logic emphasizes a shared Syro-Palestinian history and kinship, as well as a common struggle against Israeli and Western colonial aggression. Thus, my friend Muna, as a Palestinian, could boast about having taken part in the uprisings gripping the region in 2011 because her grievances as a protester reinforced rather than weakened state rhetoric and ideology. At the same time, the inclusion of Palestinians in the Syrian state project, despite the lack of formal citizenship, enables the Syrian government to solidify its surveillance and control of the refugee camps.

2 From Humanitarianism to Development

UNRWA *and Palestinian Refugees*

ON OCTOBER 28, 2005, during a community meeting in Neirab Camp, the head of UNRWA in Syria said, "For far too long, UNRWA has worked with Palestinian refugees as though it knows what is good for them, without really asking them" (field notes, October 28, 2005). This comment was made in the context of UNRWA's recent policy changes, which had centered on the agency's increasing embrace of the discourse of "development" in framing its assistance to Palestinian refugees. UNRWA's embrace of this discourse marks an attempted shift away from the agency's traditional forms of assistance, which had focused on the refugees' immediate and basic needs, toward forms concerned with their long-term, sustainable well-being (UNRWA 2005a). The official's acknowledgment indicates that it is not just the nature of the agency's assistance to refugees that must change but the very nature of the agency's relationship with them. UNRWA describes its now decade-long reform process as a move away from the paternalistic approach that had informed its humanitarian assistance to Palestinian refugees toward an approach that engages these refuges as "partners" in the effort to improve living conditions in their camps (UNRWA 2009).

That is the official narrative presented by UNRWA to explain its most recent set of policy changes concerning its role as the agency established by the UN General Assembly in 1949 to oversee international humanitarian assistance to the nearly 750,000 Palestinians who had become refugees as a result of the 1948 Arab–Israeli war. A careful examination of UNRWA's latest reform process, which was set in motion in 2004, reveals a larger and more complex picture: the process emerged from the intersection of local, regional, international, and global factors rather than as an autonomous, calculated, and coherent plan deliberately set in motion by the agency. Indeed, UNRWA's purported transition must be read within the context of dwindling economic support from UN member states; it must also be read as part of a broader shift in global refugee assistance whereby socioeconomic development is increasingly proposed as a mode of assistance in protracted refugee situations; finally, it must be read within the context of changes brought about by the advent and subsequent failure of the Oslo peace process, which began in 1993. Oslo had an effect on the views of Arab host states and Palestinian refugees regarding drastic changes to the infrastructural and socioeconomic fabric of refugee camps and in some cases had a direct effect on the landscape of the camps.

The Neirab Rehabilitation Project began in 2000, well before UNRWA's latest reform process was officially begun. It was initially limited to improving refugee housing in Neirab Camp's World War II–era barracks, which had been the only form of housing available when the camp was created in 1948. Although over time many refugees had moved out of the barracks and built their own houses nearby, about a third of Neirab's population (roughly 6,000 individuals) continued to live in the decrepit shelters. This limited version of the Neirab Rehabilitation Project was itself unprecedented: it marked the first time that the Syrian government, which had been invested in the idea of camps like Neirab maintaining their aura of temporariness, accepted UNRWA engagement in the comprehensive improvement of camp housing.[1]

By June 2004, which marked the official start of UNRWA's reform process, the Neirab Rehabilitation Project had grown to encompass the neighboring Palestinian refugee camp of Ein el Tal and had officially become a development project. As such, it had turned into an attempt to comprehensively improve both the infrastructure of the two camps and their socioeconomic life. The transformation of the project into a large-scale development effort followed UNRWA's decision to use Neirab and Ein el Tal as a laboratory of sorts for testing the feasibility of sustainable development in Palestinian refugee camps.

The Neirab Rehabilitation Project would play a major role in shaping UNRWA's new Infrastructure and Camp Improvement Program (ICIP), which was institutionalized in 2006 and is the most tangible outcome today of UNRWA's reform process. The ICIP has become a central component of UNRWA-led efforts to improve living conditions in the Palestinian refugee camps that are part of its areas of operation–namely, Gaza, the West Bank, Lebanon, Jordan, and Syria. For instance, the ICIP was the basis for UNRWA's approach in the (ongoing) reconstruction of the Nahr el-Bared camp in Lebanon, which was destroyed by the Lebanese army following the camp's infiltration by the radical Islamist group Fatah al-Islam. The ICIP was also the basis for recent improvement projects in the Rashidieh camp in Lebanon, the Arroub, Fawwar, and Dheisheh camps in the West Bank, and the Talbieh camp in Jordan (UNRWA 2008).

Emphasizing Development

Several factors help explain UNRWA's recent policy shift toward a focus on comprehensive development as opposed to emergency humanitarian assistance or basic social services in Palestinian refugee camps.

UNRWA's *Financial Crisis*

UNRWA's policy shift must be understood within the context of structural pressures on the agency. At the turn of the twenty-first century, UNRWA was facing a severe financial crisis. According to its own assessment, donations from member states were at an all-time low, poverty was on the increase in the refugee camps, and extended exile had resulted in overcrowded camps whose crumbling infrastructure was compromising their inhabitants' health and quality of life (UNRWA 2004; Hansen 2004). To address its funding crisis as well as its bleak assessment of living conditions in the camps, UNRWA organized a conference in June 2004 in partnership with the Swiss Agency for Development and Cooperation (SDC) in Geneva (UNRWA 2004), at which it finalized a Medium Term Plan, which had been the subject of conference review and discussion and which recommended that the agency turn to sustainable development as a primary mode of assistance to Palestinian refugees (UNRWA 2005a:2).

A Global Shift in Assistance to Refugees in Protracted Situations

UNRWA's purported transition toward a more developmental approach in Palestinian refugee camps "follows a broader reform process within the UN, including in agencies assisting refugees" (Misselwitz and Hanafi 2010:359). In 2003 the United Nations High Commissioner for Refugees (UNHCR) began to publicize steps it had taken to incorporate development in its policy on durable solutions for refugees (UNHCR 2003). UNHCR's reform process, which was initiated in the 1990s, came about because the agency was forced to acknowledge that protracted refugee situations were on the increase worldwide and tended to occur in the poorer countries of the global South; that governments were becoming less willing to extend asylum to refugees; and that donors were becoming less willing to fund "long-term care and maintenance–for example, provision of food rations–which such situations often entail" (Meyer 2006:2). UNHCR, which had begun formalizing its policy shift at the turn of this century, undoubtedly facilitated UNRWA's own transitioning toward development as a main form of refugee assistance.

In 2000, in parallel with its new emphasis on development, UNHCR began internally promoting community development, which calls for a participatory approach based on the inclusion of targeted communities in the planning and implementation of development projects (Calhoun 2010). In 2005, it published a handbook on how to plan and implement development projects in refugee communities. Such projects are officially part of the agency's Development Assistance for Refugees (DAR) programs. An interesting dimension of UNHCR's development approach is "the use of existing government and national structures, plans and processes as the basis for programme activities," which, UNHCR believes, will "assure national ownership and sustainability" (UNHCR 2005:vi). Thus, UNHCR's approach to development is one that seeks to incorporate refugees within their host country's national development project.

As illustrated in this book, UNRWA's vision of development echoes UNHCR's attempted shift in assistance to refugees. This is especially the case for UNRWA's promotion of development as a means to encourage sustainability and refugee self-reliance, its promotion of a participatory approach that views refugees as "partners" in project planning and implementation, and its use of existing government and national structures as a basis for envisioning and implementing development.

A Change in the Attitude of Arab Host States

A third factor behind UNRWA's recent reform process was the Oslo peace process, especially the post-Oslo climate. Officially, the main Arab host states–Jordan, Lebanon, and Syria–consider Palestinian refugee camps as temporary spaces that are to house refugees until they are able to exercise their right of return to their Palestinian homes. For this reason, they have generally opposed attempts to comprehensively transform infrastructural and socioeconomic conditions in the camps in the name of refugees' long-term well-being. While political interests also account for this position (see Al Husseini 2007), the host states have publicly framed their opposition to treating camps as permanent spaces as defense of the right of return, a right that finds overwhelming support among the refugees themselves (Al Husseini 2007). With the advent and subsequent failure of the Oslo peace process, the host states seemed to be more flexible regarding attempts to comprehensively improve camp conditions (Al Husseini and Bocco 2009; Oesch 2014).

Despite having granted Palestinian refugees a legal status similar to that of Syrian citizens, until the late 1990s the Syrian government had consistently opposed any comprehensive plan to improve living conditions in its official refugee camps. However, after several vetoes the government finally approved UNRWA's comprehensive rebuilding of the barracks area of Neirab Camp, and in 2004 the Neirab Rehabilitation Project went from rebuilding Neirab's barracks to officially becoming UNRWA's pilot development project for institutionalizing its proposed reforms.

The Syrian government not only gave its backing to UNRWA's expansion of the project into a full-fledged infrastructural and socioeconomic development effort; it became a major project participant as well. An UNRWA official whom I interviewed during my fieldwork attributed the government's change of heart to the failure of the Oslo Peace process and the realization that a solution to the Palestinian refugee issue was not close at hand. It was simply untenable, after almost sixty years (at that time) to continue to treat refugee camps as temporary spaces–a realization, he explained, that extended to other Arab host countries. This view is supported by Jalal Al Husseini and Ricardo Bocco, who argue that a major legacy of the Oslo peace process is the new "positive attitude" on the part of Arab host states toward the sustainable improvement of the physical infrastructure of Palestinian refugee camps as well as collective socioeconomic programs in them (2009:271).

It is also worth noting that representatives of Lebanon, Jordan, and Syria were present at UNRWA's 2004 Geneva Conference and that they endorsed the idea of sustainable refugee camp development. They also endorsed the argument, stipulated at the conference, that the comprehensive improvement of living conditions in the camps did not jeopardize the refugees' right of return (Budeiri 2014).

While overall there seems to have been a certain relaxation of the tendency in Arab host states to oppose changes to the physical and socioeconomic fabric of Palestinian refugee camps in the post-Oslo era, an overview of how each state has dealt with these issues over the years reveals a somewhat more complicated story.

In the case of Jordan, it was the prospect of normalization with Israel, brought about by the beginning of the Oslo peace process, that initially resulted in a change in policy with regard to the camps. Jordan holds the distinction of being the only Arab host state to have granted citizenship to its Palestinian refugee population. However, because it was important for the government that the camps remain temporary places and thus symbols of refugees' right of return (Al Husseini 2011), they were excluded from Jordan's socioeconomic development schemes. A year after signing its peace treaty with Israel in 1994, Jordan changed course and unilaterally included its Palestinian refugee camps in a national development program targeting the country's impoverished areas (Al Husseini 2011). This new openness toward comprehensively upgrading camp living conditions has continued in the post-Oslo era.

Lebanon presents a somewhat different picture from that of Jordan and Syria in its treatment of Palestinian refugees. Whereas Jordan extended citizenship to its Palestinian refugees and Syria granted them a legal status close to that of its citizens, Lebanon has generally curtailed Palestinian access to the social rights and services that its citizens are entitled to. Since the end of the Lebanese civil war in 1990, a consensus has emerged that sees the permanent settlement of Palestinians (who are mostly Sunni Muslims) as a threat to the country's fragile sectarian balance (Allan 2014; Suleiman 2010). This perceived threat has become the main factor in the current disenfranchisement of Palestinians in the country, who today face significant restrictions in employment, health, and property ownership (see Allan 2014; Peteet 2005; Suleiman 2010).

In line with its staunch opposition to Palestinian settlement, the Lebanese government has historically severely limited refugee camp expansion and reconstruction (Allan 2014; Chatty 2010). Most of the camps suffered massive destruction and some were totally destroyed over the course of the Lebanese civil war, which lasted from 1975 to 1990, but the government prohibited their reconstruction or replacement (Chatty 2010:5). In 1974, the Nabatiye camp in the south of Lebanon suffered massive destruction as a result of an Israeli raid. It was never rebuilt and its inhabitants never returned to it. Within the past decade there have been signs of the Lebanese government loosening its stringent policies toward Palestinian refugees. In 2005 it relaxed some of the restrictions on Palestinians in its labor law (Suleiman 2010). In 2009, it adopted a policy that "emphasized the necessity of improving the living condition of Palestinian refugees in Lebanon and mitigating their suffering until a comprehensive, just and durable solution is reached, based on implementing their right to return" (Suleiman 2010:16).

This apparent policy shift has remained largely symbolic and has not been accompanied by significant change in the lives of Palestinian refugees living in Lebanon (Allan 2014; Suleiman 2010). However, the post-2005 period did see a relaxation of the government's policy of banning construction material from camps (Suleiman 2010; Hassan and Hanafi 2010). This was also a period in which the government made an exception in its policy of preventing the rebuilding of destroyed Palestinian refugee camps: Nahr el-Bared, which had been destroyed in 2007 as a result of Lebanese efforts to uproot the radical group Fatah al-Islam from the camp, is in the process of being rebuilt. As mentioned earlier, this UNRWA-managed reconstruction is based on the agency's recently established Infrastructure and Camp Improvement Program, which is itself based on lessons learned from the Neirab Rehabilitation Project in Syria.

A Shift in Refugee Attitudes

Like the Arab host states, the refugees themselves have historically been concerned that their camps maintain an aura of temporariness. This can be understood as asserting their commitment to the right of return and as resistance to what they see as attempts to resolve the refugee issue through purely economic measures at the expense of political ones. For example, in Jordan it took ten years, and much persuasion by UNRWA, for Palestinian refugees living in tent camps to finally accept a move to more durable shelters in 1961 (Al Husseini 2011). There was also strong opposition in Lebanon and Syria to initial UNRWA efforts to improve conditions in the camps. Refugees in those countries organized strikes "against making any improvements, such as school buildings in camps in case this might mean permanent resettlement" (Feldman 2008b:507; UNRWA 1951). In some cases, refugees tore down houses that had been built to replace tents, and there was "widespread refusal to work on agency road-building and afforestation" (Feldman 2008b, citing UNRWA 1951). In 1960s Gaza, reactions to change were more tempered but refugees nevertheless expressed concerns "about maintaining the camps as visible symbols of displacement" (Feldman 2008b:508). Such concerns have carried over into more recent times. For example, noting in 2007 that only half of Gaza Strip residents were actually connected to the central sewerage system, Eyal Weizman states:

> When sewage overflows and "private shit," from under the ground invades the public realm, it becomes a private hazard but also a political asset. In some places, efforts by UN departments to replace existing systems of infrastructure with permanent underground plumbing have been rejected. The raw sewage affirms the refugee camp's state of temporariness and with it the urgency of claim for return. (2007:21)

The reluctance to embrace drastic change, especially when sponsored by outsiders, does not mean that Palestinian refugees steered clear of changing or modernizing the landscape of their camps themselves. However, concerns that such changes might give the impression that they were fully integrating into their host countries and no longer insisting on their right of return were always in the background. These concerns were a significant source of tension during the Neirab Rehabilitation Project, and they persist. Recent UNRWA camp improvement initiatives in Jordan and in the occupied territories faced a certain amount of resistance from targeted refugee communities (Budeiri 2014; Al-Nammari 2014).

While changes to the landscape of Palestinian refugee camps remain a touchy issue, there is a growing flexibility among refugees toward the idea of drastically altering infrastructure and living conditions. Once again, Oslo seems to have been a factor. In the occupied territories of the West Bank and Gaza as well as in Jordan, normalization with Israel and the growth that followed extended to camps near urban areas. In the West Bank and Gaza, this growth contributed to "weakening the existing taboos about camps having to be temporary spaces clearly distinguishable from cities" (Misselwitz 2009:255). Jalal Al Husseini (2011) notes with some surprise that Palestinian refugees in Jordan accepted the government's plans in the mid-1990s, following its peace treaty with Israel, to incorporate them into its national economic development agenda.

Oslo's failure also contributed to a weakening of the taboo against urban growth and major socioeconomic change in the camps. The focus on the creation of an independent Palestinian state and the marginalization of the right of return led to refugee fears, both in the occupied territories and in Arab host states, that the peace process was ultimately about achieving normalization at the expense of refugee rights (Misselwitz 2009). In the occupied territories, these fears were a source of Palestinian distrust toward the Palestinian National Authority (PNA), leading refugees to reject the incorporation of their camps into the PNA's governance structure (Misselwitz 2009). However, as it became clear with Oslo's failure that there was no imminent durable solution to the Israeli–Palestinian conflict, much less one that that might harm refugee rights, it became more acceptable to discuss comprehensive and long-term improvements: "Palestinian voices of dissent beg[a]n to challenge, with more courage and vigor, the hard line positions that rejected any physical or spatial improvement efforts in the camp" (Misselwitz 2009:314).

It is worth noting that the initial break in trust between the PNA and the Palestinian refugees in the occupied territories was not the sense that the PNA was focusing on state building rather than refugee rights but that Palestinian refugee camps had been largely left out of efforts to improve living conditions in the occupied territories following the end of the first intifada (which had taken a heavy toll on camp infrastructure) and the signing of the Oslo Accords (Misselwitz 2009). It is also worth noting that, while refugees officially distanced themselves from the PNA and its post-Oslo state-building efforts in the late 1990s, which were seen as normalization in the absence of a just solution to the refugee issue, there was an unprecedented building boom and unprecedented levels of urbanization during that period in Palestinian refugee camps in the occupied territories (Misselwitz 2009).

It is clear that one cannot reduce the historical and, to a certain extent, ongoing resistance of Palestinian refugees to outside efforts to drastically change conditions in their camps to a question of opposition to improvement. To account for the refugees' contradictory attitude and for the resistance faced by UNRWA as it attempted to institutionalize camp improvement in its areas of operation, it is necessary to take a closer look at the agency's history and the evolution of its relationship with Palestinian refugees. It is also necessary to examine UNRWA within its larger international context and pay attention to its relationship with its other stakeholders, including Arab host states, Israel, and Western donors.

UNRWA and Palestinian Refugees

In November of 1948, the United Nations General Assembly (UNGA), in response to the Palestinian refugee crisis, established the United Nations Relief for Palestine Refugees (UNRPR), which provided financial support to the various NGOs assisting refugees (Takkenberg 1998). Earlier that year, the General Assembly had tried to facilitate a political solution between the newly established Israeli state and Palestinian Arabs by appointing a UN mediator, Count Folke Bernadotte, who concluded that the exodus of Palestinians had resulted from "the panic created by fighting in their communities, by rumors concerning real or alleged acts of terrorism, or expulsion" (Takkenberg 1998:14). Bernadotte was assassinated in September of 1948 by members of the Stern Group, a radical Zionist organization, and shortly after the General Assembly adopted Resolution 194 recognizing the right of Palestinian refugees to return to their homes and their right to compensation for lost or damaged property. Resolution 194 also called for the creation of the United Nations Conciliation Commission for Palestine (UNCCP), which was established in December 1948 to continue political mediation.[2]

Today, UN Resolution 194 has become a cornerstone of Palestinian refugee advocacy for return. The right of return of individuals who have been displaced from their place of residence is also recognized in customary international law, in the four Geneva conventions, and in the Universal Declaration of Human Rights (Dumper 2007; Takkenberg 1998). For instance, according to article 13, paragraph 2 of the Universal Declaration of Human Rights, "Everyone has the right to leave any country, including his own, and return to his country" (Takkenberg 1998:234).

The UNCCP–composed of the United States, France, and Turkey–initially tried to promote the return of Palestinian refugees in accordance with Resolution 194 but failed to come up with a proposal endorsed by all parties. It then began to look into alternatives to repatriation, brushing aside the fact that the refugees themselves wanted to be repatriated. Under heavy pressure from the United States government, which privately favored the resettlement of refugees in their host countries, the UNCCP undertook an Economic Survey Mission in 1949 aiming to determine the feasibility of resettlement (Schiff 1995; Takkenberg 1998).

The survey recommended that "the United Nations carry out a program of 'public works' to employ Palestine refugees, start them on the road to rehabilitation and bring an end to their enforced idleness" (UNCCP 1949:vii). It also recommended that a new agency be created to continue providing refugees with relief and to carry out the recommended employment-generating projects. This agency, established in December 1949, would become known as UNRWA (United Nations Relief and Works Agency for Palestine Refugees in the Near East). In the meantime, the UNCCP, which had a protection mandate vis à vis Palestinian refugees, would continue to mediate Israeli–Palestinian peace negotiations, including negotiations on the refugee issue (Dumper 2007).

Although in 1950 the office of the United Nations High Commissioner for Refugees (UNHCR) was established to assist all refugees, Palestinian refugees were not absorbed in it.[3] Their exclusion was mostly due to fear from Arab states that, if included in UNHCR, Palestinians "would become submerged [with other categories of refugees] and would be relegated to a position of minor importance" (Takkenberg 1998:66). One of the major concerns was that "the . . . problem would not be adequately addressed if UNHCR's durable solutions, such as resettlement to a third country or settlement in the first country of asylum, were applied to Palestinian refugees" (Suleiman 2010:14).

During its first six years, UNRWA carried out "small-scale training and employment-creating projects," "medium-sized, government-controlled undertakings such as road building and tree planting," the "subsidization of a small number of refugees willing to resettle to Libya and Iraq to set up small businesses or farms," and "large-scale development projects" (Schiff 1995:21). Although never publicly acknowledged by UNRWA, large-scale development projects were to be the backbone of Palestinian refugee resettlement in the Middle East (Schiff 1995). For example, the United States, which was unofficially pushing for resettlement, was instrumental in devising a large-scale "water resource development" project in the Jordan Valley (Schiff 1995:36).[4] American planners expected that the project would be "sowing the seeds of cooperation among nations" and "absorbing refugee creativity and labor in a transformed Jordan Valley region" (Schiff 1995:13).

The economic development projects recommended by the Economic Survey Mission (the so-called public works program) proved unsuccessful because of political friction between participating Arab states and Israel (with regard to the large-scale water development project) and significant resistance from Palestinian refugees and leaders of the Arab host states who suspected that such projects would promote the permanent resettlement of Palestinian refugees in Arab states (Schiff 1995). In the late 1950s, UNRWA recognized that its public works program had failed and focused on continuing its relief efforts as well as offering "basic services" to Palestinian refugees, such as health and education. In the mid 1950s, UNCCP's activities had come to a standstill because of its failure to mediate a political resolution to the Israeli–Palestinian conflict.[5] This was of significance to Palestinian refugees because, in addition to its protection mandate toward them, the agency was charged explicitly with implementing paragraph 11 of Resolution 194 recognizing the right of return (Kagan 2010). With the cessation of UNCCP activities, the sole UN agency now responsible for the refugees was UNRWA, which had been given only a relief and welfare mandate.

Since the failure of UNRWA's "public works" program and the agency's subsequent focus on relief and basic services programs, its assistance has continued to shift in relation to changes in the refugee community, the expectations of host countries, the generosity of donors, and the political climate surrounding the Israeli–Palestinian conflict. Political scientist Benjamin Schiff (1995) discerns four periods in the history of UNRWA–refugee relations: UNRWA went from promoting regional economic development in the 1950s to reducing its operations to relief and basic services in Palestinian refugee communities in the 1960s. From 1967 until the early 1980s, it added emergency wartime assistance to its list of duties as refugees coped with the Arab–Israeli wars of 1967 and 1973, the Jordan–PLO war of 1970, and the Lebanese civil war, which began in 1975 and lasted 15 years. Additional refugees were created out of these wars, most notably during the 1967 Arab–Israeli conflict, which resulted in approximately three hundred thousand new refugees (Shiblak 2005).[6]

UNRWA's fourth phase was ushered in by the Palestinian intifada of 1987 and the sympathetic image Palestinian refugees were acquiring around the world. The agency witnessed an upsurge of donations from UN member states and was able to extend the scope of its activities. In the late 1980s and early 1990s, some thirty years after its public works debacle, the agency tried once again to focus some of its funds on development-oriented programs, albeit in a limited way. Successful this time, it instituted small self-support schemes including business loans and established Women's Program Centers (UNRWA 2015a).[7] In the 1990s, UNRWA also introduced (individual) shelter rehabilitation, water, and sanitation projects in Palestinian refugee camps (Takkenberg 2010).

Additionally, the fourth phase witnessed the incorporation of protection activities into UNRWA's mandate. Although protection duties had been progressively added to the mandate since the early 1980s (Kagan 2010; Schiff 1995), they increased significantly in the late 1980s and into the 1990s. For example, UNRWA officially embraced the role of witness in 1988 after the first intifada, when it added to its list of duties "protection by publicity" and took on the task of documenting human rights abuses carried out against Palestinian refugees (Schiff 1995). By 1993, the UN General Assembly was recognizing a direct protection role for UNRWA with regard to all Palestinian refugees (Kagan 2010). UNRWA now defines protection as "all activities aimed at obtaining full respect for the rights of the individual in accordance with the letter and spirit of the relevant bodies of law (human rights law, international humanitarian law, refugee law)" (UNRWA 2010:23).[8] The agency's protection duties include promoting a just and durable solution to the Israeli–Palestinian conflict; promoting refugee-respecting policies by host governments or occupying powers; delivering services in a rights-respecting manner; and integrating protection approaches in all aspects of programming (Morris 2008; UNRWA 2009). While UNRWA now considers "promoting durable solutions" as part of its protection of Palestinian refugees, it limits itself to calling for "a just resolution to the refugee question, and especially a strong refugee representation in the peace process" when referring specifically to the Israeli–Palestinian conflict (Kagan 2010:521).

I contend in this chapter that the relationship between UNRWA and Palestinian refugees has now entered its *fifth phase*, one that can be traced back to the UNRWA-SDC 2004 Geneva conference. While UNRWA managed to survive into the twenty-first century, it was facing extreme financial difficulties, prompting then UNRWA commissioner general Peter Hansen to publish a cry for help to the international community in the *International Herald Tribune* in May of 2004. In his appeal, Hansen pointed out that UNRWA used to spend $200 per refugee but that by 2004 the agency was only spending $70 per refugee. He also pointed out that voluntary donations from the international community had not kept up with the needs of refugees, leading to declining services and limited opportunities. Hansen ended with a reminder of the June 2004 conference called to plan new strategies for improving the lives of the refugees. He announced the theme of the conference as *helping the refugees to help themselves* through improved access to jobs, housing, education, and health care. (Hansen 2004; author's italics).

Shortly after the conference, in 2005, UNRWA finalized its Medium Term Plan, which had been the subject of conference review and discussion. The plan was presented as an UNRWA effort "to restore the living conditions of Palestine refugees to acceptable international standards and set them on the road to self-reliance and sustainable human development" (UNRWA 2005a:2).

This historical overview of UNRWA shows that "development" is not exactly new to the agency. In fact, UNRWA was originally created to implement small- and large-scale development schemes across the main Arab states hosting refugees, a mission encapsulated in the term "Works" in its name. Additionally, the language used in UNRWA's development schemes in the 1950s foreshadowed the language it is currently using to promote a more developmental approach in Palestinian refugee camps. Terms like *integration* and *rehabilitation*, as well as an emphasis on refugee self-reliance and economic resourcefulness, are present in both UNRWA's current vision and the vision that had guided it some fifty years earlier (also see Misselwitz 2009; Schiff 1995). However, the fact that UNRWA's 1950s development efforts were tied to a deliberate attempt to use development as a tool for refugee resettlement and as an alternative to return–a solution that the international community was officially facilitating at the time–would create an enduring trust barrier between the agency and refugees. According to political scientist Benjamin Schiff, referring to UNRWA's failed 1950s large-scale development schemes:

> Perhaps worse than the failure of the ambitious water plans, from UNRWA's standpoint, was the sapping of refugee confidence in the organization caused by the hypocrisy of proclaiming repatriation while planning resettlement. From now on, any change in UNRWA programs raised the bugaboo of a "liquidation plot" and contributed to refugee paranoia and cynicism. (1995:46)

UNRWA in Syria

The majority of Palestinian refugees I interviewed in Syria gave the most importance to UNRWA's role as a provider of social services. However, several argued either that, in addition to providing services, UNRWA had a political role or that it should have more of one. For instance, when I asked Samah, a fellow volunteer and the head of UNRWA's Women's Program Center in Neirab, what the purpose of the agency was, she said:

UNRWA is the main service provider [for Palestinian Refugees]. . . . It should offer more services than it does right now, because, honestly, it is decreasing services. For example, it should expand its services in clinics: more doctors, more education and health services; [UNRWA should] provide scholarships to study abroad, secure work opportunities [for refugees]. . . . Also it should have a political role. It should campaign and pressure the United Nations about the right of return of refugees. [UNRWA's] role is reduced to a social and humanitarian one. (Interview, December 30, 2005)

When I asked Samah's sister Muna, also a project volunteer, what UNRWA's role should be, she offered a similar answer:

[UNRWA] offers services but it's not enough. Our people are not getting what they are entitled to. But we want UNRWA to stay because as long as it remains we will be refugees. Israel doesn't want this. It wants to erase our cause [*qadiyatnā*]. . . . UNRWA should offer higher education because UNRWA is responsible for our people because higher education is very costly. UNRWA has really decreased its educational services. It used to distribute notebooks and pens to students. And its name is "relief and works agency for Palestine refugees" but most of its workers are foreigners and they have a very high salary, about five, six times what Palestinian employees earn. . . . [UNRWA's] role is that it is here to recognize the right of Palestinian refugees to return to Palestine. If UNRWA disappears, there will be settlement (of refugees in Syria), which we don't want. Also, [UNRWA] shouldn't decrease its services. It should return to the way it used to be. (Interview, December 30, 2005)

Taken together, Samah and Muna's responses are representative of perceptions held by Palestinian refugees about UNRWA that were prevalent during my fieldwork in Syria. A common complaint tied to the idea that UNRWA was primarily a service provider was that the services offered had gradually declined over the years. This complaint transcended economic differences and was often expressed by Palestinians who did not need UNRWA assistance. For example, Samah and Muna, who were both unmarried and therefore still lived in their father's household, were part of a prominent family in Neirab Camp. Their father had been a Fatah commander in Lebanon during the 1970s and 1980s, and they had several brothers who were working in the Gulf and regularly sent remittances to the family. Neither Samah nor Muna, in their mid-forties and thirties, respectively, needed UNRWA assistance for their everyday needs.

It is also worth noting that before the current war in Syria, only 6 percent of Palestinian refugees received humanitarian aid in the form of rations and other direct handouts (Takkenberg 2010), and those who qualified for it were deemed "special hardship cases."[9] Many of the refugees I interacted with were, nevertheless, critical of UNRWA's progressive decrease in its rations program. During a conversation with Bilal, a construction worker in Ein el Tal, who was by no means wealthy but was not in need of UNRWA rations, I asked why he was so opposed to the ration cuts, pointing out that many refugees were self-sufficient and that perhaps one day they all would be. Would he still defend rations then? "Yes, of course," he replied. "Us, we never took flour. My father was a government employee, and government employees don't take flour. But I defend the distribution of flour so that we remain refugees." Earlier in the interview, Bilal had explained to me that "flour is a symbol of refugeehood" (interview, June 21, 2005).

It is not unusual for outsiders and for some UNRWA staff, especially foreign ones, to reduce complaints about UNRWA's progressive curtailing of its services to a question of dependency on aid. However, as anthropologist Ilana Feldman (2007b; 2008a) argues, UNRWA humanitarian aid acquired very early on a political significance for its beneficiaries, a significance that is tied to UNRWA's definition of who counts as a Palestinian refugee and is therefore entitled to assistance. According to the UNRWA's definition, "Palestine refugees are persons whose normal place of residence was Palestine during the period 1 June 1946 to 15 May 1948, and who lost both home and means of livelihood as a result of the 1948 conflict" (UNRWA 2015b). Rations, then, functioned not simply as a tool of humanitarian aid but also as proof of the loss of one's home and consequently as proof of one's identity as a refugee. This created a situation in which "Palestinians quickly came to see this aid, not as charity, but as a right: a reflection of international responsibility for their condition" (Feldman 2007b:144, 2008a).

At a very basic level, then, UNRWA services continue to serve as proof that one was forcibly displaced from Palestine or that one is the descendant of such a person. A particularity of UNRWA's refugee definition is that it applies both to those who lost their homes and livelihoods in Palestine during the 1946–1948 period and to their descendants. With the issue of return marginalized in official negotiations aiming to end the Israeli–Palestinian conflict, registration with UNRWA and access to its services reaffirm historical ties to the Palestinian homeland as well as forced displacement from it. Thus, for political reasons, even refugees who do not need UNRWA services place importance on these services. This was often made apparent to me in Syria by Palestinian interlocutors who implied that their ability to retain their identity as refugees and therefore their political claim to the Palestinian homeland was linked to the continuation of UNRWA and its services in Palestinian refugee camps.

This link was also apparent in non-Syrian contexts. During a visit to an UNRWA clinic in Bourj al-Barajneh Camp in Beirut in 2009, one of the clinic's Palestinian doctors explained that refugees from the camp routinely scheduled health appointments even when they did not need them out of fear that if they did not use UNRWA's health services they might disappear from the agency's registration rolls.

The notion that UNRWA aid is not charity but a reflection of international responsibility for the plight of refugees continues to be a potent one in Palestinian refugee camps. It explains why I often heard refugees, usually when expressing discontent with the agency, assert that UNRWA "works" for them and therefore should be more responsive to their desires and demands, including political ones. It is not surprising that both Samah and Muna criticized UNRWA for not being more politically supportive. This was a criticism that I heard frequently from Palestinians in Syria and that often meant that UNRWA should play an active role in defending the right of return. Indeed, many of the refugees I talked to did not adhere to the separation between the humanitarian and political realms that UNRWA officially embraces. In a 2010 speech, former UNRWA general commissioner Philippo Grandi argued that UNRWA's mission did not extend to matters in the political realm:

> [The agency does not have the power to] bring about Palestinian unity and the contiguity of the West Bank and Gaza; an end to the occupation; a negotiated conclusion of the Israeli–Palestinian conflict; the establishment of a viable State of Palestine; and the realization of a just and lasting solution to refugees' plight. (Grandi 2010)

UNRWA's official philosophy of political noninterference is not shared by the many local Palestinian organizations that provide social services to Palestinian refugees living in camps, where political factions are prominent in running charities and overseeing social programs. In Ein el Tal at the time of my fieldwork, community-based charities were run by political factions such as Hamas, Fatah, and the Islamic Jihad (UNRWA and TANGO 2005); Neirab had a kindergarten for low-income families as well as a youth center linked to the Popular Front for the Liberation of Palestine (PFLP), and other Palestinian political parties sponsored youth groups; some had women's committees that were more or less active. Neirab was home to the Palestinian Charitable Organization (al-Jam'iyya al-Khayriyya al-Filasṭiniyya), whose board consisted of Palestinian Ba'th Party members and representatives of various Palestinian political factions as well as independent members (UNRWA and TANGO 2005). Generally the various political factions, whose rhetoric emphasizes Palestinian resistance, liberation, and return, were active in local attempts to provide social services to camp dwellers.

Linked to UNRWA's perceived roles as a provider of services, a symbol of international responsibility, and a source of international visibility for the "Palestinian refugee" identity, another role was emphasized by refugees during my fieldwork: that of witness to Palestinian suffering. "Really, UNRWA is the only witness to the suffering of the Palestinian people and it is the only one that can translate this suffering to the rest of the world," said Younes, a Palestinian project volunteer, during an interview (interview, January 1, 2006). The role of witness has been more or less acknowledged by UNRWA, which has documented the hardships faced by refugees in its areas of operation since the 1980s.

The importance of international organizations acting as witnesses to Palestinian suffering has been discussed by others. Anthropologist Lori Allen (2009) argues that visual media displays of suffering, bloodied, and mangled Palestinian bodies has become a means for Palestinians in the occupied territories to communicate their humanity and the justice of their cause to the outside world. Anthropologists Didier Fassin and Richard Rechtman (2009) note that, while refugees in the occupied territories have adequate local medical services, they value the presence of humanitarian organizations such as Médecins Sans Frontières because of the role they play as witnesses to their plight under Israeli occupation.

Whether it likes it or not, UNRWA is seen by Palestinian refugees as a de facto ally when it comes to publicizing their suffering to the rest of the world, maintaining their visibility as refugees–and consequently the visibility of the issue of return–and acting as a symbol of international responsibility for the Palestinian refugee situation. However, the agency is concurrently seen by refugees as not fully trustworthy and as a potential threat to Palestinian political claims. Related to the complaint that UNRWA is not politically supportive enough, a common complaint among Palestinians in Syria was that it was under the control of Western countries, specifically the United States, which happens to be the agency's biggest bilateral donor (UNRWA 2013b). A 2013 UNRWA report features the United States and the European Commission in the top two donor spots followed by twelve European countries (UNRWA 2013b). Such information leads to the common refugee argument that UNRWA is under the influence of countries whose foreign policy is generally favorable to Israel.

The following example, based on fieldwork conducted in Yarmouk in 2004, captures the disconnect between UNRWA's official understanding of its mission as nonpolitical and Palestinian refugees' expectations. Not only does this disconnect create friction between Palestinian grassroots organizations involved in efforts to improve conditions in the camps; it also plays a major role in perpetuating refugee distrust of UNRWA.

One morning in August of 2004, I met with a foreign Damascus-based UNRWA employee involved with projects in various Palestinian camps in Syria, including Ein el Tal, Neirab, and Yarmouk. The employee had recently joined UNRWA and was interested in promoting activities for youth in the camps where he worked and in establishing spaces for cooperation between locally run organizations in the camps and UNRWA. He had invited me to accompany him to a meeting with members of the Yarmouk Youth Center.[10] As is typical of youth centers in Palestinian refuge camps in Syria, this one was linked to one of the many camp-based political parties.

When we arrived, a group of Palestinians in their late teens and early twenties were in the middle of a workshop with European youth as part of a youth exchange program sponsored by a Belgian NGO. Refugees from other camps in Syria as well as from camps in Lebanon were also participating. The center was showing a documentary about living conditions in various Palestinian refugee camps in the Middle East, and we were invited to watch. The film focused on harsh living conditions and featured interviews with refugees of varying ages, all of whom emphasized how much they wanted to return to their homeland.

Afterward, youth center members and some of their European guests sat in a circle with us, and the UNRWA employee (who had invited me to the meeting) proceeded to ask them how UNRWA could help them with their social activities. The conversation quickly turned into an airing of grievances. The Palestinian participants felt that UNRWA services had declined in the Damascus and Aleppo areas. One complained that UNRWA schools were overcrowded, limiting students' ability to learn basic skills such as reading. Another lamented the fact that UNRWA had stopped distributing free school supplies such as notebooks and pencils. He also complained that refugees were not allowed to bring up topics relating to Palestinian nationalism in UNRWA classrooms. A third participant criticized UNRWA for not covering surgery costs and for not doing enough to improve the infrastructure of various camps. Finally, a participant complained that UNRWA was under the influence of the American government.

The UNRWA employee tried to address every complaint. With regard to restrictions on Palestinian nationalism in UNRWA classrooms and undue American influence, he simply replied in English that UNRWA was "a humanitarian organization that does not interfere [in] politics." To this, the Palestinian participant who made the original complaint retorted in Arabic: "But the United States interferes in everything! [*bas Amrīka btidakhal bi-kill shi!*]," drawing laughs from the rest of the group (field notes, September 8, 2004).

A few months after my visit to the youth center, I joined the UNRWA employee in planning a celebration of International Volunteer Day sponsored by UNRWA and the United Nations Development Programme (UNDP). The two-day celebration involved workshops attended by various local and international organizations, ending with a fair featuring displays by various organizations and cultural centers promoting their social activities. UNRWA and UNDP officials were worried that the Yarmouk Youth Center, which was participating in the event, might use the celebration to focus attention on political grievances in connection with the Israeli–Palestinian conflict or, more specifically, the right of return. They therefore made it clear that they did not want any political messages in its display.

The time to set up for the fair eventually came. The youth center's display consisted of Palestinian embroidery, pictures drawn by children attending the center's programs, and posters. A bright red poster advertised the center's volunteer-taught classes for camp children, a theme that fit perfectly with the goals of UN volunteer day. However, because it held the image of a Palestinian fighter wearing a *keffiyyeh* (a traditional Arab headdress that has become a Palestinian national symbol) along with the word *intifāḍa* in big capital letters, it immediately attracted the attention of a high-ranking Palestinian UNRWA employee, who demanded that it be taken down. The center complied but managed to keep the other posters up. One featured a giant gray wall with unfamiliar writing on it. I later found out that the writing was Dutch for "Take down the wall [*sloop de muur*]," a reference to the Israeli-built wall along the occupied territories. Another that had apparently escaped the Palestinian UNRWA employee's scrutiny featured the face of a young woman with fragments from a Spanish text that seemed to be from a poem or speech scribbled across her face. A close look at what appeared to be an earring revealed that the shape resembled the barrel of a gun. I was to find out later that the statement at the bottom of this poster, written in Danish, declared "Freedom struggle is not terrorism [*befrielseskamp er ikke terrorisme*]."

The UNRWA employee who had introduced me to the Yarmouk Youth Center was furious. He felt that the center's leaders had been offered an excellent chance to work with UNRWA that would have provided them with opportunities to strengthen their center but had wasted it by using the International Volunteer Day fair as a political platform. He was very disappointed in the center and vowed never to work with its members again. The leaders' views were more nuanced. While they were frustrated with UNRWA's censorship of their display, one of them, Ibrahim, made sure I understood that "UNRWA is not our enemy." According to Ibrahim, the center did not necessarily see the agency as working against it, but it definitely had a different strategy for helping Palestinian refugees, and working too closely with the agency could be harmful to its interests. Ibrahim's mixed feelings are supported by research conducted in 2006 showing that, despite their criticisms, Palestinian refugees are almost unanimously attached to the continuation of the agency (Nabulsi 2006).

One factor that helps make sense of the mixed feelings of the leaders of the Yarmouk Youth Center is that roughly 99 percent of UNRWA employees are themselves Palestinian refugees (Farah 2010). Thus, there is a significant overlap between UNRWA and the refugees for whom it was created. It is important to note, however, that foreigners–usually Westerners–hold the reins of power because they fill UNRWA's top leadership positions. Benjamin Schiff notes that "the internationals are supposed to maintain the agency's political neutrality, uphold management standards, and intervene with the host/occupying governments (in ways Palestinians, subject to local laws and political constraints, could not) when necessary" (1995:148). He also notes that "the leading local staff had to tread carefully between commitments to the Palestinians and loyalties and duties to UNRWA" (1995:145). A similar situation exists today. On the one hand, Palestinian UNRWA employees can be seen as intermediaries who make the agency's supposedly apolitical policies more palatable to Palestinian refugees, as in the case of the Palestinian employee who demanded that the Yarmouk Youth Center take down one of its posters. On the other hand, they can be seen as inserting the agency's programs into narratives that accommodate Palestinian nationalism and political claims. For example, referring to UNRWA schools in Jordan (the overwhelming majority of UNRWA teachers are Palestinian), anthropologist Randa Farah notes that lessons in Palestinian nationalism and history "went beyond what was required in the Jordanian curriculum, and in fact contravened UNRWA and state regulations," attesting to "the failure of UNRWA to mute the political dimension of refugee histories or to generate complacency" (2010:403).

To make sense of the complicated relationship between UNRWA and Palestinian refugees, especially the latter's lack of trust in the former, it is crucial to recognize that UNRWA is not a monolith. Rather, it is a hybrid characterized by the overlap of the Western-dominated political order that oversaw its creation and the very Palestinian refugees it was created to assist. UNRWA's practices are susceptible to pressure from donor countries as well as from Israel, from the Arab host states in which it operates, and from Palestinian refugees themselves. Randa Farah captures the agency's unstable boundaries:

> UNRWA is not a fixed and homogeneous institution; rather, it is an evolving body and a space fraught with contradictions, due to the fact that it is embroiled in local, regional, and international politics. The agendas and interests of various states and institutions that impinge or directly influence the Agency may collude or collide, including the interests of refugees, refugee-employees of the Agency, the PLO/PA or Hamas, donor states, Arab host-states, and Israel. Each of these actors tries to pull it in a certain direction and inscribe it with particular meanings and functions. Thus, for example, western powers (many of them UNRWA's primary donors) have generally adopted Israel's position on the refugee issue. By contrast, Palestinian refugees, including those who fall under UNRWA's mandate, regard their political and legal rights as non-negotiable. Thus, within UNRWA the interests of refugees and those of western powers are inherently contradictory. (2012:4)

The Different Perceptions of UNRWA

Acknowledging UNRWA's imbrication in local, regional, and global politics, Rex Brynen (2014) argues that it "is subject to many multiple, competing, and even incommensurate perceptions and representations" that are partly the result of the different narratives surrounding the creation and perpetuation of the Palestinian refugee problem (2014:264). From the point of view of Palestinian refugees, UNRWA's services and its continuation as an agency are partly a matter of international responsibility for the refugee problem. Such responsibility is primarily assigned to Western countries given their dominant role in the United Nations, which endorsed the partition of Palestine in 1948. Refugees also assign responsibility to Israel for the forced displacement of Palestinians in 1948 and 1967.[11] Arab host states generally share the Palestinian narrative about the causes of the Palestinian refugee issue as well as the notion that UNRWA's services and its continuation as an agency are a matter of international responsibility. This position is at least partly linked to practical considerations because Arab host states do not want to shoulder the entire cost of refugee assistance. Moreover, despite its implied solidarity with Palestinian refugees, this position does not prevent Arab host states from simultaneously viewing the refugees as a potential security risk (Brynen 2014:264).

Departing from the above narratives, the international community and, more specifically, UNRWA's major donor countries, do not provide agency funding out of a sense of collective responsibility for creating the Palestinian refugee issue but for utilitarian reasons:

> as part of their broader relations with host countries, as a way of dealing with the particular complexities caused by Hamas control of Gaza and the Israeli-Egyptian embargo [on Gaza], and as means of reducing the challenge of "radicalism" and "extremism" among refugees and within refugee camps. (Brynen 2014:269)

Furthermore:

> Few (if any) of UNRWA's major donors would regard the refugees as having any unambiguous "right of return" after three generations, and very few (if any) would regard UNGAR 194 as establishing such a right. More to the point, these are simply not issues that the Agency' major donors spend any at all time considering. (Brynen 2014:269)

Israel rejects any significant responsibility for the forced displacement of Palestinians in 1948 and 1967, arguing that Arab opposition to the 1948 UN partition of Palestine was the source of the refugee situation (Brynen 2014). Some UNRWA views emanating from Israel and from Western donor countries, and the kinds of policy initiatives that these views encourage, are especially pertinent in terms of elucidating refugees' enduring distrust toward the agency. More generally, they help explain the contradictory and ambivalent ways in which refugees have engaged and continue to engage with internationally funded projects officially aiming to improve living conditions in the camps.

For some time now, Israeli and Western critics of UNRWA have accused the agency of encouraging refugee dependency and/or political radicalization (Farah

2012). Much of this criticism is summarized in a 2009 report on UNRWA written by James Lindsay for the Washington Institute for Near East Policy, a Washington-based think tank that seeks to "advance a balanced and realistic understanding of American interests in the Middle East and to promote the policies that secure them" (The Washington Institute 2015).

Titled "Fixing UNRWA: Repairing the UN's Troubled System of Aid to Palestinian Refugees," Lindsay's report identifies several shortcomings in UNRWA operations, among them UNRWA's incomplete shift from status-as-refugees-based to need-based assistance. It sees UNRWA's curbing of its ration distribution system over the years as a step in the right direction, but laments the fact that its other programs continue to be available to all Palestinians rather than solely to those who need them.

Another major criticism in the report is that, despite remaining UNRWA's single biggest individual donor since the agency's creation, the United States has been unsuccessful in making UNRWA reflect American foreign policy objectives. Lindsay argues that the agency was initially created to serve the United States' humanitarian agenda but that it has often clashed with US policies. In this respect, the report accuses UNRWA of anti-Israel pronouncements and of endorsing engagement with Hamas, and it criticizes what it sees as the agency's support of the right of return (2009:49, 59). More generally, the report laments what it sees as UNRWA's increasing identification with Palestinian political views as opposed to holding with what is described as the agency's original mandate of promoting refugee resettlement (2009:23). Lindsay recommends that UNRWA return to its initial goal of ending the refugee status of Palestinian refugees through resettlement, to be achieved by taking Palestinians who have citizenship off UNRWA rolls (which would mainly affect Palestinian refugees in Jordan), promoting the integration of Palestinian refugees into their places of residence, and planning for Palestinians who are not able to become host-state citizens to become citizens of a future Palestinian state in the West Bank and Gaza (Lindsay 2009).

Lindsay argues that in order to achieve the goal of turning Palestinian refugees into full-fledged citizens, and thus ending their refugee status, UNRWA needs to revise its definition of a Palestinian refugee. Contrasting UNRWA's definition with UNHCR's,[12] Lindsay criticizes the fact that UNRWA interprets refugees not only as the actual refugees who were displaced as a result of the 1948 war but also as their descendants, thus contributing to the increase rather than decrease of refugees over time.

Lindsay's criticism of UNRWA was echoed in a 2011 speech by Israel's former deputy foreign minister Danny Ayalon at a conference marking the sixtieth anniversary of the Convention Relating to the Status of Refugees.[13] Ayalon accused UNRWA of perpetuating the Israeli–Palestinian conflict by not finding a permanent solution to the refugee situation. Like Lindsay, he chastised UNRWA for including the descendants of 1948 refugees on its registration rolls, arguing that while UNHCR "helps refugees resettle, the United Nation's Palestinian refugee agency helps perpetuate their status by applying unique criteria" (Keinon 2011). These views have been echoed by other Western and Israeli critics of UNRWA and have established a significant and recurring internet presence (see Brynen 2014).[14]

Criticisms such as these were reflected in a proposed amendment to the 2013 foreign appropriations bill put forth by Mark Kirk of the US Senate Appropriations Committee. The amendment sought to require confirmation of the number of Palestinians who were physically displaced from their homes in what are now Israel and the occupied territories and the number of their descendants. Senator Kirk's office reportedly explained that the amendment was to be a simple reporting mechanism aiming to clarify how taxpayers' funds were being used and would have had no effect on US funding of UNRWA (Francis 2012). However, the amendment stirred a lively debate between UNRWA's critics and defenders. For supporters, the amendment was a welcome initial step in redefining who counts as a Palestinian refugee and in putting an end to UNRWA's policy of including the descendants of those who physically fled or were expelled from Palestine in 1948 and 1967. For critics it was "just a first step in a longer effort to cut off funding for UNRWA and deny millions of Palestinians the 'right of return' to lands their parents and grandparents lost in 1948 and 1967" (Francis 2012). A May 2012 article by Jonathan Schanzer seems to give credibility to the latter view. It explains that, according to Senator Kirk's office, the aim of the proposed legislation

> is not to deprive Palestinians who live in poverty of essential services, but to tackle one of the thorniest issues of the Palestinian–Israeli conflict: the "right of return." The dominant Palestinian narrative is that all of the refugees of the Israeli–Palestinian wars have a right to go back, and that this right is not negotiable. But here's the rub: By UNRWA's own count, the number of Palestinians who describe themselves as refugees has skyrocketed from 750,000 in 1950 to 5 million today. As a result, the refugee issue has been an immovable obstacle in round after round of negotiations between the Israelis and Palestinians. (Schanzer 2012)

It is clear that Schanzer adheres to the notion that UNRWA–which he refers to as "a silent partner of the PLO"–contributes to the perpetuation of the Israeli–Palestinian conflict through its continued existence and, especially, its practice of including descendants in its Palestinian refugee count. This view, which is also reflected in criticism of the agency by Lindsay and Ayalon, is important to an understanding of the controversies surrounding the Neirab Rehabilitation Project and the skepticism with which Palestinian refugees in Ein el Tal and Neirab greeted it. It helps explain refugees' fears that UNRWA serves as a vehicle for achieving the foreign policy goals of Israel and its Western donors, specifically the United States. The argument that UNRWA's continued existence and its definition of who counts as a Palestinian refugee perpetuates the Israeli–Palestinian conflict is a matter of debate rather than consensus in American and Israeli political circles (see Brynen 2014; Francis 2012; Schanzer 2012). However, it contributes to Palestinian refugee fears about UNRWA being a tool of Western influence that is bent on circumventing a political resolution to the refugee issue by engineering the agency's gradual dissolution and putting an end to Palestinians' refugee status through permanent resettlement. Finally, the arguments made by Schanzer, Lindsay, and Ayalon illustrate the ways in which social integration and formal citizenship in a host country or in a future Palestinian state, consisting mostly of the West Bank and Gaza, are seen by critics of the right of return as mechanisms that will render this right irrelevant to a negotiated Israeli–Palestinian peace.

The views of UNRWA's critics highlight its perceived political role in upholding the political claims of Palestinian refugees, which helps explain the ironic situation in which Palestinian refugees criticize the agency for not being supportive of their political claims while Israeli and Western detractors denounce it as perpetuating those claims. The notion that UNRWA is behind continued refugee advocacy for the right of return is not particularly convincing, however, in that it does not account for why such advocacy is as strong among camp refugees as it is among noncamp refugees (see Brynen 2014). Additionally, the reality on the ground tells a more complicated story about the relationship between UNRWA and Palestinian refugees than the narratives crafted through the perceptions of the agency's various stakeholders. This reality is the focus of the next chapter, which examines the implementation of the Neirab Rehabilitation Project.

3 Ṣumūd and Sustainability

Reinterpreting Development in Palestinian Refugee Camps

IN LATE MARCH 2004, a ceremony took place in Ein el Tal to celebrate the inauguration of the first phase of the Neirab Rehabilitation Project. This initial phase aimed to build new housing in Ein el Tal, to which about three hundred families from Neirab's barracks would be moving, as well as improve infrastructural and socioeconomic conditions in the camp in general. The ambassadors of the United States, Switzerland, and Canada, the three foreign donor countries for phase 1, were invited. UNRWA officials, the Palestinian director of GAPAR, and the Syrian governor of Aleppo were also in attendance. A former UNRWA employee in the camp that day helping to set up for the inauguration, which was to take place in an open area close to the construction site for the new UNRWA-built houses, recalled the events of that morning: shortly before the trio of ambassadors were to arrive, having first stopped in neighboring Neirab Camp, a truck loaded with young men holding banners and chanting against the project appeared. The protesters got off the truck, and others joined them. They soon overwhelmed the few local bystanders who had been watching UNRWA staff set up for the inauguration. According to the former UNRWA employee, the young men were protesting against both the US ambassador's visit and the project itself primarily because of American participation.

The timing of the inauguration is crucial to understanding the events of that day, as the former UNRWA explains:

> I think the issue was the American Ambassador coming to the camps and Americans paying for this project. And I want again to remind you of the timing, and the situation of the war in Iraq. Some of the people, young people from the camp went there [to Iraq], including one guy who died there fighting Americans. I remember [that] during that period I stayed in the camp a couple of times, [I] stayed in somebody's house at night and they showed me pictures of the guerillas fighting . . . videos of the guerillas fighting against the Americans in Iraq. And so, the situation in the Middle East was not so . . . at least in Syria, wasn't very pro-American.[1]

Indeed, the inauguration of the Neirab Rehabilitation Project was taking place about a year after the US invasion of Iraq in March 2003, a move that had caused the US government to be especially unpopular not just in Ein el Tal and Neirab but in Syria and across the Arab world. As the employee noted, there were accounts of young men from Ein el Tal and other Palestinian refugee camps in Syria joining the Iraqi insurgency to fight against American troops. The employee also noted that right around the time of the project's inauguration in 2004, one of these young men, who was from Ein el Tal and whose mother was a teacher in one of the UNRWA schools, had died fighting with the Iraqi insurgency and had been mourned in the camp. He had been recognized as a martyr and a street in the camp had been named after him.

On inauguration day, as the crowd of protesters grew rowdier, Syrian police were called in to contain them. "I've never seen so many police in my life," recalled the UNRWA employee, who estimated "more than a hundred" of them. The inauguration proceeded despite the protest but was finally cut short when some of the protesters started throwing stones in the direction of the ambassadors.

It is not clear exactly who the protesters were, but a Neirab resident later told me that the protest had been organized by the Palestinian political faction Fatah al-Intifada, which was based in Ein el Tal and was opposed to the project.[2] According to other UNRWA employees who had been with the ambassadors, a main incentive was the US veto a few days earlier, on March 25, 2004, of a UN resolution denouncing Israel's extrajudicial assassination of Hamas leader Sheikh Ahmad Yasin.

While there was no similar protest in Neirab, which the American ambassador had visited prior to heading to Ein el Tal, there were reports of Neirab residents throwing stones at the ambassador's convoy. Additionally, one UNRWA employee recalled that the Neirab visit had had to be cut short because of the tension in the camp.[3]

The events just described give a sense of the tense atmosphere surrounding UNRWA's attempt to implement its vision of development in Neirab and Ein el Tal. It shows that this tension was in part related to funding for the Neirab Rehabilitation Project. Phase 1 funding came primarily from Western governments whose foreign policy on the Middle East in general and toward Palestinians in particular was extremely unpopular in the camps.[4] However, it was not just the larger regional political context that was at the source of the tension. The largely apolitical narrative of development that accompanied UNRWA's implementation of the project was also a source of refugee distrust and antagonism. By spring 2005, sustainability had become UNRWA's new buzzword, and the sustainable livelihoods approach had become a key component of its vision of development in Palestinian refugee camps. In line with this approach, the Neirab Rehabilitation Project team had decided that promoting development in Neirab and Ein el Tal first required each community to map out its existing assets. Development would be about building on these assets rather than introducing completely new technologies. Also, the local population would be involved in project implementation. In spring 2005, UNRWA had recruited about thirty Palestinian volunteers

Figure 3.1. The new UNRWA-built hilltop houses in Ein el Tal, 2005. Photograph by Nell Gabiam.

(most of them from Ein el Tal plus a handful from Neirab) to conduct an "asset mapping" of the camp.[5]

A closer look at the engagement of the project's various stakeholders with the notion of sustainable development reveals that *sustainability* is not a neutral term. First, donors for the project's initial phase in Ein el Tal were responsible for UNRWA's choice of the sustainable livelihoods approach as the main guide for the project's implementation. Second, UNRWA's emphasis on sustainability clashed with local understandings of the relationship between Palestinian refugees' past, present, and future. For vocal Palestinian detractors as well as supporters of the Neirab rehabilitation Project, the temporality through which they envisioned a meaningful future differed from the temporality in UNRWA's notion of sustainability as development that lasts "forever." For the refugees, development was not infinite but rather circumscribed by the possibility of return to the homeland.

Sustainable Development

There were two major components to the Neirab Rehabilitation Project: an infrastructural component that focused on improving the camp's built environment and a "livelihoods" component that targeted the long-term socioeconomic well-being of refugees (UNRWA 2003, 2005a, 2005b, 2007). For UNRWA, these two components were interrelated because the quality of the camp's infrastructure has "a direct bearing on the quality of life of refugees" (UNRWA 2005a:11). The project was divided into two phases: phase 1 entailed the voluntary move of 300 families from the Neirab barracks to newly built houses on land adjacent to Ein el Tal and bringing about (additional) infrastructural, economic, and social change to the camp. Phase 2 entailed rebuilding the housing in the barracks area of Neirab as well as bringing about (additional) infrastructural, economic, and social change.

When interacting with refugees, the project team avoided talking about development in broad terms as "modernization" because such an understanding encouraged the rumor that the goal of the project was to solve the refugee issue economically. Instead, team members emphasized the "portable skills" that refugees would gain as a result of the project, skills that they would be able to use in any environment. Alice, the British manager of the "social development" component of the project, explained:

> Apart from the physical rehabilitation, housing, and infrastructure, there is really nothing inside the sustainable rehabilitation program that is not portable. If you're building people's skills, education, confidence, networking abilities, social abilities, [the] ability to organize themselves, that can be taken anywhere. (Interview, April 18, 2006)

The project team's emphasis on the portability of development was not enough to quell the negative rumors. In fact, UNRWA discovered that the very concept of sustainability, which was at the heart of its development approach, was itself part of the problem. For one thing, there is no consensus on the exact meaning of *sustainability*, an evolving term with multiple connotations (Barlund 2013; Orr 2003). It first came to public notice in the 1970s and 1980s through publications in the fields of agriculture and environmental conservation (Orr 2003). The most widely used definition of sustainable development came from the 1987 Bruntland report: "Meeting the needs of the present generation without compromising the ability of future generations to do the same" (Bruntland Commission 1987). However, this definition provides significant room for interpretation, and "one of the most striking characteristics of the term 'sustainable development' is that it can mean all things to all people" (Barlund 2013).

The view that development is more likely to be sustainable if it is participatory–that is, if it draws on the local knowledge and experience of its intended beneficiaries–is now common in the field of international development. Participatory development emerged from criticism of large-scale, top-down, modernization schemes that relied solely on the expertise of Westerners. This criticism began surfacing in the 1960s and led to calls for the greater involvement of the purported beneficiaries in project planning and implementation (Francis 2001). The idea that the knowledge, skills, and interests of local communities should be prioritized gradually gained popularity and "since the mid-1980s, words such as 'participation,' 'empowerment,' 'bottom-up planning,' and 'indigenous knowledge' have become increasingly common" (Henkel and Stirrat 2001:168).

By 2004, UNRWA had decided that the Neirab Rehabilitation Project would be participatory. In a departure from previous policy, the agency began to recruit local volunteers and began holding regular community meetings with the refugees of Neirab and Ein el Tal on how to best improve camp living conditions. By 2005, sustainability was being discussed in UNRWA documents as the overarching concept in UNRWA's development vision (UNRWA 2005a). At that time, the key phrases used to frame its interventions in Neirab and Ein el Tal were *sustainable development* and, more specifically, *sustainable livelihoods approach*.

The sustainable livelihoods approach (SLA) is a participatory development method popularized in the late 1980s by Robert Chambers and Gordon Conway. It emphasizes the importance of building on existing "human, natural, financial, social and physical assets" in a community rather than introducing new technologies from the outside (Chambers and Conway 1987; UNRWA 2007:4). According to a 2007 UNRWA document:

> Instead of top-down service delivery, [the Neirab Rehabilitation Project] is a participatory process of dialogue and mobilization of refugees. This will achieve sustainable outputs which will improve the living conditions of refugees far beyond the lifespan of the project. (UNRWA 2007:4)

The document also elaborated the kinds of sustainable outputs UNRWA hoped to achieve through partnership with camp refugees:

> Through a community development strategy, education and learning opportunities will be enhanced, unemployment will be targeted, health will be improved, cooperation and collaboration amongst camp residents will increase–the overall conditions of the camp residents will be improved. (UNRWA 2007:4)

In addition to community participation, UNRWA's discourse of development linked sustainability to another key concept, self-reliance, which the agency contrasted to "dependence on assistance." According to UNRWA's 2005–2010 Medium Term Plan:

> Palestine refugees are potentially key agents for the socio-economic development of the wider Palestinian community. This potential could be achieved by providing refugees with the means to become self reliant–a goal best attained when concerned departments work closely together to end refugee dependence on assistance. (UNRWA 2005a:12)

A central argument of participatory development is that projects should enable targeted beneficiaries to carry out activities traditionally reserved for outsiders (Chambers 1994). Accordingly, one of the project team's main tasks–with the help of foreign consultants–was to train locally recruited volunteers in survey research and focus group discussions. The idea was that Palestinian refugees in Ein el Tal and Neirab were best placed to conduct an asset mapping of their own community, to figure out existing social and physical "assets" in their own camps. After completion of the mappings, UNRWA, together with local residents, would devise ways of building on these resources.

In interviews, the foreign staff supervising the Neirab Rehabilitation Project talked about SLA mostly in terms of local self-reliance. According to Henrick, a Swiss project manager primarily involved in the infrastructural component of the project, implementation in line with SLA meant to "help [Palestinian refugees] so that they can take their lives in their own hands by themselves . . . [and] . . . also recognize themselves as subjects who take initiatives, who can develop, make steps forward, with regard to different aspects of life" (interview, January 17, 2005).

Alice, the British manager of the social development component, explained:

> [Sustainable livelihoods is] a very different approach than relief where you give people things. . . . So what the SLA does is, it says, "Well this is where you're starting from, these are the issues that make you vulnerable, so let's work on those issues to overcome that, and to build on what you already have rather than what you don't have." Secondly, again, it is about building your own capacities and this is what sustainability is. If I constantly give you something, you're always going to need me to give you something. If I build your skills and your own resources and capacities, that's something that always stays with you. (Interview, April 18, 2006)

Project managers were always foreign (they came and went as the project progressed), but the project team was made up mostly of locally hired Palestinians and sometimes Syrians, and their views often echoed those of their foreign colleagues, emphasizing local self-reliance and the ability to withstand social and economic shocks. However, there were two striking differences: local staff were more forthcoming about refugee distrust toward the project and were often unable to fully separate themselves from these feelings.

When discussing challenges to the project, foreign staff mostly pointed to logistical and managerial issues such as "keeping everyone updated, explaining approaches in detail, reporting, [and] issuing complete transparency regarding everything" (interview, January 17, 2005). They also pointed to the difficulty of introducing "a new way of doing things" in UNRWA, "a new methodology" spanning the agency's different departments (interview, April 18 2006). Foreign employees rarely mentioned refugee skepticism unless specifically asked about it.

One challenge that usually emerged in interviews with local UNRWA staff–Palestinian or Syrian–was the suspicion among a significant number of refugees that the Neirab Rehabilitation Project might be a politically motivated undertaking disguised as a humanitarian effort. For instance, Hadeel, a Syrian woman in her mid-thirties who was part of the project's social development team, told me, "The second biggest problem [in getting the project off the ground] was the fear of [the refugees] that the intention of the project was to settle people as a bargain for [them to give up] the right of return" (interview, November 8, 2005). Rana, also part of the social development team, was a Palestinian in her mid-twenties. Specifically in relation to Neirab Camp, where she had been working, she told me, "There are suspicions that this project is only to make Palestinian people accept to live or stay in Syria, to forget about their right to return" (interview, June 25, 2005). Interestingly, when I asked Hadeel and Rana what they thought about these suspicions, they did not immediately discard them as foreign staff usually did. "Personally, I feel this [project] is for development," Hadeel said, but then added, "I hope it is about development, not settlement. . . ." (interview, January 1, 2006). Rana, speaking in English, was more introspective:

> First of all, I know they have the right to have these concerns and they have the right to have these suspicions because, in our long history, we have been deceived many, many times: even our leaving Palestine was by using one of these deceptions. So even I . . . sometimes I have these suspicions, but that shouldn't affect my work because as I told you the main goal for me is helping Palestinian refugees. . . . For [the refugees targeted by the project] I try–at least I tried–to make them believe in the same way I do. (Interview, June 25, 2005)

In arguing that Palestinian displacement in 1948 was the result of deception, Rana was stating a belief shared by other refugees. According to Rosemary Sayigh, a significant number of Palestinians felt that their 1948 exile from Palestine was due in large part to a lack of support on the ground from Arab armies despite pledges to intervene on behalf of Palestinian fighters. They "concluded that the Arab regimes, or individuals within them, were accomplices in an imperialist/Zionist conspiracy to remove them from their land" (Sayigh 1979:66).[6] On a broader level, Rana's comment about trying to "make [the community] believe" evoke participatory development's religious roots (Henkel and Stirrat 2001) and more generally the way that "religious ideas factor into the discourse of development" (Bornstein 2005:3). Indeed, in a separate interview, Rana again acknowledged and attempted to transcend her doubts about the outcome of the project by comparing herself to a priest: "I believe that it's the same situation. I believe that he, inside, has some suspicion, but he's still a priest so he needs to make people have a deeper belief in God" (interview, June 2005).[7]

Participation as Control

A major factor in the distrust toward the Neirab Rehabilitation Project was a set of rumors circulating in Ein el Tal and Neirab implying that UNRWA-sponsored development was not a genuine attempt to alleviate poverty but rather a political ploy by Western governments sympathetic to Israel to ensure the permanent settlement of Palestinian refugees in Syria. In the early days of the project, one such rumor was that UNRWA's emphasis on development was a sign that the agency saw the future well-being of Palestinians as firmly grounded in Syria and that the project was really a "settlement project [*mashrū' tawṭīn*]." Another was that the project, although it presented development as a matter of achieving sustainability and self-reliance, was really a means of progressively dismantling UNRWA and making the Palestinian refugee issue disappear.

Linked to the negative rumors was the claim that the project's Western donors were supporting it because they believed that Palestinian refugees would forget about the right of return once they started leading comfortable lives. The following interaction with a young Palestinian doctor from Ein el Tal who was adamantly opposed to the project illustrates some of the resistance that UNRWA was facing in the spring of 2005. As we stood in the yard of his house, the doctor pointed to the new hilltop houses where some thirty families from the Neirab barracks had already moved and asked me, "Do you know what we call it? 'The settlement' [*al-mustawṭana*]. Stop anybody walking toward the hilltop and ask him, 'Where are you going?' He will answer 'to the settlement.'" He pointed out that two of the main donors to the project, the United States and Canada, had close ties to the Israeli government. In the doctor's opinion, the project was skillfully designed by Israel's allies to ease refugees' hardships so that they would stop thinking about return. "Who are the people who usually take part in uprisings?" he asked rhetorically. "Poor people" (field notes, May 25, 2005).

As the doctor pointed out, the United States (through the Department of State) and Canada (through the Canadian International Development Agency) along with Switzerland (through the Swiss Agency for Cooperation and Development) were playing a major role as donors in the first phase of the Neirab Rehabilitation Project taking place in Ein el Tal. Donor representatives attended several donor meetings with UNRWA and GAPAR in Ein el Tal and took part in an UNRWA-organized Urban Planning Workshop in December 2005 in Neirab. According to UNRWA employees I interviewed, the donors were instrumental in UNRWA's adoption of SLA as a mechanism for development in Palestinian refugee camps. Alice, the project's social development manager, explained that the donors had insisted that UNRWA adopt this approach well after project implementation had begun:

> The donors just suddenly said, well we don't want you to concentrate on structural transformation and, you know, physical rehabilitation. We actually want

you to look at the whole livelihoods of the refugees and, you know, we need to work with the community as a whole. So it was an add-on that came two to three years into the project. (Interview April 18, 2006)

During follow-up interviews with UNRWA employees at the agency's headquarters in Amman, I found out that the Swiss donors were the ones who initially put pressure on UNRWA to adopt the SLA and that the Canadian donors followed suit. Pointing out that the US government was funding the project through the Department of State rather than USAID, its development agency, one UNRWA employee explained that the American donors were not as invested as the Canadian and Swiss donors in UNRWA's development approach. According to this employee, US funding fell primarily within the scope of US support for Israel and the US government's view of UNRWA as "an instrument contributing to creating a measure of stability in an otherwise tumultuous region" (interview, March 23, 2015).

A conversation with the American donor representative during a visit to Ein el Tal in May of 2005 supported the idea that US funding was strongly tied to concerns over regional stability. I asked about the American incentive for participating in the Neirab Rehabilitation Project. After giving it some thought, she listed three reasons:

1. It was simply not acceptable for people to live in the kinds of conditions the refugees endured in the barracks or, as she said, "in houses with holes in them."
2. The Department of State did not want to deprive refugees of the support offered to Palestinians. That is, refugees should not be excluded from projects for Palestinians and there should be no separation between Palestinians under the Palestinian authority and Palestinian refugees. The Department of State did not want to deal with "two states," one governed by the Palestinian Authority and one governed by UNRWA. It wanted to deal with Palestinians comprehensively.
3. The United States was very supportive of refugee issues in general and played a significant role in resettlement and in providing assistance, so it was natural that it contribute to such an effort.

I pressed the donor representative further, telling her about the rumors circulating in Neirab and Ein el Tal that the US government was interested in the Neirab Rehabilitation Project because it sought the permanent settlement of Palestinian refugees in Syria. She refuted this idea, asserting that the Department of State "fully supports the Palestinian right of return." She then accurately pointed out that UNRWA had brought the project to the American government, asking for help. The project had not emanated from the Department of State. At the same time, she acknowledged that any motives for supporting the project other than the three she had given me had had to do with inhibiting the rise and growth of radical movements such as Hamas and Hizbullah. Such movements, she explained, tended to thrive in environments with precarious socioeconomic conditions (field notes, May 29, 2005).

The American donor representative's comments show that development was seen by the Department of State to some extent as a political tool against Palestinian radicalism. This is yet another example of the tendency to associate radicalism with poverty, a tendency also apparent in the policies of a post 9/11 world in which "many countries, especially the United States, have viewed counter-terrorism and humanitarianism as crime-fighting partners" (Barnett and Weiss 2008:25). Furthermore, by considering Palestinian refugees in Arab host countries as ultimately belonging to a state-in-the-making governed by the Palestinian Authority, the donor representative was implying that an eventual return would be to a future Palestinian state based in the occupied territories. This understanding did in fact contravene the Ein el Tal and Neirab refugees' idea of return. The refugees were from towns and villages that are now part of the state of Israel, and when they talked about return it was in terms of those towns and villages and not a future Palestinian state that would more or less coincide with territories under the control of the Palestinian Authority. The donor's comments were a particularly telling illustration of how development–and international aid more broadly–can be used to shape political subjectivities. Among other things, "development" functioned here to make Palestinians compliant ("nonradicalized"), and tied their right of return to eventual citizenship in a Palestinian state within the 1967 borders.

Critical scholarship on participatory development points out that "participation" can be a way of bypassing existing community structures. For instance, according to John Hailey, "How much participative development owes its genesis to attempts by Western governments, and by virtue of their funding position, Northern aid donors, to limit the power and influence of political dissidents, freedom-fighters or radical Marxists?" (2001:99). Behind the donors' embrace and even encouragement of participatory implementation of a development project may have been a form of governmentality (Foucault 1991) that aims for better control over a population by bypassing or weakening established local structures, especially those that are hostile to the donor country (see Li 2007).

While the interests of various stakeholders are a part of what guides development, it is important to note that they do not necessarily define development practices or outcomes, even when they are associated with powerful entities such as project donors (Ferguson 1994; Li 2007; Mosse 2005). And while ulterior political motives imputed to the donors were a significant part of refugee distrust, not all Palestinians in Neirab and Ein el Tal saw the project as a threat to the right of return.

Palestinian Refugees Debate Sustainability

When it came to communicating UNRWA's vision of development to refugees in Neirab and Ein el Tal, UNRWA project documents written in Arabic translated "sustainable development" as *tanmiya mustadāma* (literally "continuous" or "perpetual" development) and initially summarized SLA during community meetings as the refugees' gaining skills and empowerment that would stay with them "forever" (*lil-'abad*). Local project volunteers, who had undergone training with UNRWA staff and foreign consultants, acted as intermediaries to help broadcast UNRWA's vision of development and assist with development in the wider community.

During conversations with local Palestinian project volunteers in Ein el Tal, notions of participation, self-reliance, and protection from socioeconomic vulnerability associated with SLA did come up, but so did other interpretations of sustainable development that had not been intended by UNRWA. Some volunteers talked about sustainable livelihoods in terms of sustainable employment, enrichment of sociocultural life, and social cooperation or "unity" (interview, January 17, 2006). Others tied sustainability to the more tangible effects of the Neirab Rehabilitation Project. For them the project should not be "a dream, [but something] that is executed" (interview, January 25, 2006). At the time of the asset mapping in Ein el Tal, construction had started on the new houses for the refugees from Neirab. When asked about how he understood sustainability, one of the volunteers, Bilal, said, "A house in good condition with many rooms gives the opportunity for young boys and girls to do better in their studies and reach a high level of education" (interview, June 21, 2005).

Although the Palestinian project volunteers echoed UNRWA's understanding of sustainability to a certain extent, they also attached their own interpretation. For example, some did not adhere to UNRWA's view of self-reliance as the opposite of dependence on assistance. On the one hand, UNRWA framed sustainability as a move away from "constantly [giving] things to refugees" toward self-reliance. On the other hand, it was not uncommon for Palestinian refugees to talk about development in ways that echoed UNRWA's discourse of sustainability and at the same time advocate for UNRWA's ongoing "help." For one project volunteer, Majid, sustainability meant, among other things, the "*continued* involvement of UNRWA in the community" (interview, January 17, 2006; emphasis by author). According to Bilal, "Refugees need to be self-reliant but that doesn't mean that UNRWA should distance itself from us, not help us" (interview, June 21, 2005).

UNRWA had failed to anticipate that sustainability's temporal implications would feed into the negative rumors that had been plaguing the Neirab

Rehabilitation Project since its official start in 2000. The temporality in UNRWA's framing of sustainability was an infinite one: refugees were to acquire skills and a quality of life that would endure, that would last forever. In other words, development itself would last forever; it would be self-perpetuating once refugees had become self-reliant and were capable of taking "their life into their own hands." For Palestinian skeptics, sustainability as perpetual development, which for them implied permanent settlement in Syria, was further proof that the project was part of an international conspiracy to do away with the right of return.

Sustainability's temporal implications and the discomfort they created among Palestinian refugees were apparent during the March 2005 training of local Ein el Tal project volunteers in asset mapping. Rana, the Palestinian UNRWA employee and project team member mentioned earlier, was abruptly interrupted by one of the local volunteers as she went over the project's sustainable development approach in Arabic. She had been explaining that, among other benefits, the project would provide people in the community with skills that would stay with them "forever" [lil-'abad] when a young man asked, "Why forever?" Right away understanding that "forever" and its implication of permanence had disturbed the volunteer, Rana said that the goal of the project was to create a better life for Palestinians; it was not to encourage them to stay in Syria. Rather, they would be able to take the skills and empowerment they had gained with them. She said, presumably alluding to return, "And do you think that once you return, your problems will be over? This project will empower you to deal [with them]" (field notes, April 26, 2005). During this episode, Rana, who had confided to me at the time of our interview that even she sometimes had doubts about the real intentions of the project, displayed her resolve to convince refugees in Ein el Tal of the transformational power of development (Crush 1995).

By the time I returned for a follow-up visit in Ein el Tal and Neirab in 2010, UNRWA had abandoned sustainable development as the overarching concept through which it sought to communicate its vision of development. The Neirab Rehabilitation Project's most recent (German) manager, who had assumed his duties in 2007, said that he realized that framing the project around sustainability had not been effective in garnering refugee support. "From day one sustainability was a despicable term," he said, explaining that it was too "rigid" and too easily misinterpreted by the refugee community as an attempt to bring about the permanent settlement of Palestinians in Syria (interview, October 4, 2010).

Nowadays UNRWA's preferred term for articulating its development vision is *human development*, which emerged in response to criticism of the leading development approaches of the 1980s that construed development primarily in terms of economic growth (Sen 1999; UNDP 2015). In addition to economic growth, the discourse of human development emphasizes access to social resources such as health and education, democratic governance, civil and political rights, sustainability, and security from chronic stresses (e.g., hunger) and disruptions (e.g., unemployment or conflict).[8] The project manager I spoke to in 2010 told me that there was a widespread sense among Neirab's inhabitants that the camp's youth had become depoliticized and passive about the future. He believed that human development and self-reliance tied into the way Palestinian refugees understood their daily struggles, but he acknowledged that self-reliance was not without its own controversies. It had proven problematic because of refugees' fears that it signified UNRWA's progressive disengagement from the camps. At the same time, according to the manager, refugees were receptive to the idea of self-empowerment that "self-reliance" implied as a way of solving community problems (interview, October 4, 2010).

UNRWA's change of terms was not related only to refugee reaction in Ein el Tal and Neirab. During my 2010 interview with the Neirab Rehabilitation Project's latest manager, it became clear that another incentive was funding. While the first phase of the project in Ein el Tal had been primarily funded by Canada, Switzerland and the United States, UNRWA had since then relied on several other donors to continue. The project's second phase in Neirab was funded primarily by the United Arab Emirates, Japan, and Germany, as well as the regional governments of Galicia and the Basque country. According to the project manager, SLA had not been effective in terms of "selling" the project and attracting (additional) donors. UNRWA had discovered that human development was a more popular concept in the international development community and was more effective in eliciting donor interest.

While to my knowledge there is no foreign donor–led initiative to deliberately use development as a means of ensuring the permanent settlement of Palestinian refugees in their host countries, it is evident that donors exert a significant influence in shaping development ideology and practice. UNRWA's approach is not simply an ideological one but one guided by more pragmatic interests such as funding. It is also clear from the project manager's comments that, despite trying to adapt its development discourse in ways that were more acceptable to Palestinian refugees' self-understandings, this discourse did not entirely cease to be controversial. Although human development acknowledges that political empowerment is an aspect of development, this has not translated into a mutually shared vision of development as a political project. This failure is not surprising given UNRWA's self-understanding as a nonpolitical organization, and it illustrates the limits of the agency's participatory development approach.

UNRWA prided itself on its efforts to consult with Palestinian refugees and involve them in the planning and implementation of the Neirab Rehabilitation Project. There were UNRWA employees, like the project manager, who made a genuine effort to reach out to refugees in Ein el Tal and Neirab and take into account their thoughts and opinions. However, for UNRWA, participation mainly entailed coming up with ideas at agency headquarters in Damascus or Amman and then sharing them with the refugees in the camps, as well as keeping refugees informed of each stage of the project and seeking the consent of the targeted communities for each new step. Participation did not include UNRWA and Palestinian refugees coming together to decide the categories and concepts that would frame development in Neirab and Ein el Tal or the meanings behind them.

Despite a concern that agents "step back and let the local people articulate their own reality" in development projects, the method and framework of participatory approaches are usually not in question (Henkel and Stirrat 2001:180). With regard to SLA implementation in Neirab and Ein el Tal, this meant that the approach itself, the questionnaire, the survey, and the focus group discussions were preestablished, not the result of a dialogue with the refugees. Had this dialogue occurred, it would have become apparent that the notion of sustainability as development that lasts forever did not resonate with local self-understandings. I believe such a dialogue would have been useful to explore the ways in which ardent Palestinian supporters of the Neirab Rehabilitation Project reconciled development with their identity as refugees continuing to advocate for their right of return to their Palestinian homeland.

Sustainability as Resilience

In chapter 1, I discussed how the Palestinian director of GAPAR, the Syrian agency responsible for Palestinian refugees, had attempted to bridge development in a host country with return to the Palestinian homeland: "We will not be able to return without first developing ourselves so that we can be resilient (ṣamidīn). This is how we understand [the Neirab Rehabilitation Project]. It does not compromise the right of return." He equated development with ṣumūd, an Arabic term that, in this context, can be translated as "resilience."

Understood as the ability of society to withstand unexpected disturbances, resilience is implied in dominant understandings of sustainable development (Chambers and Conway 1987; Orr 2003). For instance, at the heart of SLA is the idea that communities should determine the impediments to their ability to live secure lives and figure out ways to withstand or overcome them. However, in the GAPAR director's understanding, resilience was not sought as an end in itself, as the unquestioned and perpetual ability to withstand impediments. It was about the ability to withstand impediments so as to better actualize the political project of return. It had a dynamic aspect that tied social and economic transformation to political transformation. At the same time, it had a finite temporality because it was linked to the goal of return.

At a donors meeting in May 2005 in the UNRWA-run al-Zeeb school (named after the Palestinian village of al-Zeeb) in Ein el Tal, this sense of finite temporality was further emphasized by the GAPAR director. In addition to the donors, the meeting featured top UNRWA officials, members of the Neirab Rehabilitation Project team, GAPAR representatives, and the Syrian deputy governor of Aleppo. As part of his introductory speech, the director emphasized that Ein el Tal and Neirab were temporary places of residence for Palestinian refugees and that they would be the target of "development and improvement" *until* the return of the refugees to their original homes in accordance with UN Resolution 194. He explained that the areas inhabited by Palestinian refugees would be returned to Syrian authorities once the Palestinians had left for their homeland. He then expressed hope that the project would produce tangible results. The Palestinian refugees were in need of activities, he said; a cultural center was needed to encourage youth activities. He also mentioned that both Ein el Tal and Neirab should have an ambulance to carry people to the nearest hospital in case of an emergency: "Is it possible in the age of development, of modernization, is it normal to have people die for lack of an ambulance?" He asked that UNRWA spare no efforts in supplying the camps with ambulances. "This is a humanitarian question," he

Figure 3.2. UNRWA's al-Zeeb School with the minaret of the camp's mosque to the left, 2011. Photograph courtesy of Lex Takkenberg.

asserted. He ended by telling the meeting participants, "I hope to meet with you in our Jerusalem, in our liberated Palestine" (field notes, May 29, 2005).

In a departure from UNRWA's view, the GAPAR director saw development as finite, culminating in return (which he tied to the "liberation" of Palestine). This view was shared by other Palestinians involved in the Neirab Rehabilitation Project, including the Palestinian UNRWA staff, and by Rana, who asked Palestinian project volunteers how they expected to survive once they returned without first "developing" themselves. It was also shared by UNRWA's Aleppo "area officer," a middle-aged Palestinian refugee living in Neirab, who explained during an interview that the Neirab Rehabilitation Project was "not connected to settlement in any way":

> When the skills and experience and empowerment and training improve the person, he can move them from one place to another. He can move them to Palestine with him when refugees return. Should he stay here and remain a backwards person? When he finally gets to return to Palestine, he will find the rest of the world 400 years ahead! (Interview, January 18, 2006)

Despite this universalist approach to development, the area officer's argument that development was amenable and even useful to the eventual return of Palestinian refugees once again tied development to a finite future, to the time when Palestinians would "finally" be able to return.

Comments made by Atif, a teenage Palestinian volunteer and welder from Neirab, offer further insight into how the views of vocal supporters of the Neirab Rehabilitation Project both joined in and departed from UNRWA's development discourse. In addition to having worked as a volunteer on the project, Atif was a member of the Democratic Front for the Liberation of Palestine (DFLP), a leftist Palestinian political faction founded in 1969. As one of the most enthusiastic Neirab refugees participating in the project, he was not particularly concerned about its potential negative repercussions on the right of return. It was not only the fact that all but one political party in Ein el Tal and Neirab had come out in support of the project that reassured him[9]; that UNRWA was the main project implementer also helped ease any initials doubts. For Atif, the very existence of UNRWA was proof of the refugee status of Palestinians, and as long as outside intervention was channeled through it he was not worried about losing this status. In fact, he welcomed the Neirab Rehabilitation Project as a chance for Palestinian refugees to gain even more visibility in the international community through the various donors involved: "Any donor who helps Palestinian refugees through UNRWA gets to know them *as refugees* [author's italics]." At the same time, Atif explained that he was ready to "fight" and even "kill" anyone who would attempt to settle refugees and that Palestine and the right of return were "red lines." He then added:

The right of return is all we have left; because to be ten people in one house, the father dies, and everyone gets two square meters [of space], this is not living [I realized from having visited his family in the camp that he was describing his own situation]. We have a green ID card, but it's forbidden to travel, to go out [of Syria], to take part in activities outside, this is not living. If we were in our own country we would be very comfortable, and free from the house where all are sharing ten square meters, free from rations; we would alleviate UNRWA's load; [UNRWA] would help other people; and [he added jokingly] we would give up smoking. (Interview, November 7, 2005)

Although Atif was reiterating a shared opinion among refugees that the issue of return would have to be part of the solution to the refugee question, he did not see development as an obstacle:

There is a concept that many people believe in. It is that the fighter [*al-munāḍil*] must remain poor. This is a widespread idea in people. His economic situation must be weak so that he remains a fighter. But I say "no," the fighter, when his house is big, he has a place to practice his activities. He will be more active and he has a chance to produce something. (Interview, November 7, 2005)

Atif's explanation of his support for the Neirab Rehabilitation Project and for "development" more broadly explains why some volunteers saw no contradiction between the idea of sustainability and the idea that UNRWA should continue to "help" Palestinian refugees. Such an association seems at first glance contradictory and certainly departed from UNRWA's official understanding of sustainability as "self-reliance." However, it appears much less strange when framed by a political lens that acknowledges the importance of the collective Palestinian political struggle, rather than by a neoliberal lens that is primarily about economic self-reliance.

First, Atif attributed his support of the project to the fact that it was channeled through UNRWA; indeed, he welcomed any attempt to improve camp living conditions as long as UNRWA was in charge. Second, when he imagined a future without hardship and without UNRWA, it was a future in which return or, at least some form of Palestinian self-determination, had become a possibility ("if we were in our own country"). Despite his endorsement of "development" and his dismissal of the idea that the fighter must remain poor, development was not the fundamental change that would put an end to Palestinian suffering and it would have no bearing on the continuation of UNRWA, which would only be able to "help others" once Palestinians were able to return.

When trying to make sense of why Palestinian refugees would endorse sustainable development, self-reliance, and UNRWA's continued "help" in the same breath, the political role of UNRWA in their eyes and the political symbolism of its services in refugee camps must be taken into account. When the views of Palestinian supporters of the Neirab Rehabilitation Project are examined closely, it is clear that sustainable development includes the sustainability of the struggle for the right of return, to which UNRWA's continued "assistance," given its political dimension, is important. Here the form of assistance is not as crucial as UNRWA's continuation as an agency historically set up to assist refugees pending a political resolution of their situation. Development, by providing social, economic, and (as argued by Atif) political resilience, can also contribute to the sustainability of the project of return. What is clear in the arguments of Atif and GAPAR's Palestinian director is a refusal to separate socioeconomic improvement in Palestinian refugee camps from Palestinian political claims and a defense of the idea that development can be formulated politically (see Ferguson 1994).

Additionally, I believe that the negative rumors plaguing the Neirab Rehabilitation Project functioned primarily as means through which refugees were able to bring the political context of their hardship to bear on discussions about improving camp conditions; whether or not refugees actually believed the rumors is secondary. For this reason, it is worthwhile to return to the GAPAR director's attempt to frame development politically by linking it to the concept of *ṣumūd*. I do not focus on development as *ṣumūd* in order to argue that this concept should have framed the project. Making such an assertion would go against my previous argument that the project's guiding concepts should have emerged out of a dialogue with the refugees as a collective. Rather, my goal is to offer one example of how development might be reinterpreted more politically (Ferguson 1994), not by drawing on an abstract notion of empowerment but by grounding such empowerment in local realities and understandings.

Ṣumūd as a Guiding Concept

At its core, *ṣumūd* represents the Palestinian political strategy pursued from 1967 onward in the West Bank and Gaza (Lindholm Schulz 2003; Slyomovics 1999). As a political strategy, it emphasizes that, despite the massive forced displacements of 1948 and 1967, Palestinian society has not dissolved, and it expresses the determination of Palestinians who were able to remain on their land, or at least were able to remain in parts of historic Palestine, to stay put regardless of the pressures put on them by Israel, such as occupation, land expropriation, and restriction of movement. During the pre-Oslo era as well, *ṣumūd* informed the resolve of Palestinians living under occupation not to engage with Israeli institutions (Slyomovics 1999). Over time, *ṣumūd* was appropriated by Palestinian refugees outside the homeland and came to include the refugee experience–the ability to both resist and endure camp life as well as the unwavering commitment to the right of return (Allan 2014; Lindholm Schulz 2003; Peteet 1991; Schiocchet 2013).

With its emphasis on endurance and steadfastness, the dominant discourse of *ṣumūd* is future oriented, but it is not fundamentally about change; it is not fundamentally about changing present conditions or building a particular kind of future. Rather, as anthropologist Leonardo Schiocchet notes, within the refugee context and at a very basic level, *ṣumūd* is driven by refugee fears of "the effacement of their properties, rights, lifestyles, and, more importantly, their own identity":

> Such fears mark their understanding of themselves, which in turn position their engagement with the world. The fear of self-effacement also leads to an idealization of one's own existence as resistance. Within Palestinian refugee camps in general, being a refugee is one more element reinforcing the equation "existence = resistance" as an attribute of Palestinianness. The "existence = resistance" equation defines the sort of passive resistance that characterizes the idea of [*ṣumūd*]. (Schiocchet 2013:67)

Recent anthropological studies of Palestinian refugees point to the need to recognize more dynamic iterations of *ṣumūd* (Schiocchet 2013; Allan 2014). For example, in her work on the Shatila camp in Lebanon, Diana Allan argues for an understanding of *ṣumūd* as part of "a material pragmatism" that, while keeping refugee communities going against all odds, "is producing new forms of subjectivity and belonging" (2014:34). It is my contention that the arguments made by outspoken Palestinian supporters of the Neirab Rehabilitation Project also represent a rearticulation of *ṣumūd* as dynamic, open to change, to material transformation, and to the formation of new political subjectivities. The main idea underscoring some of the interventions of Palestinian project supporters is that the socioeconomic and infrastructural improvement in Neirab would empower both individuals and the community to be stronger advocates of Palestinian political claims and to be better prepared to actualize the project of return. According to this view, "improvement," which implies change conceived positively, is the motor of *ṣumūd*, which is about empowerment in the face of the debilitating effects of material scarcity; this in turn makes it easier to realize Palestinian political claims. Such a view merges a nationalistic understanding of *ṣumūd* with material pragmatism.

Anthropologist Leonardo Schiocchet offers another example of *ṣumūd* as imbued with a more dynamic meaning, a meaning that echoes some of the arguments made by supporters of the Neirab Rehabilitation Project. He mentions a Palestinian scholar who had been resettled from Iraq to Brazil following the upheavals caused by the American invasion. In reflecting on how *ṣumūd* has come to encapsulate Palestinian refugees' steadfast commitment to the right of return, the scholar argued for a reinterpretation of the concept as a cultivation of the "power to go" (*qudrat al-dhahab*) to the Palestinian homeland, which he felt was more effective and realistic than the static and (in his view) utopian hold on the "right of return" (Schiocchet 2013).

To make sense of Ein el Tal Palestinians' insistence on return to the homeland being part of the temporal narrative of development, one must go beyond the issue of return as an implementable right and beyond the issue of whether all refugees desire it–it is important to acknowledge its moral and existential dimensions (Khalidi 1992). For Palestinians, the right of return is also about recognition of the injustice they have suffered as a result of the Nakba and their ongoing suffering linked to it. In this moral sense, return has become a part of how Palestinian identity is understood and expressed; thus "to yield return is to yield identity" (Lindholm Schulz 2003:230). Additionally, the Nakba is not just an event in the past but one that continues in the present through a succession of new catastrophes that bear resemblance to it, including war, expulsion, mass displacement, destruction and dislocation of communities, and mass pauperization (Sa'di and Abu Lughod 2007; Sayigh 2007). As the ongoing catastrophe that prevents Palestinians from living in "normal time" like other people (Jayyusi 2007; Ramadan 2013; Schiocchet 2013) the Nakba has become all too palpable in the case of Syria, where more than half of the country's Palestinian population has been displaced by the ongoing war and close to 100 percent are receiving emergency assistance from UNRWA as of February 2015 (UNRWA 2015d).

At a very basic level, the discourse of return that permeated the engagement of Neirab and Ein el Tal Palestinian refugees with the Neirab Rehabilitation Project must be seen as an effort to ground the project in a narrative that resonates with their sense of themselves as Palestinians. Their insistence on the right of return should be further understood within an international context that gives very little importance to it. Within this international context of marginalization, refugee insistence on linking development to return should be seen as a form of everyday resistance (Scott 1985) to the apolitical ideology of development promoted by UNRWA and its donors–a resistance that is part of an "ethics and politics of refusal" (Simpson 2014), which here means the refusal to engage with narratives of improvement that fail to acknowledge and address the refugees' historical dispossession and the political claims linked to it. It is incredibly difficult for us to think or write about the refusal of "what 'sensible' people perceive as good things" (Simpson 2014:1) without seeming to portray it as an acceptance of "suffering." Ultimately, Palestinian resistance to the Neirab Rehabilitation Project must be read primarily as an attempt to underscore both the political *and* the material dimensions of Palestinian suffering rather than as an outright rejection of material improvement or as a blind attachment to the right of return.

4 "Must We Live in Barracks to Convince People We Are Refugees?"

The Politics of Camp Improvement

Aᴄᴄᴏʀᴅɪɴɢ ᴛᴏ ᴀ ᴜɴʀᴡᴀ project document released in February of 2007:

> Neirab Camp suffers from the most abysmal living conditions of all the Palestine refugee camps in Syria. The refugees in Neirab have been living for almost 60 years in dreadful and inhumane circumstances sheltered in a series of vacated army barracks. . . . Over the years, the original camp has evolved into a congested living environment with an extremely high population density offering little ventilation, sunlight or public space. This situation is particularly appalling in the area of the original barracks of the camp, where nearly 6000 of the most vulnerable refugees are accommodated under extremely harsh living conditions. (ᴜɴʀᴡᴀ 2007:4)

ᴜɴʀᴡᴀ had made several attempts in the 1990s to implement comprehensive housing improvements in the Neirab barracks, but those attempts were invariably stopped by the Syrian government. In 2000, with the position of the Syrian government having shifted with regard to comprehensive housing improvement in Palestinian refugee camps, ᴜɴʀᴡᴀ finally received the green light to proceed. Neirab would become the first camp in the agency's areas of operations since the 1950s to be the target of an ᴜɴʀᴡᴀ-sponsored large-scale housing improvement project. The lessons learned from this project would inform the institutionalization of the agency's Infrastructure and Camp Improvement Program (ɪᴄɪᴘ) in 2006.

While ᴜɴʀᴡᴀ singled out Neirab in the mid-1990s as having particularly harsh living conditions, many of the problems associated with it could be extended to other Palestinian refugee camps across ᴜɴʀᴡᴀ's area of operations. According to Muna Budeiri, deputy director of ᴜɴʀᴡᴀ's regional ɪᴄɪᴘ, "The ad hoc expansion of homes and infrastructural facilities [in Palestinian refugee camps] has often resulted in substandard shelters that are structurally and environmentally unsafe" (Budeiri 2014:191). Additionally, the absence of space for expansion as well as demographic increase forced many camps to develop vertically, leading "the camps [to become] dense, overcrowded, and hyper-urbanized settings that invariably contain large pockets of concentrated poverty and underemployment or unemployment" (Budeiri 2014:190). Finally, the combination of overcrowding and the loss of open and public spaces "negatively affected the quantity of natural light in homes and the quality of ventilation, resulting in significant adverse health effects" (Budeiri 2014:191). Citing camps such as Al Amari in the West Bank, Shatila and Bourj al-Barajneh in Lebanon, Amman New Camp (locally known as Wihdat) in Jordan, and Neirab in Syria, Budeiri warns that Palestinian refugee camps "may be approaching a tipping point, after which interventions will steadily and rapidly decrease in efficacy and the deterioration will become irreversible or if at all possible will be reparable at a high prohibitive cost" (Budeiri 2014:191).

UNRWA saw the ICIP as the answer to the housing and infrastructural problems described by Budeiri. The ICIP also represented one of the materializations of UNRWA's roughly ten-year old reform process. One of its main premises was that–emergency reconstruction notwithstanding–interventions in the camps' built environment needed to be undertaken in a holistic, integrated manner, taking into account the entirety of the camp's landscape, including its social landscape (interview, ICIP member, Amman, March 23, 2015; UNRWA 2012:199).

The ICIP also emphasized that the built environment needed to include the camps' surrounding areas, especially neighboring municipalities "to ensure that development efforts inside and outside camps are conducted in harmony and to mutual benefit" (UNRWA Camp Improvement Manual:4).[1] It further stressed that interventions in the physical and social fabric of the camps needed to be participatory and community driven because "comprehensive improvement can only take place if the local community becomes the key agent of change" (UNRWA ICIP booklet n.d.).[2]

As indicated by follow-up interviews conducted in 2015 with members of UNRWA's ICIP, and according to UNRWA's Camp Improvement Manual, the camp improvement program is still a work in progress and still a sensitive issue. Many of the challenges faced by the agency in its attempt to improve living conditions in the Neirab barracks resurfaced in subsequent attempts to improve the built environment of other camps in a comprehensive manner, framed by the discourse of development. Given the enduring sensitivity of its reform process, UNRWA's attempt to partner with Neirab's community in improving living conditions in the barracks provides a relevant ethnographic frame for thinking about what is at stake when the built environment of a Palestinian refugee camp becomes the target of development. A challenge that UNRWA faced early on and continues to face is how to conceive of improvement in a way that addresses the camp as both a physical and a social space. Another challenge was that, despite the fact that the barracks' embodied the kind of human hardship that could be eradicated through the power of development, they simultaneously played a valuable role in the camp's existence as a space of memory.

Camp Improvement in Historical Perspective

UNRWA's first attempt to improve shelters in Palestinian refugee camps dates back to the 1950s, when the agency launched is first large-scale shelter-building program to replace tents. Following the 1948 Arab–Israeli war, refugees generally set up tents or built shelters in groups and clusters of family members, clan members, and people from the same village (Budeiri 2014; Misselwitz and Hanafi 2010; Sayigh 1979). Ignoring this preexisting social and spatial arrangement, UNRWA saw the camps as a tabula rasa and envisioned new shelters laid out in the form of a grid. For example, in the West Bank in the 1950s all construction plans emanated from the same engineering office, which planned the building of the new shelters "according to a superimposed grid, divided into clearly demarcated blocks, consisting of approximately twenty individual plots and surrounded by wide streets and large open spaces" (Misselwitz and Hanafi 2010:369).

UNRWA's attempt to use a grid pattern in its housing projects largely failed. In many cases, the clusters and quarters that refugees had established based on traditional support networks prevailed (Budeiri 2014; Misselwitz 2009). After the failure of large-scale camp planning and construction projects in the 1950s, UNRWA's intervention in the built environment of camps focused mostly on repairing or renovating individual shelters (Budeiri 2014), often in the aftermath of destruction caused by war (Misselwitz and Hanafi 2010). The failure of UNRWA's comprehensive housing planning partially accounts for the fact that "the growth of Palestinian refugee camps over time has been largely unmediated" (Budeiri 2014:190). Another factor that accounts for the lack of planning is the camps' official temporariness. Following its creation, UNRWA's shelter (re)construction policy was caught between the agency's adherence to the notion that the camps were temporary and its realization of the increasing protractedness of the Palestinian refugee situation (Berg 2014). UNRWA was never able to resolve this tension, which helps explain its inconsistent efforts to address the quality of camp housing. There was never a comprehensive UNRWA plan for basic camp infrastructure services such as water, sewerage, storm drainage, and electricity. These were provided by the agency in a piecemeal, substandard fashion and were irregularly distributed (Budeiri 2014). The official temporary character of the camps also played a role in their omission from the urban planning carried out in surrounding areas (Misselwitz 2009; Al-Husseini 2011). A similar situation would prevail in Palestinian refugee camps in the West Bank and Gaza, which were largely left out of comprehensive urban development projects when the Palestinian Authority (PA) came to power in 1994 (Misselwitz 2009).

Of course, the refugees' early insistence that their camps maintain an aura of temporariness as a means of signaling their preference for repatriation also contributed to the camps' exclusion from large-scale infrastructure improvement.

Refugees' fears that such projects might signal the normalization of their situation and be exploited politically were not unfounded. Urban planning as well as housing and infrastructure improvement were all used at different times by the Israeli government as a means of either disbanding the refugee camps in the West Bank and Gaza in order to weaken refugees' resolve to return or as a tool of political pacification. After the 1967 war, the large number of refugees in the West Bank and Gaza and the continued presence of refugee camps in the area became a subject of intense debate in the Israeli government.

Discussion in the Israeli government about how to handle the refugee issue in the occupied territories led to the emergence of two major areas of consensus: one, that authorities had an ethical responsibility to improve the precarious living conditions of the refugee camps; and, two, that the concentration of refugees in camps needed to be broken up as a means of weakening refugees' attachment to their original places of residence and their desire to return to those places (Hazboun 1996; Misselwitz 2009).[3]

From 1967 until 1971, Israeli authorities engaged in a mixture of persuasion and repression in order to thin out the population of Palestinians camps in Gaza (Hazboun 1996). Initially, refugees were encouraged to move out of the camps through incentives such as emigration stipends (Hazboun 1996). This practice was ended with the intervention of the Jordanian government and the UN General Assembly, and a change of policy ensued (Hazboun 1996). Israeli authorities began housing construction outside the camps and encouraged refugees to move by offering this housing at a symbolic price and by improving public services in the new location (Misselwitz 2009). In 1970 authorities set up a secret trust fund "for the rehabilitation of the refugees outside the camps" (Misselwitz 2009:308). Initially, the fund was also used to improve the infrastructure of existing camps in the West Bank and Gaza and for community development and socioeconomic improvement, "which somewhat anticipate[d] elements of the integrated development approach adopted by UNRWA in the 2000s" (Misselwitz 2009:309). The use of the trust fund to improve camp infrastructure, presumably as part of an effort to promote the integration of refugees into their surroundings, was "almost immediately abandoned" (Misselwitz 2009:309).

Given the difficulties that they encountered in encouraging Palestinian refugees to leave their camps, Israeli authorities turned to more forceful measures, starting with a road-widening program in the camps in 1971 as a means of thinning out the population and facilitating surveillance and policing (Weizman 2007). As early as 1972, the authorities also were systematically destroying refugee homes and resettling Gaza refugees in the Sinai, in the West Bank, or in smaller camps in Gaza (Weizman 2007). Road widening was often the pretext for demolition of camp shelters and was part of a larger policy of using architectural and urban planning as tools to implement the political objective of scattering Palestinian refugees and breaking up their concentration in camps (Weizman 2007).

Like UNRWA's unofficial policy in the 1950s of combining development aid with the larger political goal of regional integration of refugees in host societies as an alternative to return, Israel's policy in the occupied territories blurred the distinction between its humanitarian goal of improving the living conditions of Palestinian refugees and its political agenda of resolving the Palestinian refugee issue on its terms.

The deliberate blurring of the boundary between humanitarian and political interests on the part of Israel and the Western-dominated international community vis à vis Palestinian refugees is crucial for understanding the historical and ongoing resistance of the refugees to improvement schemes in their camps. This is especially the case when such schemes are funded or promoted by outsiders. According to Philipp Misselwitz, on the lasting effects of Israel's refugee policy:

> Demolition, replanning, and rehabilitation became viewed [by Palestinian refugees] as synonymous with an agenda of normalization, which would eventually lead to the cancellation of [the] right of return. The politicization of planning and rehabilitation formed the context for fierce and dogmatic resistance to any proposal for the improvement of the urban fabric of the camps for years to come, whether articulated by host governments, camp communities or political activists. It significantly reduced the scope of actions available to UNRWA and other humanitarian actors to deal with the increasingly dense and congested camp fabric. Measures such as the introduction of public space, gardens, wider roads for fire engines or ambulances or new housing projects were de facto tabooed. (2009:311)

It was not until the 1990s that UNRWA reintroduced large-scale housing improvement in Palestinian refugee camps. At that point, a debate had emerged in the agency about the merits of UNRWA's existing piecemeal, technocratic approach (interview, ICIP member, Amman, March 23, 2015). Some members of the agency's Engineering and Construction Services Division argued for a more holistic approach to planning, one that would address the camp as an interconnected space and take into account its social fabric rather than treat housing as an isolated and individualized issue (interview, ICIP member, Amman, March 23, 2015). At the turn of the twenty-first century, encouraged by donors who also favored a more holistic approach and by more relaxed attitudes among refugees and host countries toward outside improvement initiatives, UNRWA experimented once again with planned large-scale housing improvement (interview, ICIP member, Amman, March 23, 2015). Neirab Camp's dilapidated World War II barracks, which had attracted the agency's attention, became the perfect testing ground for this renewed experiment.

Improving the Neirab Barracks

Even though Neirab's rectangular military barracks had been built on a grid pattern, the grid quickly disappeared as refugees extended their housing in the barracks themselves or moved out of them to build their own houses. There was no formal planning, whether by UNRWA or Syrian authorities; residents simply appropriated the space they needed to build their houses.

Echoing UNRWA's bleak assessment, the barracks had come to symbolize for many Palestinian refugees in Neirab the unacceptable in terms of what they had to endure because of their status. However, it would become apparent, once UNRWA moved to the implementation phase of construction, that the camp's residents did not view the barracks solely as a symbol of human indignity. While evoking coffins whose inhabitants were relegated to a "life of death," as Younes, the young project volunteer from Neirab, put it, the barracks had become a witness to past and ongoing Palestinian suffering resulting from the Nakba. Doing away with them would mean doing away with a key piece of visible historical proof of Palestinian forced displacement and dispossession and of their ongoing effects. Additionally, the barracks were an important component of Neirab's peculiar architectural landscape, a factor that contributed to its uniqueness as a camp, as a space that stood out from its surroundings.

Because of the sheer density of the barracks area, members of UNRWA's Neirab Rehabilitation Project team quickly concluded that no change would be able to take place without some inhabitants relocating. While the Syrian government was opposed to enlarging Neirab Camp for constructing new housing, it did agree to donate land adjacent to Ein el Tal, about a twenty-minute drive away, for this purpose. Most residents of the Neirab barracks were initially unwilling to move to Ein el Tal, despite the promise of spacious new houses in exchange for their dingy one-or two-room units in the zinc-covered barracks.[4] The project team had to organize several community meetings and visits with families to convince them that moving would be in their best interest. UNRWA set up local camp committees in both Ein el Tal and Neirab at the onset of the project to help the project team better communicate with concerned residents. Neirab's project liaison officer, Abu Hosam, usually led visits to residents. He also organized visits to Ein el Tal's new building site for those interested in moving or for those who needed further convincing.

UNRWA had assumed that struggling refugees living in crowded and run-down barracks would jump at the chance to move into spacious houses in Ein el Tal, but leaving Neirab was a difficult decision. In the fall of 2005, I participated in a survey of families from two "test" barracks that were to serve as pilots for deciding the best way to replace the barracks with better housing. My partner during most of my visits was Wisam, a project volunteer and resident of Ein el

Tal who had intimate knowledge of the barracks and the families living in them. Before the start of the project, he had been living in a one-room unit in the barracks with his wife and three children. In 2004, he and his family became part of the first group of thirty families to move to the new UNRWA built-houses in Ein el Tal.

Wisam administered the survey while I asked more general questions (in Arabic), and we both wrote down the answers, he in Arabic and I in English. The goal of the survey and the discussion questions was to get the perspective of the barracks inhabitants on their living situation and their views on how their situation could be best improved. By the time the survey was conducted, close to 300 families (the project's target number) had made the decision to move to Ein el Tal, but the project team was nevertheless interested in understanding why so many families had been reluctant to move considering the hardships with which they had to cope in the barracks.

The two test barracks were separated by a narrow paved alley and bordered the Neirab market (*sūq*). They were subdivided into contiguous housing units, most consisting of one or two rooms with a tiny adjoining kitchen and bathroom.

Figure 4.1. Children running in one of Neirab's alleys, circa 2005. Photograph courtesy of Ali Bangi.

Some also had a tiny courtyard. In a few cases, especially corner units, which tended to be bigger, families had built extra stories to accommodate their married sons, breaking the evenness of the zinc roofs. Walking away from the *sūq* into the corridor that separated the two barracks, one entered a maze of narrow alleys separating other rows of barracks and the houses surrounding them. Children could be seen running up and down the alleys, the only outside space in which they can play.

I was struck during interviews by the number of complaints about housing and, at the same time, by residents' attachment to their homes and to the camp. Residents were especially critical of congestion and the resulting lack of space. One, who had built a two-room addition on top of his father's one-room unit, complained about having to share three rooms (lower and upper unit) with eight other members of his extended family. During the interviews, which were for the most part conducted in the residents' homes, I came across a family of six living in one room with only a tiny courtyard to alleviate the crowding. Many residents also mentioned the flooding and leaking in the winter and the intense summer heat. "In the summer it's like the house is on fire," one young woman told me. The leaking was blamed on the zinc-covered wood ceilings, but the flooding was blamed on the narrow and uneven streets that separated rows of barracks housing units "stuck" to each other. "I wish I could open a window to breathe," said Mohamad, a middle-aged father of three as he pointed to the wall he shared with his neighbors. The compactness of the barracks was felt in other ways as well during the winter. "Just wait for winter. Come visit us in the winter and see the suffering we go through," Mohamad continued. "We have a neighbor who had to go to the doctor because of the pollution from the heaters." The heaters commonly used in the camps were fuel based with chimney-like pipes that stuck out from the walls of the housing, emitting smoke into the alleys.

Humidity also ranked high on the list of residents' complaints about their housing. Almost all of the houses I visited had holes, cracks, and peeling paint caused by the humidity. One resident shared a one-room unit with an adjoining kitchen and bathroom and a tiny courtyard with her husband, father-in-law, and two children. She showed me the disintegrating bathroom ceiling from which a block had recently fallen on her head and injured her while she was taking a shower. Her father-in-law slept in the camp's mosque because of the lack of space in their unit. Residents of the barracks also complained, to a lesser extent, about the lack of sunlight and ventilation. One, who lived on the lower floor of a unit that had been extended to two stories, had to turn on the lights in the middle of the day to show me the tiny two-room unit, completely hidden from the sun, that he shared with his wife and two children. In most cases, bedrooms were used as common areas during the day, with mattresses neatly stacked against the walls as a way of accommodating growing families.

Despite the run-down conditions, most residents I talked to felt a deep attachment to the barracks, partly explained by their deep attachment to Neirab Camp and to what they considered to be its rich social fabric. The support and social safety net offered by family and neighbors and the sense of security that came with close, face-to-face interaction repeatedly surfaced in interviews. One of the residents Wisam and I interviewed was Um Khaled, an older widow who was probably in her late sixties. She lived in a neatly arranged and decorated one-room unit that had been enlarged to accommodate a small kitchen and bathroom. When I asked her how she would describe Neirab Camp, she replied "[Neirab is] very nice and its people are good. They love each other and there is respect. Um Ridha was sick and everyone came to help. For example, if I get sick everyone will get up and come." She also appreciated that neighbors were always visiting each other and that she knew the vendors in the *sūq* personally, but "May Allah enlarge [this house] for us." Still, even though she hoped for a larger house, she was not interested in moving to the new housing in Ein el Tal: "No, I'm sick, I can't. Here everything is close to me, the market is close, the doctor is close" (interview, September 30, 2005).

Um Khaled wanted Wisam and me to make a special note that any changes to her unit had to acknowledge her plans to live with her son on his release from jail. Indeed, I found out that she was awaiting the return of her son, the "love of [her] heart [*ḥabīb qalbī*]," from a prison in Damascus where he was serving the thirteenth year of his sentence. "When my son left (for jail), if you could have seen how sad people were!" she told us. According to my friend Muna, her son was one of many Palestinians, recruited by the Syrian army to fight PLO troops loyal to Yasser Arafat in the 1990s in Lebanon, who ended up turning his fire against the Syrian army rather than fight fellow Palestinians (see Talhami 2001).[5]

Checking previous UNRWA statistics, I asked Um Khaled about a daughter who was supposedly living with her. I learned that the daughter had been killed in Iraq, about a year earlier, when American bombs fell on the car in which she was driving with her family. Before that, Um Khaled had lost another son in a construction accident. As she talked to us about her life and some of its tragic moments, streams of young children, teenagers (presumably her relatives), and neighbors came in and out. When Wisam and I were done, she invited me to spend the night at her place. I was tempted to spend more time with Um Khaled, but I had to tell her that I was not allowed by GAPAR to stay overnight in the camp.

I was also struck by another family's unwillingness to leave Neirab's barracks. Consisting of a widow and her seven children, this was one of the first families I interviewed. At the time and for reasons not explained to me, GAPAR director Anwar Fanous had denied me permission to go into people's homes, so the family and I sat in the library of the UNRWA-run Akka primary school in Neirab. I spoke mostly with two daughters who were particularly eager to show

Figure 4.2. Rooftop view of Neirab's barracks, circa 2005. Photograph courtesy of Thomas Ramsler.

me how dilapidated their housing was. Dressed in long black robes, their heads covered with black headscarves, they were mourning their father, who had been living in Algeria. He had been a politically active member of the Palestinian party Fatah and had died a month earlier. Occasionally wiping tears from their faces, the daughters kept urging me to come by and take a look at their housing unit and see for myself how miserable it was. The older sister, Amal, gave me an overview of her family's living situation:

> We have no one but our brother taking care of our expenses. With regard to the condition of our house, it's on the verge of crumbling down. And we truly need a larger house. Our family is very big. We have a brother in another country (Algeria). He wants to come—he and his mother (Amal's father's second wife)—they want a house. He wants to come to live here. We want a solution.... The camp in general is in very bad condition economically. It's crowded and there is no breathing space—and the worst thing is the barracks. (Interview, September 28, 2005)

Yet despite the grim situation, Amal and her sister were adamant about not being interested in the new housing being offered in Ein el Tal. They had actually signed up for it initially because Abu Hosam had "convinced" them to, but they had firmly made up their minds: they were not leaving. "I was born in this house," said Amal. "I got married but returned [she had recently gone through a divorce]. Despite all the bad conditions, I love it. I don't like to go out." Added Amal's younger sister, "If I had to live in a tent in the camp, I would prefer that to leaving. It's been thirty years since we've been living in our house. If I left, it would be as if my spirit had left me. In my opinion Neirab is better for me because we are all together" (interview, September 28, 2005).

I was eventually able to visit Amal's house once GAPAR changed its mind about my entering the barracks to interview residents for UNRWA-sponsored research. Amal and her sister had dared me to find a more miserable-looking house than theirs, and I had to agree with them. Of all the houses I visited, theirs was the most run-down. The family of seven lived in two adjoining rooms. A small kitchen and tiny bathroom were located to the right as one entered the small courtyard facing the rooms. The walls were full of cracks caused by the humidity, and the yellow tarnished paint was peeling off in areas. Aside from the mattresses stacked against the walls and the mats on the floors, the rooms were mostly barren. The kitchen and bathroom walls were riddled with holes from the effects of humidity. The house looked as if it might be ready to crumble on its inhabitants.

Nonetheless, after speaking with other residents in the barracks, I could understand why Amal and her family were unwilling to move. The extended family, as well as neighbors, acted as a crucial source of social support in Neirab, and people were reluctant to give up this support for an "isolated" life in a different place, even if that place happened to be another Palestinian refugee camp. Ironically, Neirab Camp's overcrowding, which was a constant source of complaint from its inhabitants, had resulted in a close-knit community bustling with activity where everybody knew everybody else. This was especially the case in the barracks, the most densely populated part of the camp. Neighbors were often walking in and out of each other's homes while Wisam and I were interviewing household after household. Residents would often contrast what they perceived as their "strong social relations" to life in Ein el Tal: "There, it's everyone for himself." Contrary to Neirab and its cramped landscape, Ein el Tal was made up of individual houses with yards separated by spacious streets. As an unofficial camp set up by Syrian authorities well after the events of 1948, it was the result of planned housing.

The people I talked to in the barracks repeatedly mentioned how much they loved Neirab's social interconnectedness. For many, it was a primary reason for foregoing the better housing being offered in Ein el Tal. For some, however, opposition to moving out of Neirab to another area in Syria was purely a matter of principle: "From Palestine to here and from here to Palestine. There is no alternative," insisted an older resident who was probably in his late sixties or early seventies. When I asked Mohamad, the father of three who had complained about the cramped conditions in the barracks, if he would be open to moving to Ein el Tal or somewhere else outside the camp, his response was no. "I am attached to Neirab. I will not leave it unless it is for Palestine or [because of] death." For these Neirab residents, moving necessarily meant returning to the homeland, a position that reinforced the role of the camp as a substitute for the homeland (Malkki 1995).

Residents' deep attachment to the barracks was expressed by Mai, a woman living in a two-room unit with her husband, four children, and mother-in-law. When I asked her if she would ever consider moving, she was emphatic: "No, never! I'm used to this camp. I go to Aleppo for one day and I think about when I will return. I go to Damascus for two days and I start thinking about returning. I am very comfortable here. When we were in Saudi [for a pilgrimage to Mecca], I couldn't stop thinking about when we would return. There is more security here" (interview, September 29, 2005). "Security" came up several times during interviews as one of the features of Neirab Camp that people liked the most. However, this was the security that came with the close face-to-face interactions that were characteristic of Neirab and the fact that everyone in the camp knew everyone else, or at least who they were.

I experienced this "face-to-face" sense of security over the course of my field-work. On occasions when I stayed in Neirab Camp until late at night, my friend Muna, who had been a project volunteer in both Ein el Tal and Neirab, would flag down a (usually empty) microbus (the main form of public transportation in Syria) making its way out of the camp and negotiate a fare with the driver to take me home. Before I got on board, she would sternly ask the driver which family he belonged to (both to make sure he was from the camp and to warn him that should anything go wrong his family would hear about it) and would demand he give her his cell phone number. Once the driver complied (they always did), I got get on the bus. Then Muna would make me promise to give her a call on her cell phone once I got home.

During a conversation, Atif, the teenage project volunteer from Neirab, elaborated on the sense of security Neirab's inhabitants felt. He explained that Neirab's level of generosity and thoughtfulness was unique: if someone's house caught on fire, everyone in the camp came to help; if someone collapsed on the street, people immediately came to assist. If this were to happen in Aleppo, Atif argued, nobody would do anything. During a community meeting, the project manager asked residents to describe Neirab Camp. "It's the smallest piece of land in the world with the most caring people in the world," answered one resident (field notes, September 13, 2005).

While carrying out the survey of the two test barracks, I noticed that women were much more reluctant than men to move out of Neirab, either to Ein el Tal or someplace else. Neirab's social interconnectedness and close extended family networks constituted a big part of their social life, and this was particularly important because, for many, their mobility was limited by their duties in the home. Their husbands, on the other hand, as the family breadwinners, had social networks that went beyond their life in the camp. Proximity to their (extended) family was one of the main reasons that Amal and her sister did not want to leave their dilapidated housing in the barracks.

In April 2006, as my stay in Syria was coming to an end, I went to Neirab to say goodbye to the people I had gotten to know and stopped by Amal's house. I was surprised to learn that Amal and her family had ultimately decided to move to Ein el Tal. In the months after Wisam and I had completed our research, Abu Hosam, Neirab's project liaison officer, had taken Amal and her family to see the new housing. That appears to have been a turning point. Amal told me that after seeing the new housing she and her family felt it was a good idea to move. "It's big. Plus they say the farther you are from each other the more of an effort you make to see each other," said Amal's sister, referring to family members staying behind. "Is this the kind of house one dies in?" asked Amal as she pointed to their run-down Neirab dwelling (field notes, April 6, 2006).

Refugees' reluctance to leave the barracks for new housing in Ein el Tal must be considered within the wider context of their lives in Neirab. Neirab was where they were brought together through the shared experience of exile and dispossession and the shared experience of life in the barracks, the only housing available during the camp's early years. It was also where refugees could depend on each other and, as such, was seen as a valuable social safety net. According to a survey that was part of the 2005 UNRWA-sponsored asset mapping of Neirab Camp, the great majority of camp residents turned to family or neighbors in time of need.[6] During subsequent focus group discussions, they described the support they received from family and neighbors in both material and emotional terms. Emotionally, they felt empathy toward one another, especially regarding the difficulties and constraints they shared as refugees. Only 11 percent of survey respondents reported turning to UNRWA in time of need (UNRWA and TANGO 2006).

During my interview with Anwar Fanous, he explained to me that GAPAR would never have approved of the Neirab Rehabilitation Project had the plan been to move families from the camp to an area other than a Palestinian refugee camp because of the Syrian government's insistence that Palestinian refugees, as a collective, had to be repatriated and could not be resettled in Syria. However, the reluctance of residents of the barracks to move to Ein el Tal shows that Neirab was not just any camp that could be interchanged with any other one. It was a specific place that its inhabitants greatly valued, especially in terms of the comfort and security its social interconnectedness provided them.

Even if moving en masse from one camp to another was not considered transgressive, Palestinian mass movement could be a touchy issue because it brought to the fore memories of the Nakba. During a community meeting, Atif, the teenage Neirab volunteer, made the mistake of using the word *hijra* (migration), which older refugees associated with the 1948 exodus from Palestine (Sayigh 2007), to refer to the move from Neirab to Ein el Tal. He was immediately stopped by disapproving murmurs and by fellow Neirab volunteer Muna, who lashed out, "*Hijra*? Isn't one *hijra* enough [*hijra waḥde ma bkāfi*]?" Atif sheepishly apologized and substituted *intiqāl* (move).

Having achieved its goal of persuading about 300 families to move "voluntarily" by the fall of 2005, the Neirab Rehabilitation Project team could finally set its sights on improving living conditions in the Neirab barracks. By then, and in line with the recommendations of the 2004 Geneva conference, the project had officially become participatory. The project team therefore organized a series of meetings with residents of the two test barracks as a starting point for discussions of rebuilding options.

Improving the Barracks

The community meetings included members of the project team as well as representatives of the Syrian government working for GAPAR. The team organized its first meeting for the evening of September 13, 2005. Twenty-two residents, including four women, showed up in one of the rooms of the UNRWA-run Akka school, where most project community meetings were held. They sat in rows facing the blackboard while team members sat in the front of the room facing them or at the sides. Henrick, the Swiss architect and overall project manager, opened the meeting by underscoring the importance of participation of all levels of the camp population in the search for a solution. After presenting pictures of the housing block where the families from the two test barracks lived, he opened the floor to questions. Nidal, a barracks resident, wanted to know whether funding for the project was connected to "the political situation," which set in motion the following exchange:

> HENRICK: What we are talking about are fully technical issues. After this exercise we can present a document for funding. We are addressing the project from an architectural, planning, and social point of view. We are not politicians.

> NIDAL: You are not politicians, but . . . [He is interrupted by Abu Nayef, a member of the local Neirab Camp Committee set up by UNRWA in coordination with GAPAR]:

> ABU NAYEF: Political leaders in Syria examined the project in all its aspects and gave their support. They gave more money than the donors themselves. People have been living for fifty years in miserable housing. Does improving people's housing condition mean settlement? Why should there be a necessary relationship between improving people's living conditions and

settlement? Also, those moving to Ein el Tal signed a paper saying they are in no way renouncing their right of return by moving.

NIDAL: Of course the donor countries have political goals. . . . when the donors see that the peace process isn't going well, they will stop the funds. [Nidal was articulating the argument that the project was an extension of ongoing peace talks and really a way of "solving" the refugee problem through economic integration rather than pure humanitarian goodwill].

ABU HOSAM: Suppose the donors have a bad relationship with Syria, does it change our situation? No. Let them think what they want to think, we know we will not forget our right of return.

WISAM: I am one of the people who moved to Ein el Tal. I am well known for my political activities. This project is for the improvement of living conditions and is not in exchange for the right of return. It is our right to improve our situation and live like other people. Also, it's normal for developed countries to help less developed ones. It's not necessary for development to have a political aim. (Field notes, September 13, 2005)

Wisam–with whom I interviewed residents of the two test barracks a few weeks after the meeting–was a member of the Popular Front for the Liberation of Palestine (PFLP), a Palestinian political faction with a Marxist outlook founded in 1967. He had studied communist doctrine in Moscow and Prague, where, he claimed, one of his fellow students was the son of Patrice Lumumba, the Congolese (from the Democratic Republic of the Congo, formerly known as Zaire) independence leader assassinated in 1961. Wisam was a self-proclaimed atheist well versed in the history of modern class struggle. When I told him during my 2010 visit to Ein el Tal that I had moved to Chicago, his immediate reaction was to recall that Chicago had been the site of the 1886 Haymarket labor rally.

At the time of my fieldwork, Wisam was working as a house painter but was known in Neirab and Ein el Tal as a "politician," someone who had dedicated most of his life to the Palestinian cause. A few times during our interviews or the survey, some residents expressed concern about settlement rumors. Wisam put an end to them simply by saying: "I am a politician. Do you think I would be taking part in this project if it were about settlement?" During the exchange at the community meeting, Wisam's status as a politician who supported the project was once again helpful in calming the situation. The next meeting, a few weeks later in October, was attended by representatives of eleven of the twenty-four families living in the two test barracks. Henrick had asked residents to bring suggestions about how to address the problems in the barracks, and he had come up with housing options that he thought might improve the situation. His ideas included simply renovating the existing barracks, converting them into rows of apartment buildings, and renovating only the larger and sturdier barracks units and converting the smaller and more run-down units into joint apartment buildings.

After the housing options were presented, it became clear that those who had relatively large units were not interested in exchanging them for apartments, even if doing so would mean better housing conditions in general as well as larger streets and public spaces such as parks or playgrounds (currently nonexistent). Of great importance to these residents was the fact that they could build additional stories. According to kinship rules and patterns of gendered inheritance, it is not uncommon in the Arab world for extended families to stay close to each other by expanding to accommodate married sons (daughters usually leave the household to live with their new husbands). In Neirab, it was the norm for sons to build on top of the family house once they were ready to start a family of their own. Vertical extensions were also due to the lack of space for horizontal expansion and the fact that building up was a cheaper option than buying land for building. Sizable families living in smaller and often more run-down units were more flexible about UNRWA's proposed infrastructural changes. Building vertically to accommodate sons was a difficult if not impossible task for them. They also stood to gain space if the barracks were transformed into uniform apartment buildings.

Given the mixed reactions of the residents, the UNRWA project team felt that simply renovating large housing plots that were in good shape and combining smaller plots into one or several joint apartment buildings would be the option that would satisfy most families. However, to satisfy all project stakeholders the team still had to consult with the donors, GAPAR, and the larger Neirab community.

Neirab Camp as a Laboratory for Urban Development

In December 2005, the project team organized an urban development workshop in Neirab, bringing together UNRWA representatives, Neirab community members, a representative of each of the two test barracks, UNRWA staff, GAPAR, Syrian Baʻth Party representatives (who were themselves Palestinian refugees), project donors, and "experts" connected in one way or another with urban development. The goal was to open up the discussion that had been taking place between the project team and the residents to all project stakeholders as well as to experts to arrive at a consensus on what to do about the barracks.

A major concern for donors was that any changes to the barracks result in "actual development." It was clear that they favored a solution that would revolutionize the area's landscape by providing a significant amount of public space, creating order, and promoting modern housing that would settle once and for all problems of light, space, ventilation, and humidity. These changes would be necessary in order to call the project "development."

Others stakeholders, including members of GAPAR and the Neirab community, seemed to agree. "We need to convince people that the first choice [simply renovating individual housing units in the barracks] will not solve the problem, that it will not lead to development," said Abu Hosam. For Anwar Fanous, renovation of existing housing was "just improvement of some areas." This would not, he argued, develop Neirab Camp. He also argued that project participants needed to think about the benefits to the camp as a whole and not just what individual families might feel is best for themselves (field notes, December 8, 2005). According to these views, which echoed those of the donors, development meant something new, not just an upgrade of the old.

The general consensus at the end of the workshop seemed to be that simply renovating existing barracks housing would fall short of "development" and that apartment buildings were necessary for there to be real improvement in residents' lives. Apartment buildings would do much to solve the problems of overcrowding, humidity, and lack of sun and ventilation, and would create enough space to enlarge streets and perhaps even build a small park or playground. However, the Neirab Rehabilitation Project team learned a few weeks after the workshop that GAPAR, which consisted primarily of Palestinian refugees (some of them from Neirab Camp), had changed its mind. After originally arguing that simple renovation was not real development and supporting apartment buildings as a solution, GAPAR representatives argued that the project could not deny residents ownership of a roof on which, according to "Palestinian tradition," future generations of sons would be able to build. This was the official reason for GAPAR's change of mind, but there were deeper ones.

I had the opportunity to meet with the Palestinian director of GAPAR at the agency's Damascus headquarters a few months after the urban planning workshop. I asked him how he viewed improvement in the barracks. He explained that in his understanding the project was not about revolutionizing the barracks to transform them into a model of healthy modern living. "Neirab will not become a kingdom or a city," he said. "The project is not a huge modernization project. We just want to reduce the overcrowding." He stated that he was absolutely opposed to apartments, which, ironically, would go far in reducing overcrowding: "I gave the refugees rights to the land they live on and to their roof, so how can I give a refugee the right to live on top [of another refugee]? I can improve, develop, but not change [the camp] into something else. If you replace houses with shared apartment buildings, [the camp] will become something else" (interview, April 18, 2006).

Earlier I pointed to the importance of ownership of one's roof, which enabled the household to extend vertically without having to acquire additional land. At a more general level, though, I noticed the social importance of roofs in Palestinian refugee camps regardless of whether or not they allowed household expansion. Often decorated with potted plants and flowers, roofs were a place of family get-togethers as well as a place to entertain guests. They were also where residents gathered during cool summer nights to sip tea or smoke *argīle* ("hookah" or water pipe). In these ways, the roofs were a distinctive part of Palestinian camp architecture, whether in "modernized" camps such as Yarmouk in Damascus or in more remote ones such as Ein el Tal and Neirab.

During our interview, the GAPAR director emphasized the need for Neirab to maintain its distinctiveness as a Palestinian camp, saying that his goal was not to build streets or parks but rather "to provide the minimum so that the camp remains a camp. The features of the camp should not be changed." Toward the end of the interview, he said, "The features of the camp are a way to connect to the central problem of Palestinian refugees, to their right of return. [They] are the symbol of the crime committed by Israel against Palestinians in 1948. . . . Israel [is] against things that remind it of this crime." Among these "things . . . [are] the camps and UNRWA" (interview, April 18, 2006).

Similar concerns were expressed by some Neirab residents at community meetings but not without pushback from others. During a meeting held in March 2006, a member of the PFLP-GC political faction insisted that "the camp must keep its features [*ṭabīʿa*] as a camp. . . . This camp is a community of Palestinians.

Figure 4.3. Ein el Tal rooftop decorated with potted plants, 2011. Photograph courtesy of Lex Takkenberg.

We are with development, but some people are saying, 'Take the house, all of it, and return us to Palestine.'" He was making an argument similar to the GAPAR director's, underscoring the importance of preserving the distinctiveness of the camp as a Palestinian space. He later added: "As a (political) party, we want each family to have a house and a roof. The refugee question is a political question." Abu Hosam, in response, asked, "Must we live in barracks to convince people we are refugees?" The PFLP-GC member retorted that "we have a reality that we are Palestinian refugees" and that this status had to be factored into the final decision. Neirab Camp committee member, Abu Nayef, had the last word. He said that he did not disagree about the refugee question being a political one but he had come "to talk about changing conditions in the camp" (field notes, March 30, 2006).

Such debates reveal that the issue of what to do about the barracks not only pitted the preferences of community members against those of UNRWA, the donors, or GAPAR. Neirab community members themselves were divided. For some, like Abu Hosam, the well-being of the inhabitants had to be privileged over the political interests of refugees. Others, like the PFLP-GC member, were not against development per se, but would not support it at the expense of the refugees' political interests (in this case, the camp maintaining its distinctiveness as a Palestinian space, which in his view would be compromised by modern apartment buildings). As for those who actually lived in the barracks, they tended to highlight immediate pragmatic concerns, such as the ability to use their roofs to accommodate their growing families, expanding their housing space, and improving their unit, even if a few did express concern that the project's ultimate aim was the permanent settlement of Palestinian refugees in Syria.

In sum, most of the Neirab community agreed that change was needed. The real questions, reflected in the variety of opinions, were what kind of change and how much. Do certain changes threaten the political interests of Palestinian refugees? How much weight should be given to those interests versus the overall well-being of barracks residents? For Palestinians like the GAPAR director and the PFLP-GC member, there was something threatening about the homogenizing effect of apartment buildings. During meetings, it was not unusual for Neirab residents to state that the camp should not become like any Syrian neighborhood in Aleppo as a result of the Neirab Rehabilitation Project.

The Barracks as Witness

In attempting to modernize Neirab, UNRWA generally minimized the social and political value of its identity as a camp, as a space occupied by Palestinian refugees. Neirab's barracks, its haphazardly built houses and tiny alleys, were what made it a "camp," a place that was different. The barracks, which embodied

Palestinian suffering, were a central component of the camp's existence as a space that pointed to the particular history of Palestinian refugees. Anthropologist Randa Farah (1999), who conducted fieldwork in refugee camps in Jordan, comments on the zinc-covered barracks as a defining feature of many early Palestinian camps:

> These numar al-zinco, or the zinc housing units, symbolize the refugee experience in Palestinian culture. What holds the zinco sheets in place are mainly stones and old car tires. The "zinco" appears in many if not most life histories: The "sound of "rain" in the winter as it hit the metal, leakage through cracks and crevices and unbearable scathing heat in the summer. These romanticized images are reproduced when describing "innocent" childhood memories, where despite the unbearable cold and heat, their lives had more meaning and the relations of people in the camp were closer. (Farah 1999:193)

Abu Hosam, like Farah, recognized refugees' ambiguous feelings as he remembered life in the barracks of Neirab Camp. In an article in English (with Arabic translation) published in the Neirab Rehabilitation Project newsletter, he recalled the harsh winters in the barracks during which "the rain froze before it reached the ground to form candles of ice hanging down on the edge of the zinc sheets" and that "some children and old people died from the severe cold." But "childhood doesn't know pain, but always hope. . . . What concerned me at the time was that I had to find a place to play, which was available around the barracks. The most common games at that time were marbles, football [soccer] and leap-frog . . . ." (Azzam 2005).

A conversation I heard in the fall of 2010 during my follow-up trip to Syria illustrates the deeper implications of changes to Neirab's landscape, especially when it came to doing away with the barracks. On the last evening of my visit, I met with Muna, Atif, and Nizar, all of whom had volunteered with the Neirab Rehabilitation Project in its early phases. As we sat in one of the many outdoor cafés facing the Aleppo Citadel, the conversation turned to the project's latest phase, in which UNRWA had begun rebuilding the barracks area; several barracks had already been reduced to rubble. Muna suddenly asserted: "If the barracks stayed, it would be better," calling them "a witness to the Nakba." She added: "[They] help us remember our cause [qaḍiyatnā], the presence of Palestinians in the camp, our life of poverty, our martyrs." Muna would have preferred that the barracks remain and all of their residents accommodated with new housing. Even though she acknowledged that she was being unrealistic, she explained that "when the [World Trade Center] towers fell, the United States erected a memorial; we need to have our barracks" (field notes, October 6, 2010).

Whether or not such a comparison was warranted, I believe that by linking the Nakba to the events of 9/11, Muna was trying to underscore the importance that people attribute to memorializing particularly traumatic events in their history. As Muna made clear, the barracks were a testament to the events of 1948, when around 750,000 Palestinian Arabs (out of the total population of approximately 1 million) lost their homes, livelihoods, and possessions, and became refugees. With the barracks replaced by modern apartment buildings, what would testify to the loss, desolation, and years of hardship they had endured since their forced displacement?

Neirab's barracks, as an embodiment of the traumatic past of Palestinian refugees, speak to what historian Pierre Nora refers to as "true" memory, which he distinguishes from "memory that has been transformed by history." For Nora, "true" memory is memory "which has taken refuge in gestures and habits, in skills passed down by unspoken traditions, in the body's inherent self-knowledge, in unstudied reflexes and ingrained memories" (1989:13). While sociologist Cihan Tugal questions Nora's notion of "true" memory unaffected by history, pointing out that history and memory mutually shape each other, he does recognize that "memory has a peculiar relation to the non-signifiable–to that portion of human experience that cannot be expressed lucidly in language"(2007:140). The barracks spoke to that lived, sensory, nonsignifiable aspect of memory. They were not just a material space but an affective one and as such were intimately connected to collective memory. When the crumbling barracks of Neirab Camp became threatened with disappearance, their importance as an embodiment of Palestinian suffering and as a witness to the Palestinian history of forced exile suddenly came to the forefront.

The Neirab barracks bring to mind anthropologist Kathleen Stewart's analysis of the role of ruins in the context of crumbling former coal mining camps turned into small towns in the Appalachian hills, and of Appalachians' tendency to incorporate physical remnants of the past–which Stewart refers to as ruins–into their everyday lives. These ruins, she argues, challenge assimilation into the American mainstream; they challenge "master narratives of history as progress and embody a continuously re-membered past that hits the present like a nervous shock" (1996:96). The barracks, as *lived-in* ruins, as remnants of a traumatic past embedded in refugees' present lives, can be said to have represented "an anti-progressive temporality of repetition and rupture that interrupts historical continuity" (1996:96). I believe that what was essential for those who insisted that Neirab continue to look like a refugee camp was that it continue as a space connecting its inhabitants to Palestine. It just so happened that the barracks embodied the story of loss that Palestinian refugees insist on telling. They were built during World War II, shortly before the Palestinians became refugees, not for comfort but rather to serve as temporary shelters during a period of sociopolitical instability. Despite this temporary function, the barracks came to bear the traces of a refugee return delayed time and time again. Their cracks, holes, uneven floors, and drafty zinc roofs pointed backward to the original moment of dispossession and testified to the refugees' hardship in exile. It is in this sense that the barracks contained traces of memory that "function[ed] in a manner akin to a phantom limb, in that what is felt is no longer there":

> It is a sentient recollection of connectedness experienced at the site of rupture, where the very consciousness of disconnectedness acts as mode of testimony and memory. . . . It is the ravished body that holds out the possibility of restitution, not the invocation of an illusory wholeness or the desired return to an originary plenitude. (Saidiya Hartman 1997:73)

This does not mean that nothing could or should have been done about living conditions in the Neirab barracks. Rather, I wish to emphasize the importance of memory in Palestinian refugees' self-identity (see Sa'di and Abu-Lughod 2007; Bshara 2013) and the role of the camp as a space of memory. The impending demolition of the zinc-covered barracks suddenly made clear that, along with keys, flags, land deeds, cemeteries, monuments, photographs, and artistic representations, they had become part of the material landscape of Palestinian memory (Feldman 2008b; Khalili 2005). Plans to destroy the barracks compelled refugees in Neirab to reevaluate the significance of the camp's landscape to Palestinian identity and political claims.

I also seek to emphasize the role that housing and architectural style play in articulations of collective identity and the social expression of moral values (see Smith 2008; Weizman 2011). The modern apartment buildings, for those who opposed them, symbolized assimilation into the host country and forgetfulness of one's Palestinian past. One could interpret the insistence on the part of the GAPAR director and the PFLP-GC member that Neirab continue to look like a camp as exploitation of Palestinian refugee hardship for political purposes. While their position was certainly politically motivated, recall from chapter 1 that it was the GAPAR director who, in November 2005 at a Neirab community meeting, tried to dispel widespread negative rumors about the real intent of the Neirab Rehabilitation Project and to beg the community not to let the chance of improving living conditions pass them by. It also bears mentioning that GAPAR had been initially supportive of apartment buildings as a replacement for the barracks.

The concerns expressed by GAPAR's director and the PFLP-GC member cannot be fully separated from the general uneasiness with which Palestinians in Ein el Tal and Neirab greeted the Neirab Rehabilitation Project. From the very beginning, they insisted on framing the project politically and understanding it in terms of the extent to which it might undermine Palestinian political claims. However, there was no platform for residents to fully debate these issues with all project stakeholders. When issues relating to the political interests of refugees were raised at community meetings, UNRWA employees and hired project consultants generally did not engage with them or, in the case of Henrick, simply pointed out that they were not "politicians."

An examination of other UNRWA-sponsored camp improvement projects negates the facile assumption that refugee resistance to "improvement" was simply the result of pressure or manipulation on the part of political leaders. Drawing from its experience with camp improvement projects in the Dheisheh and Fawwar refugee camps in the West Bank (which were initiated in 2007), the agency's Camp Improvement Manual states: "The most frequently reiterated fear [among refugees] is related to a widespread suspicion that camp improvement and the concept of 'strategic planning' is driven by a hidden agenda to 'normalize' the camps as permanent cities" (UNRWA 2012:32).

The reconstruction of the Nahr el-Bared refugee camp in Lebanon, under the supervision of UNRWA, is an example of widespread community support for preservation of camp specificity despite improvement plans. In the summer of 2007, Nahr el-Bared was the site of a fierce battle between the Lebanese Armed Forces and the radical Islamist (and predominantly foreign) group Fatah al-Islam, which had infiltrated the camp six months earlier (see Hassan and Hanafi 2010; Ramadan 2009). By October 2007, the Lebanese army had prevailed in the battle but the camp lay in ruins.[7]

Nahr el-Bared's refugees mobilized before any UNRWA reconstruction intervention by forming the Nahr el-Bared Reconstruction Commission for Civil Action and Studies (NBRC), a "spontaneous grassroots initiative" involving representatives of camp committees and community networks as well as external professional planners, architects, social scientists, and activists (Hassan and Hanafi 2010:38; UNRWA 2012). The NBRC drafted a reconstruction principles and guidelines document that became the basis of a partnership with UNRWA once the agency took on management of the rebuilding effort. Among the principles and guidelines was opposition to project plans to transform Nahr el-Bared into an "'ideal' camp with no relation to the camp as it existed before the conflict" (UNRWA 2012:60). The NBRC also asserted that Nahr el-Bared should be rebuilt as a "'camp' and not under any other title." Noting that camps had both negative and positive connotations (UNRWA 2012:60), among the strengths NBRC associated with the camp as a specific kind of place were "the strong social relations and fabrics, the relationship with Palestine, the right of return, [and] communal memory" (UNRWA 2012:60). Finally, while acknowledging that the destroyed Nahr el-Bared camp suffered from the lack of sunlight and ventilation as well as poor infrastructure, the NBRC nevertheless insisted that the "benefits and drawbacks" of rectifying those problems be studied in detail and serve as "the basis for acceptance, refusal or modification . . . by the community" (UNRWA 2012:61). As with Neirab, a perceived potential drawback of rectifying problems of sunlight access, ventilation, and poor infrastructure was the loss of the camp's identity and specificity. Sociologist Sari Hanafi notes that the NBRC reconstruction plan was premised on "what had existed on the ground, preserving individual housing units, neighborhoods, circulation routes and landmarks" (2010:3). He explains that "politically, the idea was to rebuild the camp as such, not as a town, therefore preserving the temporariness of the space" (Hanafi 2010:3).

Ethnographic research conducted by Adam Ramadan with residents of Nahr el-Bared further points to the importance that residents placed on reconstruction that maintained it as a Palestinian refugee space and safeguarded the project of return:

> For residents of Nahr al-Barid, rebuilding the camp means not just to reconstruct a physical living space but to remake what that place had been socially, culturally, and politically; in other words, to reconstitute the assemblage of social relations and practices that make and remake Palestinian identities. Indeed, my interviews suggest that to return to Nahr al-Barid and reassemble the camp has become an essential step along the road to eventual return to Palestine. (Ramadan 2010:57)

Roofs seem to have been a significant concern among Nahr el-Bared residents. Hanafi notes an "ambiguous desire" of the refugees "to preserve the extended-family building type as the cornerstone of the camp, where younger generations build their dwellings on top of their parents' home" (2010:3). As with concerns raised in Neirab, Hanafi explains that this desire was partly due to a concern for maintaining "the social coherence of families and village origin" (Hanafi 2010:3).[8]

The concerns of Nahr el-Bared's residents were similar not only to those articulated at community meetings in Neirab but also to those articulated by refugees during the UNRWA-led reconstruction of Jenin Camp in the West Bank, which suffered major destruction from an Israeli military incursion in April 2002. In 2003 an emergency committee (EC) consisting of "social leaders, members of the Palestinian Legislative Council, and leaders from the political parties and community centers" (Tabar 2012:50) was formed in response to UNRWA's reconstruction plans for Jenin.[9] While UNRWA argued that it would be impossible to replicate the dense interconnected architecture of the destroyed portion of the camp, the EC insisted that it be rebuilt as it had been: "Fearful of any attempt to undermine the status of the space as a refugee camp, the EC insisted that the demolished houses be rebuilt on their former sites" (Tabar 2012:51). According to Linda Tabar, behind the EC's position lay a diversity of opinion in the Jenin community about how much weight to give improvement by addressing, for example, overcrowding versus preserving "broader community interests" (2012:51). She argues, however, that the EC's position represented a consensus that had united the community, including families whose houses had been destroyed.

An additional issue that emerged in both in Nahr el-Bared and Jenin was fear on the part of refugees that modernization through infrastructural changes such as road enlargement or house construction based on a grid model would make the camp more legible and accessible to Lebanese (in the case of Nahr el-Bared) and Israeli (in the case of Jenin) authorities and serve the latter's security interests. This spatial issue was moot in Neirab, despite the camp's narrow alleys and mazelike character, which made its houses mostly inaccessible to vehicles of any kind. Given that Syrian security was already deeply entrenched in the camp through the incorporation of camp residents into the government's security apparatus and given the generally nonconflictual relationship between the Syrian regime and the refugees, concerns about road width or accessibility to outsiders were never raised at community meetings. They were also absent from government discussions because the government did not view its camps as inimical territory and because its ability to surveil the camps was not dependent on the camp architecture. These differences in the politics of the built environment as played out in Syria versus how they played out in Lebanon and in the occupied territories are a reminder that, despite commonalities, it is important to avoid homogenization and to acknowledge the specificities of different Palestinian refugee contexts.

5 "A Camp Is a Feeling Inside"

Urbanization and the Boundaries of Palestinian Refugee Identity

During an October 2010 visit to Syria, I asked project volunteer Wisam how he felt about the recent destruction of the Neirab Camp barracks. Drawing on a comparison with Yarmouk, a camp made up of modern apartment buildings which had become incorporated into the city of Damascus, he replied, "When you go to Yarmouk you say 'I'm going to Yarmouk Camp,' not 'Yarmouk City'" (field notes, October 6, 2010).

Prior to the Syrian war, Yarmouk was known as a success story of refugee integration into a host country (Kodmani-Darwish 1997; Tiltnes 2007). Located in Damascus, it was a commercial hub boasting huge open-air markets as well as modern grocery stores; its streets were lined with shops selling sweets, fashionable clothing and footwear, books, and other goods. With its three- and four-story apartment buildings, Yarmouk easily blended into its surroundings. Many of its Palestinian inhabitants were professionals working as doctors, engineers, and civil servants (UNRWA 2015f). A 2007 report from the Norwegian Fafo Research Foundation cited the camp as "one of the largest commercial centers in the country" (Tiltnes 2007:7–8). Political scientist Bassma Kodmani-Darwish agreed, describing it as "an indistinguishable part of the capital, and one of its most vibrant commercial centers" (1997:98).[1] Although it had integrated into the city of Damascus in many ways, Yarmouk was able to maintain its identity as a Palestinian refugee camp.

Yarmouk was established in 1957 by Syrian authorities to accommodate Palestinians squatting in various parts of Damascus. Prior to the current war, it was home to the largest gathering of registered refugees in Syria, approximately one hundred and fifty thousand (UNRWA 2015f). UNRWA considered Yarmouk an "unofficial" camp. The agency was more prominent in official camps, but it also provided services to unofficial camps.

Before the war, Yarmouk was generally considered to have a higher standard of living than other camps in Syria and was generally set apart from them in research studies focusing on refugee living conditions (Kodmani-Darwish 1997; Al-Mawed Mawed 1999, 2002; Tiltnes 2007; UNRWA 2015f). Several factors explain the relatively high socioeconomic status of Yarmouk's refugees. The first and biggest group of refugees who settled in Yarmouk came mostly from Palestinian cities such as Yafa and Safad and were relatively well to do. In addition, because the camp was erected on the outskirts of Damascus, it was able to partake in the area's rapid urbanization in the 1950s and was eventually physically incorporated into the city. Camp residents took advantage of Damascus' well-functioning public transportation system (which included Yarmouk) and had easy access to educational facilities and the labor market of the greater Damascus area (Tiltnes 2007). It also bears mentioning that in 1971 Yarmouk was formally integrated by Syrian authorities into the Damascus governorate (*muḥāfaẓa*) and that, like other Damascene neighborhoods, it had a municipality (*baladīyya*) (Fadhel 2012). In 1996, the Ministry of Culture built an Arab Cultural Center in Yarmouk, giving the camp the same right as other Damascene neighborhoods to have a major public cultural institution (Fadhel 2012). Finally, Yarmouk benefited from social and economic services provided by the Palestine Liberation Organization (PLO) throughout the 1960s, when the camp was considered the "political capital" of the refugees' struggle for self-determination and the right of return to their Palestinian homes (Kodmani-Darwish 1997). At a local level, Yarmouk

Figure 5.1. Yarmouk Camp before the war. Photograph courtesy of Ahmad al-Zein.

Figure 5.2. Yarmouk Street (Shar'a al-Yarmūk) before the war. Photograph courtesy of Ahmad al-Zein.

would continue to be the center of Palestinian political activism in Syria, a situation that afforded it more socioeconomic resources than other camps (Tiltnes 2007). Before the current war, the headquarters of all major Palestinian political factions were located in Yarmouk, and the camp counted numerous grassroots social and political organizations.

Space and Stigma

Prewar Yarmouk was emblematic of the generally positive relationship between Palestinian refugees and the Syrian government and people. However, while living in Damascus during my first year of fieldwork, I became aware of a discourse of danger surrounding the camp. This discourse seemed to be based on Yarmouk's identity as a Palestinian refugee camp and the stereotypes it evoked among some middle- and upper-class Syrians. In chapter 1, I mentioned that Shereen, the daughter of my Syrian landlord at the time, advised me against moving to Yarmouk because, she said, it was poor and therefore dangerous. Other Syrian acquaintances were equally concerned when they learned that I was spending time in Yarmouk or thinking about moving there. During a conversation with some Syrian friends, Basam, a graphic designer, admitted that my spending time in Yarmouk was shocking news to him as he imagined it to be a dangerous area. He then asked a question I would never have anticipated: "Do people wear shoes there?" I gave him an incredulous look, so he continued: "Or do they wear those plastic sandals?" Because he mentioned the plastic sandals, I understood that he was talking about the plastic slippers that a middle-class Damascene might wear inside his home but that a person of lower social status might wear in the streets.

Basam told me that his fear of Yarmouk probably had to do with his lack of experience with it. He then observed that, for me, being in Yarmouk was probably similar to being in "a place like Chicago." He seemed to be implying that Yarmouk was comparable to the inner cities of big American urban centers such as Chicago that are often associated with poverty, crime, and racialized ghettoes. Indeed, Basam's comparison of Yarmouk to "a place like Chicago" echoed comments made to me in the past that had racial overtones. Shereen, my landlord's daughter, ended her cautionary speech about the dangers of Yarmouk by pointing out that, from what she had seen in Hollywood movies, crime was pervasive among African Americans in the United States.

It is important to point out that despite such stereotypes a significant number of Syrians living in other parts of Damascus frequented Yarmouk's shops and commercial areas and sometimes even owned businesses in the camp. One young woman I met in 2004 whose father had owned a store in Yarmouk, spoke very fondly of the camp. I also met other young Syrians who told me they liked to shop there because of the cheaper prices. Additionally, there was a significant Syrian population living in Yarmouk. In fact, by 2011, the year that the popular uprisings started, Yarmouk's Palestinians had become a minority in their own camp, which housed approximately six hundred and fifty thousand Syrians (Bitari 2013). Despite this Syrian majority, "Yarmouk's identity has always been distinctly Palestinian, with its politics and public events focused on Palestine, and the Syrian residents themselves often becoming 'Palestinianized'" (Bitari 2013:62).

Thus, the stereotypes cannot be extended to all Syrians or even to all middle/upper class Syrians, and they usually were expressed by Syrians who were not familiar with Yarmouk. Also, they were not just extendable to other Palestinian refugee camps in Syria but to Syrian areas as well that were perceived as "poor." For instance, Lina Blin (2012) and Sari Hanafi (1996) argue that the stigmatization of the inhabitants of Syria's refugee camps is similar to that suffered by Syrians from the poor neighborhoods of Syrian towns and cities (Blin 2012; Hanafi 1996). Additionally, Blin points out that "in Syria, it is the space of the camp [which is associated with poverty] that is stigmatized and not the Palestinian population in itself" (2012:217; translation by author).[2]

The idea that it is the Palestinian refugee camp as a space rather than the Palestinian identity that is stigmatized was supported by an incident involving Saleem, a Palestinian acquaintance who was studying economics at the University of Damascus. Toward the end of my first year in Syria, I began renting a room from an elderly Syrian woman who lived in Bab Touma, a quarter in the Old City of Damascus with a significant Christian population, and had obtained permission from my landlady to have Saleem come over and help me with my Arabic. However, Saleem had asked me not to tell my landlady that he was Palestinian. When I asked why, he said, "Because she's old and she might get scared. She might think I'm uneducated and dangerous because I live in the camp."

The first time Saleem visited, my landlady was seated in the courtyard under an orange tree. After introductions, Saleem and I sat down at a table in the courtyard and proceeded to work. Later on, as I went into the kitchen across the courtyard to make us some tea, Saleem followed me, frantically asking, "What if she asks me where I'm from? What should I say? She's old and she might get scared if I tell her." I advised him to simply tell the truth. My landlady never asked Saleem where he was from while I was making tea. However, as our lesson was coming to an end, her oldest son, who according to his mother was the only Christian to have risen to the rank of general in the Syrian army, walked in. My landlady explained to him that Saleem was helping me with my Arabic. As I went back into the kitchen to wash the tea dishes, I could hear my landlady's son questioning Saleem, although I could not make out all the words of the conversation.

By the time I came out of the kitchen, the questioning had stopped. Saleem got up to leave, and as I walked him out the door, my landlady's son invited him to stay for coffee, which he politely declined. I knew this had to be a positive sign, which Saleem later confirmed. The fact that he had been invited for coffee meant the drilling session had gone well and that he was welcome in the house. Saleem later told me that he was happy he had told the truth about himself, but maintained that things could have gone either way. I asked why he thought some Syrians might be suspicious of Palestinians refugees. He explained that Syrians tended to assume that Yarmouk was like Jaramana, a refugee camp located in the Greater Damascus area (outside the city limits) and considered to be one of the poorest camps in Syria (Tiltnes 2007). According to Saleem, most of the refugees in Jaramana had little education and could be aggressive in certain situations. He then added that the situation with the Jaramana refugees was similar to that with African Americans in the United States.

These comparisons, equating (poor) Palestinian refugees living in camps to (poor) African Americans are indicative of a transnational class discourse linking space and social status. They also reflect what sociologists Michael Omi and Howard Winant have called the "contemporary globalization of racial space" (Omi and Winant 1993:8) to the extent that they are indicative of the global stereotyping of racialized groups, in this case African Americans. In one instance during my research, comparisons between Palestinians and African Americans were expressed in a positive manner: a Palestinian writer and English professor at the University of Damascus who was living in Yarmouk told me that he appreciated African American literature and liked to check out books by African American authors from the library of the American Cultural Center in Damascus. He was interested in "how people who are discriminated against identify themselves in the face of this discrimination which attempts to impose a certain identity on them." Parallels between marginalized Palestinians and marginalized African Americans and between the Palestinian refugee camp and the Black urban ghetto have appeared in other realms. For example, the documentary *Slingshot Hip Hop* (Salloum 2008) focuses on young Palestinians in Israel, the West Bank, and Gaza, who, through the experience of poverty and discrimination, come to identify with black urban youth and embrace rap music as a form of social and political critique. More recently, lines of solidarity have formed between Palestinian activists in the occupied territories and Black activists in the United States, linking police brutality against African Americans to the brutality of the Israeli occupation (Palumbo-Liu 2015).

Stereotypes about race and class aside, it is not surprising that Yarmouk, despite being viewed by social scientists and others as a success story of refugee integration, evoked images of both abject poverty and criminality in the minds of outsiders unfamiliar with it. Indeed, while humanitarian discourse propagates a representation of the refugee as helpless and destitute and relies on pity and compassion to garner support for its interventions (Boltanski 1999; Malkki 1996; Redfield 2005), refugees–and migrants more generally–are often seen as threatening by host state authorities and populations (Arendt 1973; Daniel and Knudsen 1995; Fassin 2005; Robins 2009). Syria is not the only country where Palestinian refugee camps evoke negative stereotypes among outsiders. Scholars focusing on the experiences of Palestinian refugees in Jordan, Lebanon, and the occupied territories have pointed to the tendency of nonrefugees to associate camps and, at times, refugee identity itself with pathology and/or criminality (Farah 1999; Feldman 2007b; Peteet 1996).

It is important to acknowledge that many Palestinian refugee camps, such as Ein el Tal and Neirab, were characterized by a concentration of poverty, high unemployment rates, and poor infrastructure, which helps explain their comparison to slums or ghettoes. Henri Rueff and Alain Viaro argue that the provisional status of Palestinian refugees–the fact that "host governments have had different levels of restrictions for the development of refugee camps" (2010:358) and the fact that camps have often remained isolated even when embedded in larger urban structures–has stunted their growth and impeded infrastructure improvements. Finally, as illustrated by the controversies surrounding the Neirab

Rehabilitation Project in Ein el Tal and Neirab, Palestinian refugees themselves have contributed to stunting infrastructural growth in their camps by resisting drastic changes to the camp landscape for political reasons, fearing that such changes might be perceived as relinquishing the right of return in favor of settlement in the host country. Yarmouk, for its part, had physically transformed and become urbanized to such a point that it was not unusual, at the time of my fieldwork, to hear some of its Palestinian inhabitants lament that it no longer looked like a camp. And yet Yarmouk continued to be recognized as a camp by its inhabitants as well as by outsiders. What is it, then, that made it a "camp"?

The Camp from an Ethnographic Perspective

A Camp Is a Racialized Space

Scholars have argued that a camp is a technology of containment and separation that has become part of a planetary system of segregation characteristic of the late twentieth and early twenty-first centuries (Agier 2007, 2008; Isin and Rygiel 2007). For example, anthropologist Michel Agier refers to new urban models with "gated identities" at one extreme–camps that increasingly became normalized and permanent–and "gated communities" at the other–spaces reserved for the socially privileged (2008:61). Political scientists Engin Isin and Kim Rygiel (2007) identify certain spaces as "*other* global cities [author's italics]" that share some of the characteristics of global cities and are often connected to the functioning of these cities; however, they exist first and foremost as abject spaces. Isin and Rygiel argue that one of the spaces in which "other global cities" are observable is the refugee camp, and they cite as examples UNRWA-run Palestinian camps where socioeconomic conditions are "generally poor with a high population density, cramped living conditions, and inadequate basic infrastructure such as roads and sewers" (Isin and Rygiel 2007:195).

Where did Yarmouk fit within this understanding of the camp as a particular kind of space before the Syrian war? It was not an abject space but rather one where Palestinian refugees as a whole had a relatively high socioeconomic status. Nor was it one excluded from everyday Damascene life or from the socioeconomic opportunities offered by the city. Nevertheless, by virtue of its identity as a refugee camp, it existed in the minds of some Syrians as a dangerous and destitute place, and it is partly in this sense that it overlapped with globally recognizable spaces of urban marginality (Agier 2008; Davis 2006; Isin and Rygiel 2007; Wacquant 2008a).

It should not be surprising, then, that some of the Syrians I talked to drew comparisons between poor African Americans and Palestinian refugees and implied that Yarmouk was comparable to an African American ghetto. While the two spaces emerged out of different histories and are clearly not interchangeable, there is one aspect that Yarmouk shared with present-day African American ghettos: the stigma of place (see Wacquant 2007). Furthermore, I would argue that refugee identity, like African American identity, can be viewed as racialized. Hannah Arendt saw in the post–World Wars I and II political order which was based on the sovereign nation-state, the mutation of a racially informed logic that was now targeting refugees. This logic pitted the "civilized" people of the world against those deemed to be "savages" during European colonial expansion. However, "in a world that has almost liquidated savagery," refugees appeared as "the first sign of a possible regression from civilization" (Arendt 1973:300).

Anthropologist Michel Agier (2008) argues that the contemporary imaginary through which the forcibly displaced or nationally "out of place" are stigmatized and put in segregated areas goes back to the hygienism and racial thinking typical of the nineteenth century. In her work on Palestinian refugees in Lebanon, Julie Peteet (1996) shows that in Lebanon the need to contain Palestinian "difference" in light of the country's fragile sectarian balance was central to the government's efforts in the late 1980s to confine Palestinians to camps and prevent the integration of the camps into their surroundings. While the Syrian government never forced Palestinians to live in camps, it did encourage those who were living in Syrian cities or villages to move to spaces specifically set aside for them, spaces that would become known as "unofficial" camps (see Bouagga 2014). This policy can be viewed primarily as a political strategy to prevent the integration of Palestinian refugees and ultimately as a way to pressure the international community to implement their right of return (Bouagga 2014). However, in practice it had the effect of circumscribing Palestinian identity to specific spaces that functioned as ethnic enclaves. Interestingly, an UNRWA employee, responding to a question I asked about the difference between official and unofficial camps, explained to me that UNRWA considered "any large concentration of Palestinian refugees" to be "a camp." Thus, Yarmouk's existence as a space associated with a separate Palestinian identity was part of what made it a "camp."

A Camp Is a Political Space

Given Yarmouk's physical incorporation into Damascus and the fact that it was not readily recognizable as a humanitarian space prior to the Syrian war, its visibility as a camp had come to depend less on its landscape and more on the identity and practices of its Palestinian inhabitants. According to Khadija Fadhel (2012), Yarmouk's political and symbolic dimensions in relation to Palestinian identity and the Palestinian cause were the main reasons it continued to be known as a camp: it represented both an affirmation of Palestinianness (*palestinité*) and "a political project built on the right of return" (Fadhel 2012:

312; translation by author). This affirmation and the political project of return were interrelated: advocacy for the right of return to "Palestine" presupposed the Palestinian identity of those who were advocating it. Additionally, in the current political climate, in which refugees perceive the Palestinian Authority as increasingly willing to compromise on refugee return during negotiations with Israel, "the most valuable resources that activists mobilize for the return are memories of and claims to historic Palestine" (Al-Hardan 2012:70).

The mobilization of these memories and claims bridge the political and cultural. As in other Palestinian camps inside and outside Syria, Yarmouk's streets were named after towns and villages in historic Palestine and its walls were adorned with graffiti advocating refugee return or commenting on various aspects of the Israeli–Palestinian conflict. Similarly to other camps, Yarmouk's walls also featured posters of Palestinian political leaders or *martyrs* of the Palestinian cause. One could also find in Yarmouk 'souvenir' stores selling CDs, music, posters, and other paraphernalia relating to Palestine or the Israeli–Palestinian conflict. Yarmouk's Arab Cultural Center was dedicated primarily to exhibits, plays, and music shows celebrating Palestinian identity and history.

Also testifying to Yarmouk's centrality as a Palestinian political space were the regular political demonstrations that took place in the camp over events connected to the Israeli–Palestinian conflict. While in Syria, I witnessed two massive demonstrations in Yarmouk that included flags, slogans, chanting, and parades. The first one was organized to commemorate the death of Palestinian leader Yasser Arafat in November 2004; the second one was to celebrate Israel's withdrawal from Gaza in August 2005. They were held inside the camp and brought together representatives of the numerous political factions based in the camp along with residents. While these demonstrations could be extended to other Palestinian refugee camps, Yarmouk, which happened to house the largest number of Palestinian refugees in Syria, played a central role in Palestinian political activism in Syria. It is not surprising, for example, that Yarmouk made international headlines in June 2011, a few days after Palestinians had marched to the border separating the Syrian-controlled Golan Heights from the Israeli-controlled part of the Golan in commemoration of the territories lost in the 1967 Arab–Israeli war. The protesters were fired on by Israeli forces as some of them tried to breach the border fence between the two areas, and several were killed (Kershner 2011), some of them from Yarmouk. The camp received special attention from the international press when Palestinians mourning the death of the demonstrators stormed the Yarmouk headquarters of the Popular Front for the Liberation of Palestine–General Command (PFLP-GC). Protesters believed that the PFLP-GC had incited the march to the border. They were accusing it of having manipulated the camp's youth into participating in an event they felt was much more about preserving the party's tight relationship with the Asad regime–which was in the midst of trying to quash an uprising–than concern for Palestinian rights (Kershner 2011).

During an interview, Waleed, who was in his mid-twenties and running the Yarmouk Youth Center at the time of my fieldwork, emphasized the camp's role as a center of Palestinian political activism. His situation was somewhat different from that of the majority of Yarmouk's refugees. He came to the camp because of his father's expulsion from Jordan in the 1970s for involvement in Palestinian political activism. Having come to Syria at that time, Waleed's family was not granted the same rights granted to Palestinians who had arrived during or in the aftermath of the 1948 Arab–Israeli war. They were part of a Palestinian refugee minority in Syria who were denied legal rights and status by the government. Waleed had spent time in Belgium and was married to a Belgian woman, and by the time of our interview he had managed to secure Belgian residency papers and was in the process of applying for Belgian nationality. There was no doubt in his mind that Yarmouk was indeed a camp. During our interview, he explained (in English):

> The meaning of "camp" for me is a collection of Palestinian people that are still active socially, still active politically, and connected. And I see Yarmouk Camp as most of this. And how I see this? From the beginning . . . this camp gave a lot of martyrs, in Lebanon and in Jordan, gave a lot of fighters. Until now, in Lebanon, if you go to ask in the camps, they tell you that the people of Yarmouk are the most courageous people in the fighting in Lebanon [the Lebanese civil war]. . . . For me the camp is not only barracks and poor people, no; I mean, if I come to Yarmouk one day, and I don't find any (political) posters and I don't find any (political) writing and I don't find for six months any (political) demonstrations, then maybe I will say this is not a Palestinian camp. (Interview, October 25, 2005)

For Waleed, Yarmouk's identity as a camp had to do with its particular atmosphere of political activism. Contrary to an idea commonly articulated by Palestinian refugees themselves as well as others, he saw no connection between such activism and material deprivation. He argued that those who equated material hardship with Palestinian refugee identity were "stupid." Later in our interview, he said:

> When I was without papers I did not want to [have] children because why will I [have] another miserable one without papers? Not able to move, to study, to work? Just to increase the [number of] miserable Palestinian people? No, I want more good people, more educated people with more chances, more artists, more [cultured] people. Those people can fight. Not [just the Palestinians with] Kalashnikovs and the miserable ones. (Interview, October 22, 2005)

A Camp Is a Feeling Inside

Despite Yarmouk's role as a bastion of Palestinian identity and political activism, its spatial and socioeconomic incorporation into Damascus had some refugees fearing that it was dangerously close to losing its identity as a Palestinian refugee camp and becoming "undone" in the city (Agier 2008:173). "Look at Yarmouk, it looks nothing like a camp," said a leader of the Popular Front for the Liberation of Palestine (PFLP) who was based in Yarmouk during a 2004 interview. He pointed to the camp's commercial areas, its modern multistoried apartment buildings, and the fact that Syrians were now living there. "Where is the 'Palestinian?'" he asked (interview, April 19, 2005). The PFLP leader explained that he was not advocating that Palestinian refugees live in miserable conditions, but he felt it was important that the camps remain recognizable as camps "from the outside." These comments were very similar to those made by GAPAR's Palestinian director and by Palestinians in Neirab in responding to UNRWA plans to modernize the camp's barracks area.

Despite the concerns just mentioned, I encountered Palestinians in Yarmouk who brushed off fears about the camp's changing landscape, offering a slightly different understanding of what makes Yarmouk a "camp." Generally, residents I talked to who defended its identity as a camp drew on understandings that went beyond or transcended landscape and socioeconomic resources. Ibrahim, a founding member of the Yarmouk Youth Center, explained (in English) his understanding of Yarmouk as a camp in emotional terms and in the context of the 1948 displacement and dispossession of Palestinians:

> Look, I'm Palestinian. I'm a Palestinian refugee; my father is a Palestinian refugee also. My father was born in Palestine, was kicked out of Palestine. But I spent my childhood in this camp, which teaches me that I have to return to Palestine. The camp for the refugee is a symbol of return, you see, that's why we like to keep this name "the camp." Whatever it is, it's still a camp from inside. Inside the people it's a camp. And [it] is the symbol of returning: Ok, I'm here in this camp so I will return. (Interview, February 10, 2005)

For Ibrahim, the camp also connoted suffering, but suffering understood primarily in terms of the historical trauma of displacement and exile and the longing to return to one's home:

> The word camp represents just a period of time within which we are suffering and this is why, always, I like to say "the camp." The camp is the basis of how I see my situation: Ok I'm living in a camp that means that I suffered; my family suffered before me, and we are still suffering. We have to return because it's a camp; it's not our own world. (Interview, February 10, 2005)

The camp as a temporal space as well as a space of emotional longing came up in other conversations I had with Yarmouk residents. Saleem, whom I mentioned earlier in this chapter, was not worried about Yarmouk's changed landscape or its incorporation into Damascus. He saw these changes as a positive step in his life as a Palestinian refugee. I asked him what Yarmouk symbolized for him:

> I consider Yarmouk a part of me. We were born in the camp and our family members were born in the camp and raised us here. Today, the landscape of the camp has improved to the point where there no longer are traces of suffering and we now have houses instead of tents and we have businesses and jobs and are not dependent on [outside] help like we used to be in the past. This is why we like the camp a lot. And even if one day I have enough money to buy a house outside of the camp in a better neighborhood, maybe I'll buy the house, but I won't give up my house in Yarmouk, inside the camp, because I was born here and I want to stay here in the camp and I will stay until I return to my country, Palestine. (Interview, August 26, 2004)

For Saleem, Yarmouk was a camp for the simple reason that it was populated by Palestinian refugees. In this sense, the camp was a part of him but he was also a part of it. As with Ibrahim, the camp was also a transitory space, the existence of which signaled an eventual return to one's home/homeland (see Ramadan 2010). These two dimensions, nationalistic and temporal, were linked by an internal feeling of not fully fitting into one's current surroundings. Saleem's uncle, whom I also interviewed, emphasized this understanding of the camp as an emotional condition shared by a group of people:

> A camp is not only buildings. It's a social state; it's a feeling you have inside. We live in Syria; we have good relations [with Syrians], but we feel a sense of exile [*ightirāb*]. Even if I lived in a castle I would still feel like a refugee and that my homeland is Palestine. I prefer to live in a dirty area in Palestine rather than in a castle outside Palestine. Our situation in Syria [having a status similar to that of Syrian citizens] does not cancel [*yulghī*] our relationship with the land. It is rare for people to give up their sense of national belonging. (Interview, September 26, 2004)

Yarmouk is useful in thinking about the implications of UNRWA-sponsored development in Palestinian refugee camps and the uneasiness with which some Palestinian refugees reacted to the agency's modernization plans for their long-term well-being. The issue of Palestinian refugee camps remaining identifiable as such went beyond whether refugees should live in barracks, apartment buildings, or UNRWA-built houses with yards. Ultimately, it was about their ability to live in an environment in which they could articulate their particular vision of history, their sense of themselves in the present, and their particular aspirations for the future. Was the notion of the "camp" necessary to such an environment? To answer this question, it is useful to examine the scholarship that has focused on the meaning of the camp as a space set apart from other spaces.

The Desert, the Camp, and the City

Anthropologist Michel Agier argues that Palestinian political identity rests on a double foundation:

> The memory of lost land [is] kept alive by the reiterated recollections of elders, and the confinement of refugees to the outside-sites of the camps. The camps need to keep the symbol intact of expected return, and therefore form the appropriate framework to express suffering, paralysis and non-existence. (Agier 2007:174)

And yet, as Agier points out, Palestinian refugee camps are transforming:

> For years they have undergone an urbanization that is at the level of social organization comparable to the economic practices and material dimension of what we know of urban peripheries around the world. The distinction between the city dweller and the refugee hangs by a thread. (Agier 2007:174)

Agier argues that, although the camp and the city are different worlds, they overlap in that features associated with cities are found in camps. Like cities, camps defy notions of autochthony and rootedness. Additionally, the precariousness and instability of camp life open up a space for "the formation of new subjectivities," another phenomenon associated with cities. Finally, given the increasingly protracted nature of refugee situations, camps currently tend to be built according to an urban planning approach that allows them to grow and serve practical needs beyond the emergency stage (Agier 2008). Thus, for Agier the space of the camp holds the promise of transformation into the city, but this promise is unfulfilled because of the refugees' precarious legal and social status and the confining character of the camp: "The town is in the camp but only in the form of attempts that are constantly aborted," (Agier 2008:65). . . . "The camp is comparable to a town but this status is unachieved. Everything is potential but nothing develops, no promise of life is really fulfilled" (Agier 2008:59).

If for Agier the camp cannot substitute for the city, it can "come undone" in the city, in the sense that the social and material barriers that hold its inhabitant back can disintegrate (Agier 2007:172). As a result, the displaced and the refugees cease to be "victims" and become "subjects" (2007:173). For Agier, the refugee camp is an intermediary space between the stale, remote, and empty desert and the socially and politically vibrant city. If refugees are to completely overcome the social and political limitations placed on them by virtue of their identity, the camp as a space must "come undone" so that "only the principle of asylum" is maintained (2007:175). Here, Agier is pointing to the depoliticizing effect of camps that, as humanitarian spaces, are set up to manage populations and attend to their immediate needs rather than encourage their inhabitants' independence, resourcefulness, and political emancipation (also see Weizman 2011).

Noting that "three symbolic landscapes of exile stand out in Palestinian literature: the desert, the city, and the refugee camp," Barbara McKean Parmenter offers a slightly different interpretation of the camp and the city as they relate to Palestinian identity (1994:50). In a departure from Agier, who sees the city as a liberatory, Parmenter says that "the city is a frequent setting and symbol of Palestinian homelessness in the literature of older and younger writers alike. When poets write of Palestine they usually name specific towns and villages. The city of exile, however, often remains anonymous, a technique that emphasizes the sense of detachment and placelessness" (1994:60) Thus, *the exile city is much like the desert* in its placelessness. The superficiality which Palestinian writers encounter there is akin to the barrenness of the desert" (1994:60; author's italics).

The refugee camp, according to Parmenter, is a much more ambivalent space. Like the desert and the city, it represents "the placelessness of Palestinian experience . . . [and] yet in some instances, [it] is also a potent symbol of resistance and steadfastness" (1994:63). Furthermore, it "is not a homogenous space, alien and meaningless like the desert and city. The Palestinians who live in the camps have shaped them into their own places" (1994:66). Parmenter concludes that "the desert and city form the antipode of the Palestinian sense of place and mark its outer bounds. The refugee camp is an intermediate landscape in which a sense of place is delicately maintained and strengthened" (1994:69).

It could be argued that the goal of the Neirab Rehabilitation Project was to assure Palestinian refugees of their "right to the city" (Harvey 2008) and to address the status of Neirab and Ein el Tal as "unachieved" towns, as spaces that had become urbanized but still lacked many of the features associated with modern towns or cities, including self-government (Agier 2008:58; Weizman 2011). On the one hand, refugees living in camps have an uneasy relationship with what Parmenter (1994) refers to as the "placelessness" of the city, its superficiality. On the other hand, with the Palestinian refugee issue remaining unresolved and the camps having become de facto permanent spaces, it becomes more tenuous for refugees to resist changes to the camp landscape in the name of preserving their history of forced displacement, their visibility, and their political advocacy around the right of return. One way for refugees to reconcile changes to the landscape of their camps with their Palestinian identity and the right of return is to interpret the space of the camp in a more flexible and abstract manner, emphasizing the affective, cultural, and temporal boundaries of Palestinian refugee identity and delinking material conditions from political claims.

In the case of Yarmouk, delinking meant that precarious infrastructure and social hardship were no longer the main elements testifying to historical injustice. Rather, this injustice became embodied in political activism, which was itself linked to the production of a separate Palestinian identity. This delinking of the refugees' material conditions from their political claims was also noticeable in some of the local rhetoric concerning the Neirab Rehabilitation Project. As mentioned earlier, Wisam downplayed the significance of the barracks to Neirab's identity by pointing to thoroughly urbanized Yarmouk: "When you go to Yarmouk, you say I am going to 'Yarmouk Camp,' not 'Yarmouk City.'" Although this answer implied a contrast between the camp and the city, it also suggested that the features that make a camp distinct go beyond its level of urbanization.

Another instance of the delinking of Neirab's material conditions from its identity occurred during the conversation between Atif, Muna, and Nizar that I mentioned in chapter 4. Muna's comment, "If the barracks stayed it would be better," was only the beginning of a much longer conversation that showed that the flexible attitude of some of Yarmouk's residents about their refugee identity in relation to the landscape of their camp was held by some Neirab residents as well. Indeed, Muna's words set off a debate in which she and Atif and Nizar, who had joined us in Aleppo on an October evening at an outdoor café, took part. Like Muna, Atif and Nizar were from Neirab and like her they had worked as volunteers on the Neirab Rehabilitation Project. Another similarity that all three shared was the fact that none of them had grown up or was living in the barracks area.

Unlike Muna, both Atif and Nizar downplayed the role of the physical structure of the camp as witness to the Nakba, emphasizing other ways of keeping the memory of Palestinian displacement and dispossession alive. According to Nizar, "What is important is that that this area [Neirab] should be called 'Neirab Camp.'" For him, a "camp," whether it was made up of "buildings, barracks, or high buildings . . . refers to the fact that we are still refugees, we have our rights, and the most important right is the right of return. The name camp means our stay is temporary."

"Leave one barrack to be a witness to the Nakba" Muna retorted. "The barracks are gone. There is nothing left to show how people used to live."

According to Atif, who was also skeptical of Muna's viewpoint, "The biggest witness to the Nakba is [Resolution] 194 which protects the right of return." He later added: "The barracks are not the only witness [to the Nakba]; international law is a witness, the presence of UNRWA is a witness."

"How long should people have to live in barracks?" asked Nizar. He questioned Muna on whether she thought children would be negatively affected by growing up in "modern houses." "No; they won't forget" Muna replied; she apparently did not agree that Palestinian refugees would "forget" about Palestine and about the right of return once they started living the comfortable lives promised by the Neirab Rehabilitation Project. Still, she wanted at least one barrack to remain "so that people from outside see how we live, witness our suffering." Atif responded:

> People, when they are able to rise out of poverty, become educated, become doctors, engineers, if material conditions get better, they can improve their condition, they can improve their cause [*qaḍiyya*]. It is not necessary to live in barracks, to stay poor, to remain committed to Palestine. The Palestinian land remains in our heart; our accent is Palestinian; our heritage [is Palestinian]. (Field notes, October, 2010)

For Ibrahim, Salim, and Nizar, the notion of the camp was important primarily as a nominal category rather than as an expression of physical and material conditions. For Atif and Waleed, the notion of the camp was tied to specific cultural and political practices. For Muna it was tied to the ability to testify to the suffering of the Nakba and the ongoing suffering engendered by it. Saleem's uncle and Ibrahim underscored that the notion of the camp had affective dimensions. Both Agier and Parmenter point to the camp as a specific kind of space that is distinguishable from the city, and Parmenter notes that in the Palestinian literary imagination the camp is more conducive than the city to building a meaningful community in exile.

If one takes into account all of the understandings of the camp evoked so far in this chapter, it appears that the notion of the camp is useful to the creation of a space of difference, a space that, for historical and political reasons, is not able to be assimilated. Despite the disempowering and depoliticizing effects of the camp, especially when conceived in humanitarian terms (Agamben 1998; Agier 2008), some of the ideas articulated above implied that there are ways of producing the camp as a space of difference without concurrently advocating physical isolation or jeopardizing social and political fulfillment. Is there is a way for the camp to be an exceptional place without being a space of exception (Agamben 1998)? Further examination of Yarmouk Camp, including the effects of the Syrian war on the camp, helps elucidate this question.

Yarmouk as an Exceptional Place

Yarmouk is one of the Palestinian refugee camps most affected by the ongoing war in Syria. It became engulfed in the fighting between Asad's troops and anti-government rebels in December of 2012, and geography played an important role in its fate: the camp happened to be on the path of Syrian rebels advancing from conquered territory in the south and attempting to lay claim to Damascus. After Syrian rebels infiltrated the camp, government troops responded by shelling it. As the fighting escalated, causing severe destruction and mounting civilian casualties, an increasing number of Palestinian refugees (as well as the Syrians who had settled in the area) fled. By February 2013, an estimated 70 percent of the camp's

Palestinian population was gone (UNRWA 2013a). Until June 2013, UNRWA was able to provide emergency assistance to the Palestinians who remained. In July 2013, however, the camp was sealed off from Damascus by the Syrian government, effectively barring any assistance, including food and medicine, from reaching the roughly eighteen thousand Palestinians (out of total prewar refugee population of approximately one hundred and fifty thousand) still trapped inside (Amnesty International 2014a; UNRWA 2015g). According to a 2014 Amnesty International report, "Scores of civilians [from Yarmouk] are reported to have died as a direct result of the siege or as a result of attacks by the Syrian government forces," with starvation, lack of adequate medical care, and shooting by snipers said to be the three main causes of death (Amnesty International 2014a:4). Around April 2013, Syrian authorities cut Yarmouk's main power supply (Amnesty International 2014a), and as of June 2015 the camp had been without electricity for two years and without municipal water for about eight months (SREO 2015).[3] During some of the harshest periods of the siege, for example between fall 2013 and January 2014, many residents were forced to subsist on a diet of leaves or weeds, which they foraged at the risk of sniper fire (Amnesty International 2014a). Conditions were so dire that a fatwa was reportedly issued by local sheikhs that allowed residents to eat cats and dogs (Amnesty International 2014a).

The publicity garnered by such hunger and starvation (Al Jazeera 2013a; UNRWA 2013a; Wood 2013) was somewhat effective in forcing the Syrian regime to ease restrictions against humanitarian assistance, and in mid-January 2014 intermittent food distribution began (Amnesty International 2014a). An agreement reached in early 2014 negotiated by representatives and supporters of the Syrian regime, armed opposition groups vying for control of Yarmouk, and members of the Ramallah-based Palestinian Authority further contributed to easing the humanitarian crisis: hundreds of sick and wounded civilians, together with some family members, were allowed to leave the camp (Amnesty International 2014a). However, the distribution of food and medical supplies remained inconsistent and was often cut off by fighting in the area.

On April 1, 2015, Yarmouk was invaded by ISIL (the Islamic State in Iraq and the Levant), which quickly claimed control of most of its territory. Syrian authorities responded with heavy shelling (Al Jazeera 2015; The Telegraph 2015; SREO 2015) Yarmouk's residents became caught in a three-way conflict between ISIL, the Syrian government, and local Palestinian fighters from Yarmouk's Aknaf Beit el-Maqdis, a group with alleged ties to Hamas that is opposed to both the government and the Islamic State (SREO 2015). Some of Yarmouk's residents were able to flee to the surrounding rebel-held Syrian neighborhoods of Yalda, Babilla, and Beit Saham (ICRC 2015). On April 7, 2015, UNRWA spokesperson Chris Gunness declared in a radio interview that while conditions in Yarmouk were already "appalling" before the ISIL invasion, the camp had "descended even further into unimaginable levels of inhumanity" (NPR 2015). In June 2015, the SREO, an independent, nonpartisan research center based in Gaziantep, Turkey, released a report stating that, according to Yarmouk residents, no humanitarian organizations, including local ones, had been operating in the camp since the ISIL invasion (SREO 2015). As of February 2016, UNRWA is still being denied access to the camp, with its last food distribution there in March 2015 (email exchange with UNRWA representatives, September 22, 2015; NPR 2015; UNRWA 2015; UNRWA 2016).

Postwar Yarmouk comes closer to evoking the Agambian notion of a space of exception than it does to any of the meanings laid out in this chapter. Although this notion is problematic in that it inadequately accounts for some of the main features that made Yarmouk a camp in prewar Syria, it is relevant to an understanding of the dramatic reversal of the refugees' fortunes as a result of war.

Drawing on the work of German political theorist Carl Schmitt, Giorgio Agamben (1998) uses the term *space of exception* to describe a space where law has been suspended and where inhabitants live only a "bare life," devoid of any social or political significance. What is emblematic of this space is that the treatment of those who inhabit it depends not on the law but on the goodwill of those who have power over it (1998). In such a space, fact and law become blurred and "anything is possible" (Agamben 1998).

Camps in prewar Syria were not characterized by the suspension of law. The vast majority of Palestinian refugees were protected by Law No. 260, which granted them most Syrian citizenship rights. At the same time, one could argue that prewar Yarmouk lent itself to an understanding of the camp as a space of exception–not as a reality but as "an ever-present possibility" (Caton and Zacka 2010:209), one that looms more strongly over particular groups such as the stateless and refugees.

Besieged Yarmouk has indeed become a place where "anything is possible." To what extent has its identity as a camp contributed to this state of affairs? Syrian towns and neighborhoods have also suffered government-imposed as well as rebel-imposed sieges as a result of the war, but Palestinians I interviewed in March and April 2015 argued that no siege has been as long-standing and as thorough as Yarmouk's. This assertion is supported to a certain extent by Amnesty International, which notes that in comparison with other Syrian areas the siege of Yarmouk "has been particularly prolonged, has had the harshest impact, and has caused the largest number of deaths from starvation" (Amnesty International 2014a:4). Palestinians I spoke to also argued that although the besieged residents of Yarmouk could technically get food from surrounding rebel-controlled areas, this food costs three to four times what it costs elsewhere in Damascus and its surroundings, placing it out of reach of most residents (also see Amnesty International 2014a). Finally, they pointed to a common phrase heard in surrounding Syrian neighborhoods as access to food became more difficult: "The goods of the country for the people of the country [*kheir el-balad la ahl el-balad*]." Several of the Palestinians I interviewed told me that for the first time in their lives they felt a fundamental difference between themselves and Syrians.

Additionally–and this is an area where Agamben's arguments are also relevant–Syria's extension of legal rights and protection to most Palestinians did not come from a sense of legal obligation; the government can stop this legal protection at any time. And, as Waleed's story indicates, some Palestinians in Syria do not have any kind of legal status. There is no effective global or international system that can force a government to grant rights to post-1948 Palestinian refugees or prevent it from taking those rights away. For instance, Palestinian refugees in Iraq, who used to benefit from a wide array of social rights, including affordable housing and access to public education and employment, found these rights, as well as their very lives, in jeopardy in the aftermath of Saddam Hussein's downfall, when some segments of the Iraqi population turned on them, pointing in part to their status as "foreigners" (Human Rights Watch 2003).

In their study of the juridical and political dimensions of Palestinian refugee camps in Lebanon, Hanafi and Long point out that as a way to punish the Palestinian political leadership for its support of Saddam Hussein during the first Gulf War, the League of Arab States amended its Casablanca Protocol, whose initial goal was to ensure that Palestinian refugees in Arab host states would be guaranteed certain civil rights, such as the right to employment and the right of movement. The protocol now states that the status of Palestinian refugees should be determined at the national rather than the Arab level, prompting Hanafi and Long to conclude: "Under the prevailing interpretation of international law, the 'rights' of Palestinians were not so much *rights* as *privileges* that could be revoked with little ceremony and without justification [italics in the original]" (2010:144–145).

Even those Palestinians who acquired citizenship in their host country are at risk of losing their legal privileges from one day to the next. According to Human Rights Watch, the Jordanian government has been quietly stripping some Palestinians of their Jordanian citizenship, using criteria that leave roughly two hundred thousand Jordanian Palestinians vulnerable (Human Rights Watch 2010).

The global vulnerability of Palestinians because of their statelessness and their refugee status has been further highlighted by the war in Syria. In the early days of the war, and unlike their Syrian counterparts, Palestinians (many from Yarmouk Camp) were frequently turned back when trying to cross into neighboring Arab countries. Jordan, and Egypt in particular–and Lebanon to a lesser extent–were accused of arbitrarily denying Palestinians entry at certain times (Erakat 2014; Human Rights Watch 2012). Additionally, Jordan was accused of arbitrarily detaining Palestinian refugees who had gained entry into the country, and Egypt (which is not an UNRWA area of operation) was accused of denying them basic rights such as those enshrined in the 1951 refugee convention and the UNHCR statute (Erakat 2014).

Almost since the beginning of the war, fleeing Palestinians have been barred from Jordan; they face deportation back to war-torn Syria if they attempt a border crossing (Human Rights Watch 2014). As of January 2014, they are usually unable to obtain entry visas to Lebanon at the border, and so many are forced to cross into the country illegally, making it difficult for them to build stable lives (Amnesty International 2014b). Additionally, the Lebanese government has stopped renewing the residency permits of Palestinians from Syria who are on its territory, meaning that most of these Palestinians are living in fear of being arrested and deported (Amnesty International 2014b; interview, UNRWA employee, Lebanon, March 30, 2015).

While relevant to an understanding of Yarmouk as a camp, especially in light of the Syrian war, the Agambian concept of the camp as a space of exception should not blind us to other ways in which Yarmouk was and is exceptional. Before the war, the camp was exceptional in the way it combined socioeconomic integration into Damascus and its status as a major commercial center with an enduring identity as a refugee camp known for political activism around the Palestinian cause. Additionally, as it has suffered under siege, warfare, and destruction, its inhabitants have shown tremendous resourcefulness, sometimes paying with their lives. One example of this resourcefulness is the several schools that were established by besieged residents once the camp was cut off from the rest of Damascus and from UNRWA services (according to the founder of one of these schools who eventually fled to Turkey and whom I interviewed in spring 2015, UNRWA closed its schools in Yarmouk in December 2012). These "alternative schools" have functioned throughout the siege, and at the end of the 2013–2014 academic year, as a result of negotiations between UNRWA and the Syrian government, Yarmouk high school students were allowed to leave the camp for a week to take their exams in Damascus (interview, UNRWA employee, Amman, March 22, 2015). Residents with medical knowledge and volunteers have been able to keep the Palestine Hospital (Mashfa Filasṭīn), the only hospital in Yarmouk that has not been destroyed, open and running despite a chronic lack of equipment and supplies. Volunteers have mobilized to collect trash and distribute food and drinking water.[4] These examples are a reminder that, even in the most disempowering and inhumane situations, individuals have a capacity for agency and resourcefulness (Ticktin 2006).

In this chapter, I have tried to go beyond hegemonic understandings of the refugee camp, which tend to reduce it to social marginality, powerlessness, and material scarcity, while still acknowledging the vulnerability of the refugee's status (and, in this case, statelessness) on both a local and a global scale. I have shown that neither Yarmouk's socioeconomic and infrastructural changes over the years nor its incorporation into Damascus managed to strip it of its identity as a "camp." The example of Yarmouk underscores the fact that a camp is not simply a physical space. Camp boundaries are produced and reproduced by refugees through their sociocultural practices, including political activism around the Palestinian cause. The boundaries are also embodied by the refugees themselves, given that their Palestinian identity in itself has come to signify the temporariness of their stay and their commitment to return. Finally, an important aspect of Yarmouk's enduring identity as a camp, despite integration into the city, lies in its function as an affective space. For some of the Palestinian refugees I interacted with, the camp as a site of suffering was not just a physical, tangible space; it was also an emotional space, a "feeling inside." It was a feeling of difference connected to a sense of exile and to the memories of the Nakba and the suffering it unleashed. It was also a feeling of injustice that translated into collective political activism around the Israeli–Palestinian conflict and, more specifically, the right of return. Finally, I have shown that Syrian citizens are part of the camp constituted as a separate and meaningful space. For some middle- and upper-class Syrians, the camp as a "feeling inside" took the form of fear arising from the social stigma attached to refugee camps, which were assumed to be poor and therefore dangerous and so to be avoided. In light of these different conceptualizations of the Palestinian refugee camp, it no longer seems strange that Yarmouk in prewar Syria was seen by some as a vibrant commercial area where the physical traces of past suffering had all but disappeared, and at the same time seen by others as a poverty-stricken, dangerous no-go zone; or that it was touted by some as an example of successful refugee integration into the host country and yet continued to exist as a "camp."

Prewar Yarmouk Camp is useful to thinking about how to reformulate the camp as a particular kind of refugee space that is not excluded from the advantages conferred by citizenship or by the realm of the city and at the same time, is amenable to a "politics of the displaced" (Weizman 2011:61). However, postwar Yarmouk reminds us of the enduring vulnerability of refugees and stateless persons and of the ease with which Yarmouk went from being recognized as an exceptional space to being primarily recognizable as a space of exception.

Conclusion

Beyond Suffering and Victimhood

WHEN I TOLD my friend Saleem, who lived in Yarmouk Camp in Damascus, about the rumors circulating in Neirab and Ein el Tal that the Neirab Rehabilitation Project was a ploy to make refugees "forget" about their homeland, he replied simply, "Tell them that we are living well here and we have not forgotten." It often struck me that if the Neirab Rehabilitation Project were to achieve its goals, at least as far as UNRWA was concerned, Neirab and Ein el Tal could very well end up looking somewhat like prewar Yarmouk. However, as Saleem pointed out, Yarmouk's Palestinian refugees had not forgotten. Yarmouk might have become integrated into Damascus and might have acquired hundreds of thousands of Syrian residents, but it was still a distinctively Palestinian space.

If one thinks of memory not as an attempt to recover the past but as an attempt to "underscore the loss inscribed in the social body and embedded in forms of practice" (Hartman 1997:75), then it can take many forms. Despite having physically and economically merged into Damascus, Yarmouk had managed to maintain a distinctively Palestinian feel mainly through the social and political engagement of the refugees who lived there, their cultural activities that celebrated their Palestinian heritage, and their creativity in inscribing Yarmouk's changing landscape with reminders of their identity as refugees and Palestinians.

Yarmouk's landscape of apartment buildings even proved amenable to perpetuating the "Palestinian tradition" of sons inheriting the roof from their fathers. Often, different families occupied different sections of the building; it could be said that sons still lived "on top" of the familial home. Sometimes an extended family owned the whole building, with different family branches living on top of one another.

What the example of Yarmouk shows is that infrastructural modernization and socioeconomic transformation did not lead to a loss of refugees' political consciousness or Yarmouk's identity as a Palestinian refugee camp. However, transformation did come, primarily from the refugees themselves; it was led by them, and it was incorporated into the political work of creating a meaningful community of Palestinians who maintained a connection to their past and advocated a just resolution to their refugee status.

In Ein el Tal and Neirab, which had never had the kinds of resources that were available to Yarmouk, the promise of improvement came in the form of an UNRWA-sponsored development project funded primarily by Western donors whose foreign policy sometimes clashed with the refugees' political aspirations. UNRWA's participatory approach implied that Palestinians in Ein el Tal and Neirab would play a major role in changing the living conditions in their camps (presumably for the better) and do so in a way that would safeguard their common interests as Palestinian refugees. The outcomes of the Neirab Rehabilitation Project in both camps were mixed with regard to the improvement of refugees' social and material conditions. In terms of setting up an enduring structure of trust and partnership between UNRWA and Palestinian refugees, the project was a quasi-failure (this will become clear later on).

The Outcome of the Neirab Rehabilitation Project

The Neirab Rehabilitation Project was in its second phase, focusing on Neirab, when the popular uprisings began in March 2011. The project came to a halt as the country moved toward full-fledged war in the summer of 2012. By the time of my last follow-up visit to Syria in October 2010, most of the Neirab barracks had been destroyed and UNRWA was in the process of replacing them with new housing.

During my visit, the project's most recent (German) manager explained that UNRWA had given up on the grand idea of razing the entire barracks area to make room for sprawling apartment complexes, which would have created significant space on the ground and drastically modernized the camp's landscape. In the end, UNRWA, with the support of GAPAR and the Neirab community, opted for a mixed approach that entailed consolidating smaller and more run-down units in the barracks into clusters of apartment buildings and simply renovating larger barracks units. This approach enabled the camp to keep much of its original layout as well as the distinct character given to it by its mazelike intertwining alleys–something that the manager felt was important to camp residents (interview, October 4, 2010). He told me that, in line with the wishes of Neirab refugees, one barrack would be left untouched and standing, as "witness" to the hardships the refugees had experienced as a result of their forced displacement (interview, October 4, 2010). As Muna had advocated during her heated debate with fellow project volunteers Atif and Nizar, this "last barrack standing" would be become a memorial of sorts, marking the transition of the barracks from a space of *lived memory* to a space of history.

By January 2011, shortly before the start of the uprisings, a few apartment units had been built. A new school had also been built and a health center and a sanitation station were under construction. Most of the "social development" side of the project, however, had yet to materialize (ICIP pamphlet n.d.; ICIP booklet n.d.; interview with member of UNRWA's Infrastructure and Camp Improvement unit, March 23, 2015[1]). By 2010, the year of my last follow-up visit to Neirab, a youth skills training and employment center, funded by the European Union, had been created. UNRWA had planned to create community-based organizations in the camp "in order to run and maintain the achievements of the project cycle," but these plans had been interrupted by the war (UNRWA ICIP pamphlet).

The first phase of the Neirab Rehabilitation Project, which took place in Ein el Tal, was completed in 2007, well before the uprisings and subsequent war. In accordance with project plans, approximately three hundred families from the Neirab barracks had moved to the completed new houses in Ein el Tal,[2] which, in addition to providing these families with upgraded and more spacious accommodations, helped relieve the barracks' overcrowding. Overcrowding in general and in the barracks more specifically had been a major complaint revealed by UNRWA's asset mapping of Neirab. Initial problems with water supply to the new housing seemed to have been solved with the construction of a nearby water tower, and the existing water distribution system had been improved with new

Figure 6.1. Destroyed Neirab barrack with new, almost completed apartment building in the background, 2011. Photograph courtesy of Lex Takkenberg.

Figure 6.2. New apartment buildings in Neirab Camp, 2001. Photograph courtesy of Lex Takkenberg.

Figure 6.3. EU-funded Youth Training Center, Neirab Camp, 2011. Photograph courtesy of Lex Takkenberg.

piping. Additionally, Ein el Tal's roads had been repaired and paved, and a camp-wide sewerage system had been installed.

Another major change resulting from the project was that the camp's hilly interior had become accessible to public transportation. Also, the project was able to secure a permanent space in the camp for a childcare center started by Ein el Tal residents. Through the project's efforts, there was also now a soccer field in the camp, built in response to a major community complaint about the lack of activities for youth (in practice, these changes benefited only male youth). Another major complaint revealed by UNRWA's asset mapping had been that the camp's UNRWA clinic only functioned half-time. By the time of my 2010 visit, it was functioning on a full-time basis.

Ein el Tal residents I talked to during my October 2010 follow-up trip over-whelmingly expressed satisfaction with the camp's infrastructural changes. They also noted with satisfaction that by the end of the project's first phase, stores selling basic goods had increased, saving residents the trouble of having to go all the way to Aleppo for daily necessities.

Figure 6.4. New water tower in Ein el Tal, 2011. Photograph courtesy of Lex Takkenberg.

Figure 6.5. New soccer field in Ein el Tal, 2011. Photograph courtesy of Lex Takkenberg.

Palestinians who had left Neirab for Ein el Tal were not necessarily impressed by the project improvements in their new home, however. While conducting follow-up research in spring 2015 among Palestinians who, because of the war, had fled Ein el Tal and Neirab for Turkey, I heard news that questions the idea that a group's material and social conditions can be improved by moving them to a different place. It appears that a number of families who had moved from Neirab's barracks to the new houses in Ein el Tal simply could not get used to life in their new camp and had moved back to Neirab.[3] Fatima and Maysoun, two Palestinian women and former inhabitants of Ein el Tal's new houses, whom I interviewed in the town of Kilis in southern Turkey, told me that after a few years they had chosen to return to Neirab even though this meant they had to rent a place to live. Maysoun and her husband had managed to rent their house in Ein el Tal for a short period, but Fatima and her husband had left theirs empty. According to the women, a significant number of families who had moved to Ein el Tal had returned to Neirab by the time of the uprisings.

Ein el Tal's physical and social layout was not conducive to the kind of sociality Fatima and Maysoun had enjoyed in Neirab, and it was the main reason for their decision to return. According to Fatima, "There wasn't much social activity [in Ein el Tal]. We were used to having everything near us, including our families. The majority of [my] family stayed in Neirab and there is a big distance between the two camps so there were a lot of difficulties in our daily lives" (interview April 7, 2015). For her part, Maysoun could not get used to Ein el Tal's spread-out and sparsely populated landscape, and she complained that there was no school or pharmacy at the top of the hill, where the new houses had been built (interview, April 7, 2015).

Other outcomes of the Neirab Rehabilitation Project in Ein el Tal were not particularly successful. One was the creation of an "employment office" to answer the lack of stable employment that had been one of the major problems listed by Ein el Tal residents during asset mapping. An employment advisor had been hired to help residents with job searches and professional networking in the greater Aleppo area.[4] However, lack of funding led the employment office to close by 2009, two years after the project's first phase had officially come to an end. Additionally, plans to build an Ein el Tal community center had not materialized. During an interview, a member of the Neirab Rehabilitation Project team explained that UNRWA had shelved plans for the center because its vision of a community-run center was at odds with GAPAR's insistence on having some form of control. He believed that it had perhaps been a bit naïve on UNRWA's part to promote independently run and community-based organizations in the first place, given that there is not really an independent civil society sector in Syria.

Finally, it can be said that the Neirab Rehabilitation Project had never galvanized either Ein el Tal or Neirab's population around the idea of partnering with UNRWA on issues relating to the long-term socioeconomic well-being of Palestinian refugees. The community-based organizations that the project had helped to create in early 2006 in Ein el Tal had all but dissolved by the time of my 2010 visit, and the momentum gained from refugee involvement in the project's first phase had withered. There are several reasons for this state of affairs. One of them is UNRWA's vast and hierarchical bureaucracy. For example, because there were no sports facilities in Ein el Tal, in early 2006 the newly formed "sports group," with the help of the project team, requested the use of UNRWA's al-Zeeb School playground after hours. This effort turned into a long and eventually, unsuccessful ordeal. Receiving initial permission from URNWA required weeks of lobbying various high officials at UNRWA's Damascus-based education department. However, barely a month after permission was finally granted, the sports group had to return the key for which it had struggled because a high level UNRWA employee had decided that the group had not followed proper procedures in obtaining it.[5] In the summer of 2009, a former member of the now defunct sports group informed me that the group was never able to regain access to the key.

According to a UNRWA-commissioned project evaluation report regarding the community based "library group," "It took advocating, over 20 meetings, letters, etc., for a period of six months for the Neirab Rehabilitation Project team and the 'library group' to finally get permission for the community to use an empty school room to develop a community library" (Byrne 2006:5). Regarding bureaucratic obstacles, a 2006 UNRWA-commissioned project evaluation report states: "[Refugees] were not, and did not feel, involved or empowered. Because staff and communities were too removed from planning, decision-making and monitoring, there hasn't been a sense of ownership [of the project]" (Byrne 2006:1).

Another obstacle to UNRWA's ability to forge a strong partnership with refugees in Ein el Tal and Neirab was the project's relationship with its volunteers, who had been recruited during the project's early phase. The project team did not make a concerted effort to maintain a close relationship with the volunteers it had recruited for the asset mappings once their services were no longer needed. Such an effort would have helped with subsequent community involvement and trust building. I knew of at least two asset-mapping volunteers in Ein el Tal who resented the project team because, in their view, it had made use of them and then discarded them once the job was done and their services were no longer needed. "You [the Neirab Rehabilitation Project team] have abandoned us," one female former volunteer said, complaining that she hadn't heard from the team since the end of the asset mapping in Ein el Tal (interview, January 25, 2006). Another female former volunteer, Ilham, was deeply hurt, especially given the project's encouragement of "social development," because she had put on an embroidery exhibit in Ein el Tal on her own and had received no visits or acknowledgment from the project team. Ilham was also upset because her brother, also a former volunteer, had gotten into a serious car accident and it had been weeks before anyone from the team had come to visit him.

These volunteers believed that they had helped the project team get the Neirab Rehabilitation Project off the ground. They had seen their relationship with the team as one of mutual help and support channeled into the goal of improving conditions in the camp, and they had expected it to continue once the asset mapping was completed. UNRWA had failed to recognize the personal dimensions of a "participatory" project such as the Neirab Rehabilitation Project, which reached into the everyday lives of the refugees of Ein el Tal and Neirab. The resentment of the volunteers underscores the work that still needs to be done for a sense of equal partnership to develop between UNRWA and refugees. It is easy to overlook the refugees' contributions to the project given that UNRWA had initiated the project and had disproportionate access to power and resources. However, a philosophy of mutual help and support toward a shared goal would have been more productive than one that implicitly reaffirmed UNRWA as the "helper" and the refugees as "those being helped."

Finally, that the "social" (as opposed to "infrastructural") component of the Neirab Rehabilitation Project had not produced any noticeable results had to do with what has been presented in this book as the disconnect between UNRWA's officially nonpolitical outlook and the political lens through which the refugees understood their lives. Wisam had played an active role in setting up the UNRWA-sponsored community-based organizations in Ein el Tal. I asked him about the dissolution of the organizations, which had been central to the project's "social development" goals. He pointed to a difference of vision between refugees and UNRWA:

> They [UNRWA] didn't want activities that have to do with the land [of Palestine], with the right of return, [activities] that talk about your [Palestinian] history, activities that have to do with holding on to Palestinian rights [*tamassuk bil-ḥuqūq al-filasṭīniyya*] or any activity having to do with Palestinian resistance. They want activities [that reflect the Christian saying] "if someone hits you on your cheek, turn the other cheek." (Interview, October 6, 2010)

As an example, Wisam recalled that UNRWA employees had ultimately prohibited the newly formed community-based organizations from hosting an official celebration of Land Day in Ein el Tal in April 2006, while the first phase of the project was still ongoing. Land Day (yawm al-'arḍ), which is observed on March 30, had been instituted after the 1976 killing of six Palestinians from the Galilee area of northern Israel during a protest against the Israeli government's plans to confiscate Palestinian land to build Israeli settlements. Today, it commemorates not only those killings but also continued Israeli dispossession of

Palestinians. The community-based organizations had been planning a Land Day celebration for some time and had been hoping to host it at UNRWA's al-Zeeb School. By March 2006, the music group had a repertoire of songs that it was ready to perform and the cultural group had organized art classes that produced enough drawings and paintings for an exhibit. These groups had planned to use Land Day to show the fruit of their work. Additionally, the winners of the soccer tournament organized by the sports group were to receive their medals at the celebration.

UNRWA officials, deciding that Land Day was too political, refused to sponsor the celebration in Ein el Tal. The refugees on their own could not host it because there was no available public venue other than the al-Zeeb School in which to hold a large-scale event, so the community-based organizations eventually gave in and agreed to put on a simple "cultural" celebration where they could display their work.

The celebration took place on a Saturday afternoon in late April, a few weeks after the official Land Day holiday (UNRWA officials had made sure that it would not coincide with the Palestinian holiday), on the playground of the al-Zeeb School. Shortly before the event started, the usually empty streets of the camp filled with families heading to the school, where chairs had been set up in front of a performance stage. It was the first time that I had seen Ein el Tal as a whole embrace an activity sponsored by the Neirab Rehabilitation Project (and, by extension, UNRWA). It seemed as though the project was finally conquering the skeptics in the community and that the community was finally warming up to it.

Several members of the project team were present. One of them was a foreign project assistant who had lobbied her UNRWA superiors to allow Land Day to be celebrated and had been told that she was naïve to think that UNRWA would ever agree to this. And yet this was exactly the kind of celebration that was taking place: the music group sang patriotic Palestinian songs, one of them entitled "Land Day," when the land mourns the Palestinians who have fallen during the struggle for liberation. The backdrop to the stage featured a Palestinian flag in the center with a *keffiyyeh* below it. Pinned to the flag was a portrait of Syrian President Bashar al-Asad, which was surrounded by a picture of the Dome of the Rock mosque in Jerusalem, a map of historic Palestine, and a painting of Palestine in the form of a woman. Between the painting and the portrait of Asad was a portrait of a young Palestinian man from Ein el Tal, possibly a teenager, who had become a *shahīd* (martyr) for dying in Iraq while fighting against the American occupation. The culture group exhibit had the common theme of Palestinian blood being shed in the struggle for liberation. In many of the paintings, Palestine was depicted as a tree deeply rooted in the soil.

Although they had agreed not to call it "Land Day" so they would be able to use UNRWA resources, the community-based organizations had actually

Figure 6.6. Land Day celebration in Ein el Tal.

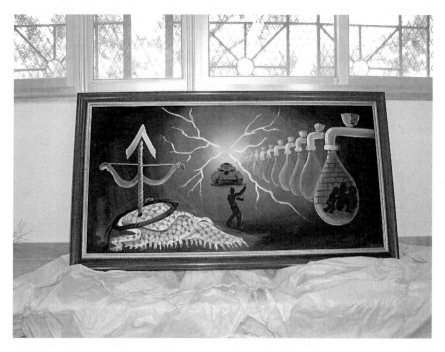

Figure 6.7. Land Day art exhibit. (The drops dripping from the faucets symbolize Palestinian blood.)

organized the very first camp-wide celebration of Land Day in Ein el Tal and had done it with the help of the Neirab Rehabilitation Project. It was through its partnership with these recently created organizations that, for the first time, the project team had been able to engage the entire Ein el Tal community. The irony, however, is that this partnership had developed around a celebration that officially–at least as far as the UNRWA field office in Damascus was concerned–had not taken place.

The Land Day celebration, which could not be acknowledged as such, embodied both the limitations and the possibilities of the Neirab Rehabilitation Project. By not acknowledging the Palestinian refugee issue as primarily a political one, UNRWA inevitably put a certain distance between itself and the community and failed to fully represent it. At the same time, by embarking on a "participatory" approach that included project beneficiaries in decision making and implementation, the agency inevitably reinforced a space where its "nonpolitical" approach could be transgressed.

Development and the Right of Return

As the Land Day celebration shows, it was difficult for UNRWA to mobilize significant Palestinian refugee support around the reforms it had set in motion without articulating a vision of progress that incorporated the refugees' particular history of exile and dispossession and their attachment to their right of return. Furthermore, the agency needed to acknowledge and engage with refugees' fears that the Neirab Rehabilitation Project sought to eradicate the past and encourage the settlement of refugees in the host country as *the* solution to their predicament. These fears were not irrational. "Development" connotes normalcy and "rehabilitation" actually means "to return to a normal state." UNRWA's 2005 Medium Term Plan had argued that "development" could not truly take hold in Palestinian refugee camps until the Israeli–Palestinian conflict came to an end (UNRWA 2005a). This argument was based on the assumption that at least some, if not all, refugees would remain in the camps after a resolution to the conflict was achieved. This assumption linked development with settlement.

While seemingly incompatible, the goals of improving conditions on the ground and refugee return should not have to lead to an "either/or" scenario. In line with Alex de Waal's rejection of a "technical-political dualism" (1997:2), improving living conditions understood as comfortable housing, professional skills, greater employment, and a richer social life, does not have to mean a loss of political consciousness. Statements by Palestinian refugees such as "Neirab must retain its features as a camp," need to be unpacked. They do not necessarily mean that Neirab must remain poor or that those living in the barracks had to sacrifice their well-being for the sake of the Palestinian cause. What was important to

Neirab residents was that the Neirab Rehabilitation Project not jeopardize their identity as Palestinian refugees. The issue was not that Neirab had to look a certain way or had to fit the model of an "authentic" refugee camp, whatever that may be. Rather, the issue was one of *difference*.

The resistance that UNRWA faced with the Neirab Rehabilitation Project and the resistance it continues to face with other camp improvement projects testify to a tension between development in the host country and the project of refugee return, which I believe cannot be fully transcended. It is the product of the collision of two different and at times incompatible approaches to apprehending and addressing social inequality in the space of the Palestinian refugee camp. One approach consists of a politics of suffering whereby suffering is part of the political struggle and becomes a means for attaining political rights and legitimacy. The other is based on a politics of citizenship that, in line with the vision of the Neirab Rehabilitation Project, sees development as a vehicle for achieving rights to the city and implicitly promotes greater integration into the host country.

The politics of suffering that has traction in Palestinian refugee camps, effective or not, is more conducive to imagining the possibility of return than is the politics of citizenship. The former is predicated to a large extent on a historical and emotional bond with the land of Palestine, from which the refugees were exiled, and the project of return to it. The hardships of refugees are seen as a result of the dislocation from their homeland, and only reunification with the land they fled or were expelled from will allow them to truly overcome their suffering. The politics of citizenship is state-centered. Substantive citizenship will allow refugees to overcome their suffering, and development is a means of achieving this goal. Socioeconomic integration into a state, wherever it happens to be located, rather than return to the homeland is what is important here.

The politics of citizenship has also served as the main framework through which Israeli–Palestinian peace has been pursued at the international level. The assumption behind international efforts to solve the conflict, starting with Oslo, is that an independent Palestinian state in the area that coincides more or less with the occupied territories is the key to a peaceful and successful outcome. This is not an outcome that favors the right of return of Palestinian refugees to their villages and towns of origin, which are located in present-day Israel. US officials involved in various Israeli–Palestinian peace efforts have generally implied that return means to a newly created Palestinian state alongside Israel, if such a state were to be created (Dumper 2007; Takkenberg 1998).

The notion that the natural place for Palestinian refugees is a Palestinian state within 1967 boundaries rather than their historic homes is reaffirmed by James Lindsay in his 2009 report on UNRWA written for the Washington Institute for Near Eastern Policy. In the event that a Palestinian state does not come into being, a politics of citizenship means that refugees ideally acquire the formal citizenship of their countries of residence or, at the very least, achieve an advanced level of social integration in those countries. Social integration, after all, ensures that refugees have at least some of the rights associated with citizenship, and it can be a conduit to full, formal citizenship. Such an approach sidesteps the return of refugees to their historical homes as a part of solving the refugee issue.

The tension between the politics of suffering and the politics of citizenship that has been analyzed in this book does not apply only to the Neirab Rehabilitation Project or the issue of camp improvement, more generally. Recognizing this tension is important to an understanding of the current predicament of Palestinian refugees in Syria. The Syrian war has brought to the forefront Palestinians' vulnerability as a (de jure) stateless people. While their Syrian counterparts, armed with passports, are able to find refuge in neighboring countries, stateless Palestinians are often prevented from doing so; when they are able to cross borders, they are frequently detained and denied the basic rights applying to refugees (Erakat 2014; Al-Majdal 2014, 2015). As formal citizens of a sovereign country, they would have an easier time of escaping the war by crossing into neighboring countries and would probably receive better treatment once over the border.

At the same time, current events in Syria highlight the power of suffering in eliciting particular kinds of political interventions. The suffering that Palestinians are currently experiencing as a result of the war (especially in their treatment when they attempt to seek refuge across borders) has resulted in calls by academics, journalists, and politicians for granting them the right of return to their Palestinian homes (Baroud 2012; Sayigh 2013; Levy 2014). These calls illustrate that suffering, especially if perceived by outsiders as catastrophic, has the capacity to legitimize certain political claims (such as the Palestinian claim to the right of return) that are marginalized in the context of formal politics.

The point here is not to weigh the politics of suffering, which continues to have traction in Palestinian refugee camps, against the politics of citizenship, which tends to inform official Western-dominated efforts to solve the Israeli–Palestinian conflict (and the related Palestinian refugee issue). It is also not to downplay the emancipatory potential of a politics of citizenship. Rather, it is to show that these two ideas have different implications when it comes to addressing the right of return of Palestinian refugees. UNRWA efforts to bring development to Palestinian refugee camps, however well intentioned, tend to fall within the framework of a Western-dominated and state-centered understanding of progress. The uneasiness and tension described in this book come from the fact that such an understanding privileges the rights associated with citizenship at the expense of the right of return.

The Camp as a Laboratory of Knowledge

During a follow-up interview conducted in Amman in spring 2015, a member of UNRWA's Infrastructure and Camp Improvement Program (ICIP) made it clear that the ICIP still has a long way to go to become fully integrated into UNRWA's normal activities and fully accepted in the agency's other departments (education, health, relief and social services, microfinance, and emergency response). The employee acknowledged resistance on the part of employees in other areas to the idea of participatory, community-led camp improvement.[6] In addition to UNRWA's official self-understanding as a "nonpolitical" agency and the pressure it faces from some of its Western donors concerned with muting Palestinian political activism, this state of affairs acts as a barrier to UNRWA and Palestinian efforts to find common ground as partners in improving living conditions in Palestinian refugee camps.

However, there are signs within the agency, and especially within the ICIP, that the agency is a bit more willing than it was at the beginning of its reform process to engage with refugees as political subjects. UNRWA's *Camp Improvement Manual*–a compilation of lessons learned not only from the Neirab Rehabilitation Project but from subsequent camp improvement projects in the West Bank, Jordan, and Lebanon begun in 2007 and after–offers some examples.[7] For one, there is now greater public acknowledgement of the political sensitivity of UNRWA camp improvements: "[They do] not intend to change the political status of Palestine refugees, affect their right of return or change the legal basis of recognized camps" (UNRWA 2012:3). For another, improvement "will not affect the status of [Palestinian] refugees including the right of return" (UNRWA Camp Improvement Manual:9). Finally, in an apparent attempt to quell rumors that development is a tool for ending UNRWA services and dissolving the agency, according to the manual improvement "will not be . . . at the expense of UNRWA core services but [will] seek to attract additional donor support" (UNRWA 2012:9).

There have been attempts by individuals working in the ICIP, either as employees or partners, to creatively address the tension between the politics of suffering and the politics of citizenship. For example, as part of its improvement projects in the southern West Bank camps of Dheisheh and Fawwar, in 2012, UNRWA began a partnership with an organization called Campus in Camps on a series of projects funded by the German government. Campus in Camps is an experimental educational program based in Dheisheh Camp in Bethlehem in the West Bank founded by Palestinian architect, urban planner, and researcher Sandi Hilal and Italian architect, urban planner, and researcher Alessandro Petti. Conceived as a camp-based university for exploring and producing "new forms of representation of camps and refugees beyond the static and traditional symbols of victimization, passivity and poverty" (Campus in Camps 2015), it aims at "transgressing, without eliminating, the distinction between camp and city, refugee and citizen, center and periphery, theory and practice, teacher and student" (Campus in Camps 2015).

According to a Palestinian architect who is a member of Campus in Camps and worked as a consultant for UNRWA's West Bank camp improvement program from 2008 to 2014, the idea for Campus in Camps emerged from discussions organized by the ICIP and refugees in the southern West Bank. The architect explained during an interview in spring 2015 that a major issue in these discussions was the feeling among camp refugees, especially younger generations, that they did not own their own narrative:

> Our young generation is not even given the possibility to live fully their present . . . this comes very strongly from the young generation: "How can we live our own history and not [a history that is] necessarily based on our grandfather's history? We would like to own our own narration, own our discourse." This was the need that came out of the young generation. They say: "all we are doing is being activists, inside NGOS, running to show people misery all over the place, and we don't own our own life, our own narration." So this was the need that came out of the camp improvement [discussions with young refugees]. (Interview, May 19, 2015)

Because the issue of self-representation was considered a major one, UNRWA had commissioned the urban planning department at Al-Quds University in Jerusalem to propose a program that would address self-representation within the context of camp improvement. The resulting proposal became Campus in Camps, which, although a collaborative effort with the ICIP in the West Bank and first implemented in Palestinian refugee camps, has remained independent from UNRWA and has been adopted in contexts other than the Palestinian one.[8]

Among the various collaborations between the ICIP and Campus in Camps is the new plaza in Fawwar Camp in the West Bank. The idea originated with the ICIP and was then discussed with Fawwar's residents and implemented through Campus in Camps. Initially some residents mounted fierce opposition to the idea of a plaza because the absence of public spaces, a common feature of Palestinian refugee camps, is a deliberate attempt to fortify residents' self-identification as refugees, as displaced and stateless (Kimmelman 2014). Nevertheless, continuing discussions with Fawwar refugees produced creative ways to change the architecture of the camp to benefit residents without fundamentally changing the camp's identity. In the end, an L-shaped space was built to represent a "roofless house" with walls. While the walls addressed the issue of privacy, which was important to women residents, the lack of a roof imbued the space with the symbolism of temporariness. Also, the walls were constructed of concrete, a material that, like a tent, is easily accessible and malleable. Residents had preferred concrete to stone because they believed "the site should retain a link with the makeshift, 'temporary' architecture of the houses surrounding it" (Kimmelman 2014).[9]

A house without a roof represented Palestinian refugees' particular relationship to the public and the private sphere. In contrast to cities, refugee camps are not spaces where the public and private spheres are completely distinguishable–Palestinian refugees do not legally own their houses, so not only is there no public space in the camp; there is (from a legal perspective) no private property, either. "Concepts like shared space, inside and outside, are blurred" (Alessandro Petti, cited in Kimmelman 2014). The roofless house signals that the plaza is not a private, individual space but rather one of "collective privacy and ownership" (Kimmelman 2014).

At the core of the philosophy that guides Campus in Camps is the idea that the camp is a space that produces knowledge, not a space that is simply an object of knowledge. For example, the "Tree School" was a collaborative learning effort of the refugees in Dheisheh Camp in the West Bank and Grupo Contrafilé, an art collective based in Bahia, Brazil. As its logo, the Tree School project used the African baobab tree. The project was grounded in the idea of a continuously moving school that is not based on national boundaries and does not have a national curriculum (Campus in Camps 2015). Its purpose was to "[draw] analogies and [identify] similarities between two exceptional spaces, Brazilian Quilombos, which are communities . . . established by enslaved Africans and Afro-descendents fleeing their oppressors, and Palestinian refugee camps" (Campus in Camps and Grupo Contrafilé 2014). The Tree School was part of an ongoing effort to "cultivate and produce knowledge that emerges from regions of the world that rarely communicate despite the fact that they have very much to learn from one another. Particularly in this historical moment, following the revolts in Arab and South American cities, these 'two worlds' share similarities in terms of social justice and equality" (Campus in Camps and Grupo Contrafilé 2014).

Through the Campus in Camps lens, camps can be viewed as productive spaces of exile that generate alternative and new modes of being, knowing, and doing. They can be viewed as laboratories for imagining alternative forms of urbanism and citizenship, for imagining new political subjectivities (see Allan 2014). They are not to be understood simply as the negative of the ideal city. As specific spaces, they have advantages as well as shortcomings. In accordance with this understanding, the city ceases to operate as a unidirectional model for improving camp life; it stands to learn from the camp and from the refugees who populate it.

Toward a New Global Humanitarian Order?

Today Ein el Tal lies in ruins and phase 2 of the Neirab Rehabilitation Project, taking place in Neirab, has been cut short by the war in Syria. Furthermore, UNRWA is in crisis mode in most of its areas of operation because of the repercussions of the Syrian war across Syria's borders and because of the situation in Gaza. However, UNRWA has neither abandoned its development discourse nor its Infrastructure and Camp Improvement Program. In fact, in April 2015 the agency announced that it was embarking on its latest improvement project, in Deir el Balah Camp in Gaza (ReliefWeb 2015), even though it had declared an emergency situation in Gaza following Israel's bombing campaign there in July 2014 and has sent out multiple appeals for financial assistance from the international community to help it address this situation (UNRWA 2015j). The Deir el Balah project is going forward against the backdrop of the UN Conference on Trade and Development (UNCTAD) report that Gaza might become uninhabitable by 2020 because of de-development caused by years of blockade and the three military operations conducted there by the Israeli government in the past six years.[10]

UNRWA's plans in Deir el Balah appear strange only if the story of its foray into development is seen as a linear narrative in which a roughly ten-year-old ambitious reform process seeking to institutionalize development in Palestinian refugee camps has came up against unfolding wars and crises across the agency's areas of operation in the Middle East. If one does not start in the last decade but looks at UNRWA's history from its creation, a different narrative unfolds, one in which crisis, relief, and some form of development have always coexisted. This coexistence includes refugees' active role in the urbanization and modernization of their camps, while rejecting change coming from the outside out of fear of normalization, but which actually played an active and important role in the urbanization and modernization of their camps.

It could be argued that the war in Syria has actually rendered UNRWA more, not less, relevant when it comes to development. Indeed, UNRWA's history of development has placed the agency at the forefront of current global debates regarding humanitarian assistance to refugees. As argued in an earlier chapter, the notion that development, as opposed to minimal relief assistance, should be the response to protracted refugee crises has gained traction in the past twenty years in UNHCR (Office of the United Nations High Commissioner for Refugees), which is the main organization providing refugees assistance worldwide (UNHCR 2003).[11] This is primarily because, like the Palestinian refugee crisis, which dates back to 1948, refugee crises are increasingly becoming situations of protracted displacement. According to UNHCR, the average period of time one now remains a refugee is seventeen years (UNHCR 2004).

The unfolding Syrian refugee crisis has placed a renewed emphasis on development as a form of refugee assistance. This time, however, it is not about more development as emergency refugee situations become long-term displacement. Rather, it is about development being used as a direct response to crisis. The unprecedented number of refugees from Syria, the expectation among the international community of a drawn-out Syrian war, and the pressures that the crisis is exerting on the resources of Middle Eastern host countries as well as those of donors to emergency relief efforts have led the United Nations to devise a "Regional Refugee and Resilience Plan" that was set in motion in 2015 (UNHCR and UNDP 2015).[12]

The Regional Refugee and Resilience Plan (3RP) brings together two hundred humanitarian and development partners, including governments, UN agencies, and national and international NGOs (UNHCR and UNDP 2015). Led by UNHCR and the United Nations Development Programme (UNDP), the 3RP seeks to provide a coordinated response to the Syrian refugee crisis in Lebanon, Jordan, Turkey, Iraq, and Egypt. According to UNHCR and UNDP representatives, it is "a unique and coordinated initiative aimed at bringing about a scaling up of resilience and stabilization-based development and humanitarian assistance to cope with the crisis" (UNHCR and UNDP 2015:6). It will not only address the needs of refugees fleeing Syria but also provide "self-reliance opportunities through livelihood support for vulnerable people" in neighboring countries that are receiving refugees (UNHCR and UNDP 2015:18). In this both emergency relief and development are required, with the latter acting as a stabilizing tool to address "the adverse socio-economic effects that the Syria crisis has on communities in countries neighboring Syria" (UNHCR and UNDP:7–8).

The ideas at the core of the 3RP are being echoed in the broader global humanitarian discourse. The notion that development must play a greater role in humanitarian crises is at the center of preliminary meetings being held in preparation for the next World Humanitarian Summit, which will take place in Istanbul in May 2016. The summit is a UN initiative to bring the global community together to "commit to new ways of working together to save lives and reduce hardship around the globe" (WHS 2015). In a November 2015 speech to the General Assembly, António Guterres, then United Nations High Commissioner for Refugees, asserted that:

> One key element in ensuring the world effectively responds to humanitarian crises is a much closer link between humanitarian and development interventions . . . Development actors – supported by development budgets – have to work side by side with humanitarians from the very beginning of each crisis, to help us prevent further conflict, to support host communities and to pave the way for durable solutions for refugees. (UNHCR 2015)

With protracted refugee situations becoming the norm rather than the exception in the twentieth-first century, emergency humanitarian aid and development assistance have become entwined in new ways. UNRWA was created in the late 1940s in a moment of crisis to provide relief to Palestinian refugees and promote development in host countries (symbolized by "Works" in the agency's name). After the debacle of its "works" mandate in the 1950s, the agency reverted to basic relief assistance with the exception of its education program. In the

1980s, it introduced microfinance. And in the early 2000s, it attempted to institutionalize the comprehensive infrastructural and socioeconomic development of camps as a regular form of refugee assistance. These periods were often punctuated by major crises, such as the 1967 and 1973 Arab–Israeli wars; the 1975 civil war in Lebanon; the 2003 US invasion of Iraq, during which more than half of the Palestinian refugee population (numbering about thirty-five thousand) was forced to flee (Charles 2012); the expulsion of most of Kuwait's approximately 450,000 Palestinian refugees after the Palestinian leadership threw its support behind Saddam Hussein's annexation of Kuwait (Haddad 2010); the expulsion of thousands of Palestinians working in Libya by Mouammar Gaddafi as retribution for the Palestinian leadership's signing of the Oslo accords (BADIL 2010); and the massive social and infrastructural destruction brought about by Israeli bombing campaigns in Gaza in the last six years.

From the long-term perspective of the events just described, the war in Syria can be seen simply as a new chapter in a long history during which UNRWA has moved from emergency humanitarian relief to basic health and social services and back and has, at times, attempted more developmental forms of intervention. UNRWA has had more than sixty years of experience juggling a situation of protracted displacement characterized by stretches of stability as well as recurring crises. During this time, it has occasionally attempted to address the long-term future of Palestinian refugees despite the continued lack of a political resolution to the Palestinian refugee situation. Now the agency can position itself as a model in global debates about how to effectively combine emergency and nonemergency assistance in refugee crises. UNRWA employees I interviewed at the agency's Amman headquarters in the spring of 2015 were especially proud that they have been able to maintain their education program in Syria throughout the war, with some UNRWA schools doubling as shelters for internally displaced Palestinians.[13]

The current global humanitarian concern with integrating development in the response to refugee crises is further evidence that in the twenty-first century protracted refugee crises are becoming the new normal. Although the Palestinian refugee situation is unique in many ways, as detailed in this book, it has also become banal in some respects. Palestinians are now part of a growing global population living outside the formal boundaries of the nation-state in spaces that force us to rethink the relationship between crisis and normality, between temporariness and permanence, and between the camp and the city.

Epilogue

AT THE TIME of writing (February 2016), the war in Syria has claimed two hundred and fifty thousand lives and resulted in over one million injured (OCHA 2016). More than six million people are internally displaced, and over four million have sought refuge in neighboring countries (OCHA 2016).

Palestinians have not been spared. UNRWA estimates that over two-thirds of Syria's prewar Palestinian population of approximately five hundred and sixty thousand are internally displaced (UNRWA 2016a); 95 percent of the Palestinians who are still in Syria are receiving sustained humanitarian assistance (UNRWA 2016a). Palestinians who have fled across Syria's borders are mostly in Lebanon (42,000), Jordan (17,000), Egypt (4,000), Turkey, and, increasingly, Europe (UNRWA 2016a). It is difficult to separate the numbers for Turkey and Europe, given that many of the Palestinians who reach Turkey eventually continue on to Europe. This is illustrated by 2016 UNRWA statistics, which state that "over 50,000 [Palestinian refugees from Syria] have been reported in Turkey and Europe" (UNRWA 2016a:38).[1]

In the early days of the war, much was made in the press about attempts by Palestinians in Syria and their political leaders to assert their neutrality. Such attempts have proven tenuous (Bitari 2013; Hassan 2012). What can be said with some certainty is that as of February 2016 Syria's Palestinians, as a collective, have managed to avoid being lumped with one side or the other. During ethnographic research that I conducted in spring 2015 with Palestinians from Ein el Tal, Neirab, and Yarmouk now residing in Lebanon, Turkey, and the United Arab Emirates, refugees consistently mentioned how, as early as 2012, the Syrian regime, acting through Palestinian political factions such as the PFLP-GC and Fatah al-Intifada, distributed weapons to young men in the camps. The official purpose was to create civilian militias known as *lijān sha'bīye* to protect the camps as clashes erupted in neighboring areas. However, according to my interlocutors, these *lijān sha'bīye*, commonly referred to as *Shabīḥa*, were simply an extension of the armed elements supporting the Syrian regime. As such, their main role was to enforce pro-regime sentiment and prevent the camps from falling under the influence or control of either the opposition or the rebels. These refugees also claimed that both the regime and various rebel groups were now actively recruiting Palestinian refugees.

Most Palestinian refugee camps have been affected in one way or another by the uprisings and subsequent war in Syria. Many, including Khan Eshieh, Sbeineh, al-Huseiniyeh, and Dera'a, in the south, have suffered significant shelling, destruction, and the massive displacement of their population (Bitari 2013; UNRWA 2015e). Of the camps featured in this book, Yarmouk and Ein el Tal have been the most adversely affected by the war.[2] According to UNRWA, in 2014 it was able to distribute food aid to Yarmouk for only a third of the year (2015g). Additionally, the camp's remaining residents continue to live without electricity and running water. Following the April 1, 2015, invasion of Yarmouk by ISIL (the Islamic State in Syria and the Levant) several thousand Palestinians were able to flee to the neighboring rebel-held neighborhoods of Babilla, Yalda, and Beit Saham (UNRWA 2015g). They have received UNRWA assistance in the form of food, drinking water, and medical services (UNRWA 2015d). Several thousand others remain trapped in Yarmouk, which has been inaccessible to UNRWA and other humanitarian organizations since the invasion (SREO 2015; UNRWA 2015d, 2015i). In February 2016, UNRWA was finally able to provide humanitarian assistance to some Yarmouk residents through a distribution point in the neighboring area of Yalda (UNRWA 2016b).

Perhaps because Ein el Tal was a much smaller camp (six thousand Palestinians compared to Yarmouk's prewar one hundred and fifty thousand) and because, unlike Yarmouk, it was not embedded in a major urban center, its destruction and the suffering unleashed by the war have received virtually no attention in the international media. On April 26, 2013, armed opposition groups entered the camp and forcibly displaced its entire population (UNRWA 2015e).[3] As with Yarmouk, geography was a factor in Ein el Tal's fate. According to UNRWA employees and Palestinian refugees I interviewed in spring 2015, its location on a hill offering views of the outlying areas, including the city of Aleppo, attracted the rebels relatively early in the conflict. Ein el Tal also happens to be situated between a major hospital (al-Kindi) and a government prison, two sites that have been at the heart of ongoing battles between government and rebel forces (interviews, Ein el Tal Palestinians in Turkey, April 2015). Displaced Ein el Tal residents found refuge in neighboring Neirab Camp, in UNRWA facilities, and with host families in the cities of Hama, Homs, and Latakia–all of which have Palestinian refugee enclaves (UNRWA 2015h; interviews, Ein el Tal Palestinians in Turkey, April 2015). Some ended up in the University of Aleppo dormitories, which were set aside for them by Syrian authorities (interviews, Ein el Tal Palestinians in Turkey, April 2015). Some who had fled Ein el Tal subsequently returned to the camp (with the permission of the rebels, who still occupy it) because of their inability to find safe shelter in another part of the country (interviews, Ein el Tal Palestinians in Turkey, April 2015). However, by spring of 2014 those who had returned fled again because of continued fighting between troops loyal to the Asad government and the rebels occupying the camp, which resulted in regular shelling of the camp.

As of February 2016, Ein el Tal remains empty of civilians. The camp suffered major destruction as a result of repeated efforts by the Syrian government to wrest control of it from the rebels. Alaa, one of the Palestinians who returned to Ein el Tal after it was overtaken by rebels in May 2013 but ultimately fled to Turkey in early 2014, showed me pictures as well as a video he had taken of the destruction. I was able to see the many houses, including those built by the Neirab Rehabilitation Project, reduced to rubble. Surprisingly (or perhaps unsurprisingly), the new water tower, which had been built by the Syrian government as part of the project, was still standing amidst the ruins.

The Palestinians from Ein el Tal whom I interviewed in Turkey were all members of families who had returned to the camp a few months after being forced out by the rebels because the Syrian neighborhoods in which they had sought refuge were caught in intense fighting. By spring 2014, they were fleeing again, this time because of relentless shelling by government forces attempting to retake the camp. Escape to Turkey seems to have been a "choice" of last resort. Having exhausted all means of finding safe shelter in other parts of Syria, they paid smugglers to help them cross the Turkish border clandestinely (Turkey is one of the many countries that does not grant visas to Palestinian refugees).

These Palestinians can be found mostly in the Turkish border towns of Gaziantep and Kilis, but there are others scattered across border towns such as Antakia, Mersin, and Mardin. A few are in Istanbul. Those I interviewed had arrived in Turkey in early 2014. Initially, the Syrian opposition government abroad took charge of the refugees, providing them with food and blankets, giving them cash assistance toward rent, and helping them find employment. It even opened a camp near the town of Kilis for the most vulnerable refugees but the camp was closed by the Turkish government for security reasons (interview, Palestinian representative of the Syrian opposition government in Turkey, April 6 2015). The opposition government abroad has since then opened a new camp for Palestinian refugees in the city of Mardin (interview, Palestinian representative of the Syrian opposition government in Turkey, April 6 2015; AGPS 2015) The presence of active members of the opposition government abroad in Turkey and their engagement with Palestinian refugees is not surprising. Turkey's foreign policy has been extremely critical of the Syrian government and supportive of the opposition groups, which include Palestinians.

In April 2015, I interviewed a Palestinian representative of the opposition government in charge of assisting Palestinian refugees from Syria who are now in Turkey. He told me that at least eight thousand Palestinians had crossed into Turkey, with the majority coming from camps in the south such as Yarmouk and Dera'a, and he estimated that only about one thousand Palestinians in Turkey were from Neirab and Ein el Tal. However, he pointed out the difficulty of determining exact numbers of refugees given that a significant number of them intend to continue to Europe.

Palestinians who have managed to cross the border do not face the risk of deportation by Turkish authorities, but they do live in precarious socioeconomic conditions. Because Turkey does not figure among UNRWA's areas of operation, Palestinians residing there are ineligible for UNRWA assistance. Even though they should technically fall under the auspices of UNHCR, the Palestinians I interviewed claimed that they have had no access to UNHCR-sponsored assistance (which is distributed through the Turkish government) either. Meanwhile, they have lost most of the assistance they used to receive from the Syrian opposition government abroad. Its representative in charge of assistance to Palestinian refugees explained that with the war now entering its fifth year, funds for humanitarian assistance have dried up.

Neirab Camp is one of the few Palestinian refugee camps in Syria that has been able to maintain a semblance of normalcy amidst the violence and chaos unleashed by the war. Although for several months in spring 2013 it was surrounded and partially blockaded by rebel forces attempting to enter it, it was never overtaken (UNRWA 2015h). According to my Palestinian interlocutors in Lebanon and Turkey, the pro-government *shabīḥa* played a critical role in keeping the rebels out of the camp, which is located near a Syrian military base and airport. As of February 2016, the situation inside is relatively calm and the camp remains firmly under government control.

As for the refugees of Ein el Tal, Neirab, and Yarmouk who are the subject of this book, I have not been able to stay in touch with all of them, but I have managed to keep up with a few.

My friend Muna remains in Neirab, and we continue to have phone conversations from time to time. Ahmad Radwan, the project volunteer from Ein el Tal, is living in Damascus with his wife and daughter. He moved to the capital after finding employment with UNRWA around the time that the uprisings began. According to one of Ahmad's neighbors, whom I interviewed in the Turkish border town of Kilis in 2015, Ahmad's family house, which I had visited almost daily and where I had eaten many meals while working in Ein el Tal, was destroyed in the fighting. Ahmad's parents and siblings, who had been forced out of Ein el Tal in April 2013 along with the rest of the camp's population, are currently living in the dormitories of the University of Aleppo.

Wisam, the project volunteer who was originally from Neirab Camp but had moved to a UNRWA-built house in Ein el Tal, returned to Neirab when Ein el Tal was taken over by rebels in April 2013. He was subsequently arrested in Neirab by Syrian authorities and spent two months in jail as punishment for his behavior in Ein el Tal, where he was still living when anti-Asad rebels began to encircle the camp in spring 2013. Wisam's first offense was organizing a committee to negotiate with the rebels so they would not enter the camp and would allow it to remain a neutral space. His second offense was going into rebel-held neighborhoods to purchase flour in order to supply the camp with bread during periods when the camp was cut off from Aleppo because of the fighting.

For his activities, Wisam was accused by Syrian authorities of collaborating with the opposition and was beaten and tortured while in Jail. He was freed thanks to the intervention of his political faction, the PFLP (Popular Front for the Liberation of Palestine). He left prison with a broken and infected leg and while seeking medical treatment discovered that he has serious heart and kidney problems. Wisam fled to Turkey and spent about two years in the city of Mersin. In August 2015, with assistance of smugglers, he took a boat from the Turkish city of Izmir to Greece with a group of other refugees from Neirab Camp. His journey lasted thirteen days: from Greece he travelled through Macedonia, Serbia, Hungary, Austria, Germany, and Denmark, mostly by car but walking for long stretches. His son, who had arrived in Sweden two years earlier using a fake passport he had bought from smugglers, met him at the Copenhagen train station.[4] Wisam now lives in Sweden with his son and daughter-in-law and their two children.[5] I spoke with him on the phone shortly after he arrived in Sweden. He does not see himself living in Syria again. He might go back one day to visit but, as of now, he only sees himself living "either in Europe or Palestine."

Atif, the teenage volunteer from Neirab, is now in his late twenties and is living in Berlin, Germany. He had not intended to migrate to Europe after war broke out in Syria. Instead, he got married and began building a housing unit for him and his wife on top of the family home. Around that time, he developed health problems, including chronic pain that prevented him from working. He was not able to finish the house. He and his wife got divorced in spring 2015. Feeling powerless to improve his health and financial situation and living in "constant fear" because of the war, he decided to travel to Europe. He arrived in Germany in late October 2015, after a harrowing three-week journey. Smugglers arranged for a bus to take him and about 60 other Palestinians from northern Syria to the Turkish border, a trip that required going though regime as well as rebel checkpoints. From Atif's description, it appears that those manning the checkpoints had an understanding with the smugglers and that money was part of it. Fighters at the checkpoints seemed aware of the group's destination and did not try to stop them, but the group was lectured by ISIL members who control the northern Syrian village of Al-Bab, on the way to the Turkish border. Atif said, "They asked us: 'Where do you want to go? You want to go to an infidel country, a country of nonbelievers? Stay here in the Islamic state. The state of pride, the state of Islam. You'll get married here, we need resources, we need workers, why do you want to go to the country of non-believers?' We didn't say a word and just nodded our heads."

After crossing clandestinely into Turkey, Atif and about 60 other people were put in a small boat that normally carries 30. He reached Greece about one hour later. From there, he continued on to Macedonia, Serbia, Croatia, Slovenia, Austria, and Berlin, Germany. His voyage included walking for tens of miles at a time–some of it in pouring rain and freezing temperature–buses, and trains. Toward the end of the journey, he and the Palestinian, Syrian, Afghan, and Iraqi men, women and children he was traveling with spent close to 20 hours straight under heavy rain in an open air stadium where Slovenian authorities had ordered them to wait until buses came for them to take them to Austria, the last country before Germany.

When Atif finished detailing his journey to me over the phone in November 2015, I asked him how he had felt when he left Neirab. I had not realized just how sensitive of my question was. Here is an excerpt from his answer:

> I felt so bad, I left my mother, I left my siblings, I left the people with whom I grew up, I left my best friends, I left the camp where I have memories, personal struggles. . . . Sitting in the alleys of the camp, in the narrow streets, that was meaningful to me. Attending [friends'] wedding celebration [in the camp], that meant a lot to me. I use to love these things. . . . We were forced to leave the camp because of the situation we faced, we didn't choose to [leave the camp]. . . . That's the problem of the human being who has no home. This is our problem, as Palestinians, that we have no home. The tragedy that we had in 1948 still affects us today. Until today I'm a refugee. From one place to another. From poverty to poverty. I'm not happy that I left the camp. . . . I left my youngest brother without saying goodbye. My brother is serving in the [Syrian] military, mandatory [military] service, I left without saying goodbye to him. I didn't see him. I left my nieces and nephews. I left everything that's beautiful in the camp and traveled.

Waleed, the leader of the Yarmouk Youth Center, fled Yarmouk for Lebanon in late 2013 for "security reasons" (interview, March 29, 2015). He continues to head the center from Beirut. The center has remained active despite the siege. At the time of our interview, Waleed estimated that there were about ninety volunteers affiliated with the center who were still working inside the camp. Several other volunteers had been arrested or killed by the Syrian government, but Waleed tells me that they were targeted on a personal basis and not for any center affiliation. After reaching Beirut, Waleed was able to turn the Yarmouk Youth Center into a formal, Beirut-based NGO. Since then, the center has received a significant amount of funding from international organizations seeking to provide aid to Yarmouk but unable or unwilling to enter Syria. These funds are being used to provide food and other services to Palestinians in Yarmouk as well as in other parts of Syria (as in the case of other humanitarian organizations, the external staff of the Center have had no access to Yarmouk since the ISIL invasion in April 2015).

Without going into detail, Waleed explained that he is now able to go back and forth between Lebanon and Syria and that the Yarmouk Youth Center is one of the few "local" organizations assisting civilians that officially operates in both government- and rebel-held areas. Until April 1, 2015, The Yarmouk Youth Center, through coordination between its leadership outside the camp and volunteers trapped inside, had been providing food and some medical supplies to Yarmouk's besieged residents; running classes and activities for children; handling waste collection and disposal; and operating a water truck that provides drinking water to camp residents (interview, March 29, 2015).

My friend Saleem, who appears in chapter 5 and who helped me with my Arabic when I was living in Damascus, had finished his studies in economics at the University of Damascus and had found a job in the United Arab Emirates before the start of the uprisings. He now lives in the Emirates with his wife (who is also a Palestinian from Yarmouk) and children. His brother, who remained in Yarmouk, was kidnapped in 2012 and has not been heard from since. Saleem suspects that the Syrian government is behind the kidnapping, but he is holding out hope that his brother is still alive. In 2013, he was able to fly his mother and youngest sister, who had fled Yarmouk for a safer area in Damascus, to the Emirates.[6] His sister obtained Emirati residency after marrying one of Saleem's Palestinian friends, and his mother was granted residency on humanitarian grounds after a two-year effort on the part of her son.

Finally, my Syrian landlady's son, the army general who had questioned Saleem one summer evening in 2005 in the courtyard of his mother's house, was killed, along with other prominent members of the Syrian government, in a rebel bomb attack in summer 2012.

As I write, the situation in Syria shows no sign of improvement and the impression I was left with during my spring 2015 interviews was one of hopelessness and disillusionment. My Palestinian interlocutors did not expect to return to Syria any time soon, if ever. For some, Syria will never be the same, meaning that they are never "going back" regardless of what happens: "Antaha el-filasṭīniyyīn fi Sūria [It's the end of Palestinians in Syria]" the most pessimistic tell me, sometimes adding that they have now lost two homelands. Others tell me that if the Palestinians who have left or will leave do return one day, it will not be with the favorable legal status that characterized the prewar era. They think that Palestinians in Syria will become "like the Palestinians of Lebanon."

Most Palestinians I spoke with expressed disillusionment with Arab leaders, almost all of whom have closed the borders of their states to them[7]; with their Palestinian leaders, including the Palestinian Authority and the Palestinian political factions, who they feel have done practically nothing to protect them from the violence of the war or to support them in their struggle to find refuge from it; and with the international community, which they feel does not care about them. They do not understand why many European countries are quick to grant refugee status to refugees arriving from Syria, but make it impossible for these refugees to arrive through secure and legal channels, putting them at the mercy of smugglers and forcing them to risk their lives on the open seas in old, flimsy, overloaded boats.

Ten years ago, when I was conducting fieldwork in Syria, citizenship was not an issue in my conversations with Palestinian refugees, whereas the right of return was a recurring theme. However, during my spring 2015 interviews with Palestinians displaced to Syria's neighboring countries, several talked about the importance of having a passport, preferably a Western one. Despite their criticism of what they see as the hypocrisy of European asylum policies, they believe that their only hope of finding stability, and ensuring that it does not disappear from one day to the next without warning, is to immigrate to Europe and obtain a Western passport. Some have family members who have already made the risky clandestine journey by boat from Egypt, Libya, or Turkey to Europe. Several tell me that they do not care about a Western passport for themselves but want their children to have passports so they can live secure lives and move freely. Now that survival and stability have become priorities, these Palestinians have appropriated the politics of citizenship but in doing so they have also reinterpreted it to fit a Palestinian narrative. An added benefit of a European passport, they say, is that with it they have a chance to go to Palestine.

Notes

Introduction

1. The exclusion of Palestinian refugees from UNHCR's mandate was mostly due to fear expressed by Arab states that, if included, the refugees "would become submerged [in other categories of refugees] and would be relegated to a position of minor importance" (Takkenberg 1998:66) A major concern was that "the Palestinian refugees' problem would not be adequately addressed if UNHCR's durable solutions, such as resettlement to a third country or settlement in the first country of asylum, were applied to [them]" (Suleiman 2010:14).

2. The number of Syrian refugees is based on UNHCR's estimates.

3. Refugees expressed this anger during UNRWA-organized focus group discussions seeking to assess living conditions in Ein el Tal, an initial step to extending the Neirab Rehabilitation Project to that camp.

4. This assessment is echoed in the literature on social suffering, which explains that it results "from what political, economic, and institutional power does to people and, reciprocally, from how these forms of power themselves influence responses to social problems" (Kleinman et al. 1997:ix).

5. "Anwar Fanous" is a pseudonym. Palestinian refugees as well as UNRWA employees typically referred to high-positioned GAPAR officials involved with the project by their full (formal) name.

6. Suffering as stoicism is emphasized in anthropologist Liisa Malkki's 1995 work on Hutu refugees in Tanzania. She shows how these refugees interpreted the hardship they faced on a daily basis in the camps as a necessary step in a purifying process that would prepare them for their eventual return to their native Burundi. Similarly, anthropologist Donald Moore (2005) shows how suffering is seen as a necessary and legitimizing process for displaced Zimbabwean farmers from the Kaerezi region seeking to recover land seized from them during the British colonial era. These farmers understand their struggle through the slogan "Suffering for territory [*kutambudzikira nyika*]," which recognizes the debilitating effects of colonial land dispossession on Kaerezians but is at the same time emblematic of their struggle to regain their land.

7. I have changed the name of the youth center to protect its identity.

8. The title deputy director is reserved for the head of UNRWA in a particular host country.

9. A notable exception is Yarmouk.

10. My research in Syria was primarily funded by a Fulbright scholarship.

11. Formal interviews carried out with Ein el Tal and Neirab residents involved mostly individuals who worked with the Neirab Rehabilitation Project as volunteers.

12. I carried out four interviews with UNRWA staff and twenty-four interviews with Palestinian refugees from Syria as part of this fieldwork.

13. I carried out twenty-four individual interviews and four group interviews with Palestinian refugees from Syria as part of this fieldwork.

1. Informal Citizens

1. This number is based on the most recent information posted on UNRWA's website. http://www.unrwa.org/sites/default/files/2013042435340.pdf, accessed May 25, 2015.

2. These numbers are based on UNRWA statistics. http://www.unrwa.org/where-we-work/syria/camp-profiles?field=16, accessed December 15, 2014.

3. Before the Syrian uprising of 2011 and subsequent war, Yarmouk Camp had the largest Palestinian refugee population, estimated at 150,000 people.

4. In 1921, the British would divide the Palestine mandate by creating the territory of Trans-Jordan (which later became the Hashemite Kingdom of Jordan) on the east bank of the river Jordan.

5. *Ba'th* means "resurrection" in English.

6. Like Syrian men, Palestinian men are required to serve two years of military service in the Syria-based Palestine Liberation Army (jaysh taḥrīr filasṭīn).

7. A *laissez-passer* is a travel document, usually issued by a state government or an international organization such as the United Nations, that can be used in lieu of a passport.

8. Conversation with a resident of Yarmouk Camp, Fall 2004.

9. Most of this information was collected from conversations with Abu Hosam, one of the first inhabitants of Neirab Camp.

10. This number includes Palestinians living in the immediate vicinity of the official limits of Neirab Camp.

11. The numbers were gathered from the *City Mayors* website. http://www.citymayors.com/statistics/largest-cities-density-125.html, accessed March 29, 2011.

12. This was corroborated more or less by another UNRWA employee, who claimed during an interview on October 5, 2010, that the idea for the Neirab Rehabilitation Project had come from GAPAR itself.

13. Personal communication, UNRWA official, March 15, 2011.

14. Syrian forces completed their withdrawal from Lebanon on April 26, 2005, in accordance with UN Resolution 1559, which was adopted on September 2, 2004, and which called for "all remaining foreign forces to withdraw from Lebanon." http://www.un.org/Docs/sc/, accessed February 6, 2014.

2. From Humanitarianism to Development

1. Before the Neirab Rehabilitation Project, the only form of housing improvement that UNRWA had undertaken in Palestinian refugee camps in Syria was the rehabilitation of existing shelters on an individual basis.

2. Paragraph 11 of Resolution 194, issued by the UN General Assembly on December 11, 1948, "resolves that the refugees wishing to return to their homes and live at peace with their neighbors should be permitted to do so at the earliest practicable date, and that compensations should be paid for the property of those choosing not to return and for loss or damage to property which, under principles of international law or equity, should be made good by the governments or authorities responsible" (UNGA 1948).

3. Information about when UNHCR was established is from the organization's website.

4. This effort was also known as the Johnston Plan, after American ambassador Eric Johnston, who acted as a mediator between Israel and the neighboring Arab countries of Lebanon, Jordan, and Syria.

5. The UNCCP has never been formally abolished.

6. Most of these Palestinians fled the West Bank and ended up in Jordan.

7. According to UNRWA, Women's Program Centers provide "Palestine refugee women with unique, socially acceptable venues in which they can socialize and participate in educational, cultural, and recreational activities. The WPCs also offer skills training, microloans, advice, and education, helping women to become more self-reliant (UNRWA 2015a).

8. As noted in its Medium Term Plan, UNRWA adopted this definition from the UN's Interagency Standing Committee (UNRWA 2009).

9. The Special Hardship Case program was introduced by UNRWA in 1978 to " [provide] a cushion of support to the neediest families among the refugee population" (UNRWA 2006:22). Eligibility is determined by a number of criteria, including the level of economic distress and whether there is a "healthy" adult male between the ages of nineteen and sixty who is a member of the household (UNRWA 2006).

10. I have changed the name of the center to protect the identity of its members.

11. The 1967 Arab–Israeli war pitted Egypt, Jordan, and Syria against Israel. As a result of that war, approximately three hundred thousand Palestinians from the territories of Gaza and the West Bank became refugees, with most of them fleeing to neighboring Arab countries. They were not allowed by Israel to return to their Palestinian homes after the cessation of hostilities (Shiblak 2005).

12. UNHCR, in accordance with the 1951 Convention on Refugees, defines a refugee as any person who

> owing to well-founded fear of being persecuted for reasons of race, religion, nationality, membership of a particular social group or political opinion, is outside the country of his nationality and is unable or, owing to such fear, is unwilling to avail himself of the protection of that country; or who, not having a nationality and being outside the country of his former habitual residence as a result of such events, is unable or, owing to such fear, is unwilling to return to it.

http://unhcr.org.au/unhcr/index.php?option=com_content&view=article&id=179&Itemid=54, accessed January 4, 2014.

13. The celebration took place on July 28, 2011 in UNHCR offices across the world. http://www.unhcr.org/4e31627f6.html, accessed May 12, 2015.

14. Brynen points mostly to You Tube videos and internet blogs as examples of this recurring internet presence.

3. Ṣumūd and Sustainability

1. This information is the result of a Skype conversation with the former UNRWA employee on April 19, 2011.

2. Fatah al-Intifada is known to be an overtly pro-Syrian government political faction, having fought along with the Syrian government in Lebanon against Palestinians loyal to Yasser Arafat's Fatah. On the one hand, it is perplexing that they would so strongly object to a project that had government support. On the other hand, the government might have viewed it as useful to have an ally vocally criticize American participation in the project, thus creating some distance between itself and the US government.

3. I had not yet arrived in Syria at the time of these supposed incidents in Neirab, but I heard about them after my arrival from an acquaintance in Damascus as well as an UNRWA employee and Palestinians in Neirab.

4. I am referring specifically to the American and Canadian governments here.

5. The asset mappings for both Ein el Tal and Neirab consisted of a quantitative household survey questionnaire and community-level focus group discussions, both administered or led by local Palestinian volunteers who had undergone UNRWA-sponsored training in asset-mapping methods. Questions about each camp's assets centered on education, health, employment, economic assets and savings, and coping mechanisms (UNRWA and TANGO 2005, 2006).

6. According to anthropologist Rosemary Sayigh (1979), there is some evidence to support the notion that Arab armies were not serious about their commitment to military intervention during the 1948 war on behalf of Palestinian Arabs.

7. Rana is of a "Muslim background" but it is possible that, perceiving me as someone of a "Christian background," she used the word *priest* to make sure I got her point.

8. This assessment is based on information from UNDP's webpage.

9. According to Atif, the faction Fatah al-Intifada had been the only one to oppose the Neirab Rehabilitation Project.

4. "Must We Live in Barracks to Convince People We Are Refugees?"

1. I received the manual, which is undated, from employees of UNRWA's ICIP when I met with them for interviews in Amman in spring 2015. It first appeared in 2008 and has been progressively updated. My version was updated in 2012.

2. UNRWA's ICIP booklet, "Partnering with Refugees: Toward a Better Living Environment until Their Rights Are Fulfilled," is undated. I acquired it from employees of UNRWA's ICIP when I met with them for interviews in Amman in spring 2015.

3. Early debates about how to handle the refugee issue in the occupied territories centered around four main schools of thought: opposition to any form of resettlement; transfer and resettlement of Gaza refugees in Gaza to West Bank villages and towns; improvement of refugee living conditions in the areas of residence and facilitation of their integration into the socio-economic structure of the occupied territories; and adherence to UN resolutions on refugees (Hazboun 1996; Misselwitz 2009).

4. An UNRWA survey found that by April 2003, eight months after construction of the first twenty-eight houses began in Ein el Tal, only 21 percent of some of Neirab's worst-off residents were interested in leaving the barracks (UNRWA 2003). The initial construction and the survey took place before the 2004 Geneva conference that ushered in UNRWA's official endorsement of participatory development in Palestinian refugee camps. This helps to explains why the survey was conducted after rather than before construction had begun.

5. According to political scientist Ghada Talhami in her 2001 book *Syria and the Palestinians: The Clash of Nationalisms*, the Arafat-led PLO, unwilling to accept its demise in Lebanon and subsequent exile in 1982, attempted to reestablish itself by infiltrating Lebanon's refugee camps. At the same time, the Syrian-backed Shi'ite militia Amal was gaining ground in the south of the country and attacking refugee camps, citing the camps' continued armed presence as a threat. Syrian troops, who were opposed to the PLO regaining strength in Lebanon, joined in attacks against the refugee camps and enlisted the help of Palestinian anti-Arafat factions (which included Palestinians based in Syria). When the fighting began, however, the anti-Arafat Palestinian factions switched sides, joining PLO forces loyal to Arafat in the camps and fighting against Amal and the Syrians.

6. Seventy-four percent of respondents reported turning to family; 56 percent reported turning to neighbors (UNRWA and TANGO 2005).

7. As noted by Hanafi and Hassan (2010), the camp's entire population fled during a series of temporary cease-fires.

8. Another reason for this desire was that "ease and cost-effectiveness are significant for a marginalized community that is not allowed to legally own property in Lebanon" (Hanafi 2010:3).

9. Similarly to the Neirab Rehabilitation Project, the Jenin project predated the institutionalization of UNRWA's ICIP but played a role in shaping it.

5. "A Camp Is a Feeling Inside"

1. This is not to say that there are no areas in the camp that are run-down or that poverty is nonexistent. According to Fafo (Norwegian Institute for Labor Research) in a 2006 report, 20 percent of Yarmouk residents qualify as "poor" (Tiltnes 2006).

2. Focusing on the Homs refugee camp, Blin points out that the camp's spatial marginality is often evoked through the image of heavy drug use among camp-dwelling Palestinians, an image that is extended to Yarmouk.

3. According to SREO, there are functioning generators in the camp but because of the cost of fuel they are very sparsely used (SREO 2015).

4. This information is based on interviews conducted with Palestinian refugees from Yarmouk now living in Lebanon, Turkey, and the United Arab Emirates in March and April 2015.

Conclusion

1. The pamphlet, which summarizes various projects conducted by UNRWA's Infrastructure and Camp Improvement Program (ICIP), accompanies the booklet *Partnering with Refugees: Towards a Better Living Environment until their Rights are Fulfilled*. It has no publication date.

2. I am not able to speak to the social adjustment and integration of the families who moved from the barracks to Ein el Tal–these issues were not a part of the Neirab Rehabilitation Project that I was able to study.

3. I received conflicting accounts of the number of families who (in the prewar period) chose to return to Neirab from the new houses in Ein el Tal. Although some interviewees said that at least half or more of all families had chosen to move back within a year or two, one interviewee said that only a small number had done so.

4. I am not able to comment on how successful the employment advisor hired by the Neirab Rehabilitation Project was in helping Ein el Tal residents with professional networking and employment during his tenure.

5. This information is based on a conversation with a Neirab Rehabilitation Project team member.

6. Similarly, UNRWA's *Camp Improvement Manual* acknowledges that one of the obstacles in the way of camp improvement is that some agency employees are resistant to the idea of involving refugees in the planning and implementation of camp improvement projects (UNRWA 2012).

7. The manual was last updated in 2012.

8. See for example the Tree School Project in Bahia, Brazil. http://www.ibraaz.org/projects/89, accessed May 23, 2011.

9. Alessandro Petti, founding member of Campus in Camps, explained in an interview the decision to build the wall in concrete: concrete is very adaptable and accessible to anyone. It can be easily purchased, assembled, and used, he said, and in that sense it is almost like a tent. Also, most tents today are made of concrete.

10. See http://unctad.org/en/pages/newsdetails.aspx?OriginalVersionID=1068 and http://unctad.org/meetings/en/SessionalDocuments/tdb62d3_en.pdf, accessed December 1, 2015.

11. The exclusion of Palestinian refugees from UNHCR's mandate was mostly due to fear in Arab states that if included the Palestinian refugees "would become submerged [with other categories of refugees] and would be relegated to a position of minor importance" (Takkenberg 1998:66). A major concern among Arab states was that "the Palestinian refugees' problem would not be adequately addressed if UNHCR's durable solutions, such as resettlement to a third country or settlement in the first country of asylum, were applied to [them]" (Suleiman 2010:14).

12. The number of Syrian refugees comes from UNHCR estimates.

13. It must be noted however, that several UNRWA schools have closed or been destroyed as a result of the war.

Epilogue

1. According to statistics published on February 19, 2016, by the Action Group for the Palestinians of Syria, 71,000 Palestinians have reached Europe as of December 2015 (AGPS 2016).

2. At the end of July 2015, the Office of the UN Secretary General made the surprising decision to remove Yarmouk from the list of besieged areas in Syria, on the advice of the Organization for the Coordination of Humanitarian Affairs (OCHA), which argued that humanitarian aid had reached Yarmouk civilians who had crossed into the surrounding areas of Yalda, Babilla, and Beit Sahem (Dyke 2015). This decision is puzzling given that regular interruptions in water and food supplies (sometimes for months at a time) continue to affect Yarmouk, Yalda, Babilla, and Beit Saham (UNRWA 2015i). Additionally, although movement between Yalda and Yarmouk is possible, going from one to the other is dangerous and individuals who try to cross between the two do so at the whim of the government forces and other armed groups. It must be noted that Yarmouk's surrounding rebel-held areas are themselves encircled by Syrian regime troops, preventing the camp's inhabitants from moving beyond those areas (email exchange with UNRWA representatives, September 22, 2015).

3. The main rebel groups mentioned in interviews with refugees displaced from Ein el Tal are the FSA (Free Syrian Army) and Jabhat al-Nusra, and it seems that the two groups occupied the camp at different times. I noticed, however, that my interviewees tended to refer to all rebels as the Free Syrian Army (Jaysh al-ḥur), making it hard to obtain exact information about the rebels' identity.

4. The passport was fake in the sense that it was someone else's; it belonged to a citizen of a European country.

5. Wisam's wife died of a prolonged illness shortly after the uprisings began. He remarried, but his second wife stayed in Turkey.

6. Saleem's father passed away from natural causes before the uprisings began.

7. According to the Palestinians I interviewed, Sudan was the only country that as a matter of general policy was still giving visas to Palestinians.

References

Agamben, Giorgio
  1998 Homo Sacer: Sovereign Power and Bare Life. Stanford: Stanford University Press.
Agier, Michel
  2008 On the Margins of the World: The Refugee Experience Today. Cambridge: Polity Press.
  2007 From Refugee Camps to the Invention of Cities. In Cities of the South: Citizenship and Exclusion in the 21st Century. Barbara Drieskens, Franck Mermier, and Heiko Wimmen, eds. Pp. 169–176. Beirut: Saqi Books.
AGPS (Action Group for the Palestinians of Syria)
  2016 Palestinians of Syria in Numbers and Statistics until 18 February 2016. http://www.actionpal.org.uk/en/post/2848/news-and-reports/palestinians-of-syria-in-numbers-and-statistics-until-18-february-2016, accessed February 20, 2016.
  2015 49 Palestinian Syrian Families in the Turkish city of Kilis Demand through the AGPS to Help Them and to Settle Their Situation. April 23. http://www.actionpal.org.uk/en/post.php?id=975, accessed November 8, 2015.
Akram, Susan, Michael Dumper, and Michael Lynk
  2011 International Law and the Israeli-Palestinian Conflict: A Rights-based Approach to Middle East Peace. New York: Routledge.
Al-Hafiz, Mai Abd al-Kader
  2006 Ayūnak aʻla al-safīna: riwāya [Your Eyes onto the Ship: A Story]. Printed by author.
Al-Hamarneh, Ala
  2002 The Social and Political Effects of Transformation Processes in Palestinian Refugee Camps in the Amman Metropolitan Area (1989–99). In Jordan in Transition. G. Joffé, ed. London: Hurst & Co.
Al-Hardan, Anaheed
  2012 The Right of Return Movement in Syria: Building a Culture of Return, Mobilizing Memories for the Return. Journal of Palestine Studies, 41(2):62–79.
Al Husseini, Jalal
  2011 The Evolution of the Palestinian Refugee Camps in Jordan: Between Logics of Exclusion and Integration. In Villes, pratiques urbaines et construction nationale en Jordanie [Cities, Urban Practices and National Construction in Jordan]. Pp. 181–204. Beirut: Presses de l'Ifpo. http://books.openedition.org/ifpo/1742, accessed October 13, 2014.
  2010 UNRWA and the Refugees: A Difficult but Lasting Marriage. Journal of Palestine Studies 40(1):6–26.
  2007 The Arab States and the Refugee Issue: A Retrospective View. In Israel and the Palestinian Refugees. Eyal Benvinisti, Chaim Gans, an Sari Hanafi, eds. Pp. 435–464. Berlin: Springer.

Al Husseini, Jalal, and Ricardo Bocco
  2009 The Status of the Palestinian Refugees in the Near East: The Right of Return and UNRWA in Perspective. Theme issue, "UNRWA and the Palestinian Refugees 60 Years Later," Refugee Survey Quarterly 28(2–3):260–285.
Al Jazeera
  2015 ISIL Seizes Most of Syria's Yarmouk Camp. April, 5. http://www.aljazeera.com /news/2015/04/isil-seizes-syria-yarmouk-refugee-camp-150404135525226.html, accessed July 2, 2015.
  2014 Aid Enters Besieged Palestinian Camp in Syria. January 18. http://www.aljazeera .com/news/middleeast/2014/01/aid-enters-besieged-palestinian-camp-syria -201411815539107398.html, accessed January 18, 2014.
  2013 Death and Starvation in Syria's Yarmouk. December 28. http://www.aljazeera.com /news/middleeast/2013/12/starvation-syria-yarmouk-20131228151752853749.html, accessed December 29, 2013.
Allan, Diana
  2014 Refugees of the Revolution: Experiences of Palestinian Exile. Stanford: Stanford University Press.
Allen, Lori
  2009 Martyr Bodies in the Media: Human Rights, Aesthetics and the Politics of Immediation in the Palestinian Intifada. American Ethnologist 36(1):161–180.
Al-Majdal
  2015 Special Issue: Palestinian Refugees from Syria: Ongoing Nakba, Ongoing Discrimination. Issue 57, summer.
  2014 Special Issue: Palestinian Refugees from Syria: Ongoing Nakba, Ongoing Discrimination. Issue 56, autumn.
Al-Mawed, Hamad Said
  2002 Mukhayyam el-Yarmouk: Muqārajāt fi Sosiologia el-Mukhayyam el-Filasṭīni [Yarmouk Camp: Comparative Sociology of the Palestinian Camp]. Damascus: Dar el-Shajara.
  1999 The Palestinian Refugees in Syria: Their Past, Present, and Future. International Development Research Center, Ottawa.
Al-Nammari, Fatima
  2014 Talbiyeh Camp Improvement Project and the Challenges of Community Participation: Between Empowerment and Conflict. In UNRWA and Palestinian Refugees: From Relief and Works to Human Development. Sari Hanafi, Leila Hila, and Lex Takkenberg, eds. Pp. 206–220. New York: Routledge.
Amnesty International
  2014a Squeezing the Life out of Yarmouk: War Crimes against Besieged Civilians. March 10. file:///Users/nellgabiam/Desktop/Syria_report_Squeezing_the_life_out _of_Yarmouk.pdf, accessed July 2, 2015.
  2014b Lebanon Barring Palestinian Refugees. July 1. http://www.middleeasteye.net /news/amnesty-international-lebanon-barring-palestinian-refugees-2115521885, accessed May 5, 2015.
Anderson, Benedict
  1983 Imagined Communities: Reflections on the Origin and Spread of Nationalism. London: Verso.

Apthorpe, Raymond
    1997 Writing Development Policy and Policy Analysis Plain or Clear: On Language, Genre and Power. In Anthropology of Policy: Critical Perspectives on Governance and Power. Cris Shore and Susan Wright, 43–59. London: Routledge.
Arendt, Hannah
    1973 The Origins of Totalitarianism. New York: Harcourt, Brace and Co.
Asad, Talal
    2003 Formations of the Secular: Christianity, Islam, Modernity (Cultural Memory in the Present). Stanford: Stanford University Press.
Azzam, Mohamad
    2005 From the North of Palestine to the North of Syria: The Move of Palestine Refugees to Aleppo (chapter 1). Communication: Neirab Rehabilitation Project Newsletter, November.
BADIL (Resource Center for Palestinian Residency and Refugee Rights)
    2010 The Palestinian Crisis in Libya 1994–1996 (An Interview with Bassem Sirhan). Al Majdal 45 (winter). Pp. 44–49.
Bar'el, Zvi
    2014 Caught between Syria's Regime and the Rebels, Palestinian Refugees Are Starving to Death. Haaretz. http://www.haaretz.com/news/middle-east/.premium -1.566601, accessed January 18, 2014.
Barlund, Kaj
    2013 Sustainable Development–Concept and Action. United Nations Economic Commission for Europe (UNECE). http://www.unece.org/oes/nutshell/2004-2005 /focus_sustainable_development.html, accessed May 27, 2013.
Barnett, Michael, and Thomas G. Weiss
    2008 Humanitarianism: A History of the Present. In Humanitarianism in Question: Politics, Power, Ethics. Michael Barnett and Thomas G. Weiss, eds. Pp. 1–48. Ithaca: Cornell University Press.
Baroud, Ramzy
    2014 Starving Refugees: How We Disowned Palestinians in Syria. Counterpunch. January 9. http://www.counterpunch.org/2014/01/09/starving-refugees/, accessed February 26, 2016.
    2012 Nakba Revisited: Tragedy of Syria's Palestinians and Centrality of the Right of Return. Palestine Chronicle. http://www.palestinechronicle.com/nakba-revisited -tragedy-of-syrias-palestinians-and-centrality-of-right-of-return/#.Uj9rPiTo87A.
Benbassa, Esther
    2010 Suffering as Identity: The Jewish Paradigm. London: Verso.
Berg, Kjersti Gravelsæter
    2014 From Chaos to Order and Back: The Construction of UNRWA Shelters and Camps, 1950–1970. In UNRWA and Palestinian Refugees: From Relief and Works to Human Development. Sari Hanafi, Leila Hilal, and Lex Takkenberg, eds. Pp. 109–128. New York: Routledge.
Berlant, Lauren
    1997 The Queen of America Goes to Washington: Essays on Sex and Citizenship. Durham: Duke University Press.

Bitari, Nidal
   2013 Yarmouk Refugee Camp and the Syrian Uprising. Journal of Palestine Studies
      43(1):61–78.
Blin, Lina
   2012 Entre Ici et Là: Intégration et Comportement Politique des Réfugiés Palestiniens
      de Syrie. [Between Here and Theres: The Integration and Political Behaviour of Pal-
      estinian Refugees in Syria]. In Les Palestiniens entre Etat et Diaspora: Le Temps des
      Incertitudes [Palestinians between State and Diaspora: The Time of Uncertainty].
      Jalal Al Husseini and Aude Signoles, eds. Paris: ISSMM-Karthala.
Boltanski, Luc
   1999 Distant Suffering: Morality, Media and Politics. Cambridge: Cambridge Univer-
      sity Press.
Bornstein, Erica
   2005 The Spirit of Development: Protestant NGOs, Morality, and Economics in
      Zimbabwe. Stanford: Stanford University Press.
Bouagga, Yasmine
   2014 Aux marges d'Alep: les camps de réfugiés palestiniens [On the Margins of
      Aleppo: Palestinian Refugee Camps]. In Alep et ses territoires [Aleppo and its
      Territories]. Jean Claud David and Thierry Boisière, eds. Presses de l'Ifpo (Institut
      Français de Proche-Orient).
Brand, Laurie
   1988 Palestinian Refugees in Syria: The Politics of Integration. Middle East Journal
      42(4):621–637.
Bruntland Commission
   1987 Our Common Future. United Nations World Commission on Environment and
      Development. http://en.wikisource.org/wiki/Brundtland_Report, accessed 27 May 2013.
Brynen, Rex
   2014 UNRWA as Avatar: Current Debates on the Agency–and Their Implications. In
      UNRWA and Palestinian Refugees: From Relief and Works to Human Development.
      Sari Hanafi, Leila Hilal, and Lex Takkenberg, eds. Pp. 263–283. New York: Routledge.
Brynen Rex, and Roula El-Rifai
   2007 Palestinian Refugees: Challenges of Repatriation and Development. New York:
      I. B. Tauris.
Bshara, Khaldun
   2013 For a Paradigm Shift: A Psychoanalytical Approach to Refugees' Memory and
      Spatial Practices. In Palestinian Refugees: Different Generations but One Identity.
      Sunaina Miari, ed. Pp. 121–145. Palestine: Ibrahim Abu-Lughod Center for Interna-
      tional Studies, Birzeit University.
Budeiri, Muna
   2014 Dynamics of Space, Temporariness, Development and Rights in Palestine
      Refugee Camps. In UNRWA and Palestinian Refugees: From Relief and Works to
      Human Development. Sari Hanafi, Leila Hilal, and Lex Takkenberg, eds. New
      York: Routledge.
Byrne, Aisling
   2006 Final Evaluation Draft Report. Unpublished UNRWA report.

Calhoun, Craig
  2008 The Imperative to Reduce Suffering: Charity, Progress and Emergencies in the Field of Humanitarian Action. In Humanitarianism in Question: Politics, Power, Ethics. Michael Barnett and Thomas G. Weiss, eds. Pp. 73–97. Ithaca: Cornell University Press.

Calhoun, Noel
  2010 UNHCR and Community Development: A Weak Link in the Key of Refugee Protection? New Issues in Refugee Research. Research Paper No. 191:1–19.

Campus in Camps
  2015 Official website. http://www.campusincamps.ps/about, accessed April 30, 2015.

Campus in Camps and Grupo Contrafilé
  2014 The Tree School. http://www.ibraaz.org/usr/library/documents/main/tree-school_digital-book_v04.pdf, accessed May 23, 2015.

Caton, Steven C., and Bernardo Zacka.
  2010 Abu Ghraib: The Security Apparatus and the Performativity of Power. American Ethnologist 37(2):203–211.

Cave Damian, and Dalal Mawad
  2012 Deadly Attack on Palestinian Camp in Syria Could Shift Palestinian Allegiance to Rebels. New York Times. http://www.nytimes.com/2012/08/04/world/middleeast/syria-assault-palestinian-camp-damascus.html, accessed October 3, 2012.

Chakaki, Mohamad
  2006 Beyond Tears, Blood and Olive Trees: Palestinian Refugee Identity and Its Implications for the Sustainable Development of Palestinian Refugee Camps. Master's thesis, School of Forestry and Environmental Studies, Yale University.

Chambers, Robert
  1994 The Origins and Practice of Participatory Rural Appraisal. World Development 22(6):953–969.

Chambers, Robert, and Gordon Conway
  1987 Sustainable Rural Livelihoods: Practical Concepts for the 21st Century. Brighton, UK: Institute of Development Studies at the University of Sussex.

Chandler, David G.
  2001 The Road to Military Humanitarianism: How the Human Rights NGOs Shaped a New Humanitarian Agenda. Human Rights Quarterly 23(3):678–700.

Charles, Tom
  2012 Ongoing Nakba: The Plight of Palestinian Refugees in Iraq. Jadaliyya. February, 6. http://www.jadaliyya.com/pages/index/4264/an-ongoing-nakba_the-plight-of-palestinian-refugee, accessed November 15, 2015.

Chatty, Dawn
  2010 Introduction. In No Refuge: Palestinians in Lebanon. Working Paper Series No 64. Refugee Studies Centre, Oxford University. Pp 3–6.

Cowan, Michael, and Robert Shenton
  1996 Doctrines of Development. New York: Routledge.

Crisp, Jeff
  2003 UNHCR, Refugee Livelihoods and Self-Reliance: A Brief History. PDES Background Documents. www.unhcr.org, accessed August 30, 2010.

Crush, Jonathan
   1995 Imagining Development. In Power of Development. Jonathan Crush, ed.
      Pp. 1–23. New York: Routledge.
Daniel, E. Valentine, and John Chr. Knudsen, eds.
   1995 Mistrusting Refugees. Berkeley: University of California Press.
Davis, Mike
   2006 Planet of Slums. New York: Pluto Press.
De Waal, Alexander
   1997 Famine Crimes: Politics and the Disaster Relief Industry in Africa. Bloomington:
      Indiana University Press.
Drieskens, Barbara, Franck Mermier, and Heiko Wimmen
   2007 Cities of the South: Citizenship and Exclusion in the 21st Century. Beirut: SAQI.
Dumper, Michael
   2007 The Future for Palestinian Refugees: Toward Equity and Peace. Boulder: Lynne
      Rienner.
Dyke, Joe
   2015 Yarmouk No Longer Besieged, UN Rules. IRIN News. July 24. http://www.irin
      news.org/report/101781/yarmouk-camp-no-longer-besieged-un-rules, accessed
      August 13, 2015.
Erakat, Noura
   2014 Palestinian Refugees and the Syrian Uprising: Filling the Protection Gap during
      Secondary Forced Displacement. International Journal of Refugee Law. 26(4):
      581–621.
Fadhel, Khadija
   2012 Recomposition socio-spatiale d'un camp de réfugiés Palestiniens à Damas; le
      cas de Al-Yarmûk [Socio-Spatial Recomposition of a Palestinian Refugee Camp in
      Damascus: The Case of Al-Yarmouk]. In Les Palestiniens entre état et diaspora: Le
      temps des incertitudes. Jalal Al Husseini and Aude Signoles, eds. Paris: ISSMM-
      Karthala.
Farah, Randa
   2012 Keeping an Eye on UNRWA. Al-Shabaka Policy Brief. http://al-shabaka.org
      /sites/default/files/policybrief/en/keeping-eye-unrwa/keeping-eye-unrwa.pdf, ac-
      cessed January 11, 2014.
   2010 UNRWA: Through the Eyes of Its Refugee Employees in Jordan. Theme issue,
      "UNRWA and the Palestinian Refugees 60 Years Later," Refugee Survey Quarterly
      28(2–3):389–411.
   1999 Popular Memory and Reconstructions of Palestinian Refugee Identity: Al Baq'a
      Refugee Camp in Jordan. Ph.D. dissertation, Department of Anthropology, Univer-
      sity of Toronto.
   1997 Crossing Boundaries: Reconstruction of Palestinian Identities in al-Baq'a Refu-
      gee Camp, Jordan. In Palestine, Palestiniens–territoire national, espaces commu-
      nautaires (les cahiers du Cermoc no. 17), Beirut: Cermoc.
Fassin, Didier
   2012 Humanitarian Reason: A Moral History of the Present. Berkeley: University of
      California Press.

2005 Compassion and Repression: The Moral Economy of Immigration Policies in France. Cultural Anthropology 20(3):362–387.

2002 La souffrance du monde. Considerations anthropologiques sur les politiques contemporaines de la compassion [The Suffering of the World: Anthropological Considerations on Contemporary Polities of Compassion]. Evolution Psychiatrique 67:676–689.

Fassin, Didier, and Richard Rechtman

2009 Palestine. The Empire of Trauma: An Inquiry into the Condition of Victimhood. Didier Fassin and Richard Rechtman, eds. Pp. 189–216. Princeton: Princeton University Press.

Fearon, James

2008 The Rise of Emergency Relief Aid. In Humanitarianism in Question: Politics, Power, Ethics. Michael Barnett and Thomas G. Weiss, eds. Pp. 49–72. Ithaca: Cornell University Press.

Feldman, Ilana

2008a Governing Gaza: Bureaucracy, Authority, and the Work of Rule 1917–1967. Durham: Duke University Press.

2008b Refusing Invisibility: Documentation and Memorialization in Palestinian Refugee Camps. Oxford Journal of Refugee Studies 21(4):498–516.

2007a The Quaker Way: Ethical Labor and Humanitarian Relief. American Ethnologist 34(4):689–705.

2007b Difficult Distinctions: Refugee Law, Humanitarian Practice and Political Identity in Gaza. Cultural Anthropology 22(1):129–169.

Ferguson, James

1999 Expectations of Modernity: Myths and Meanings of Urban Life on the Zambian Copperbelt. Berkeley: University of California Press.

1994 The Anti-Politics Machine: "Development," Depoliticization, and Bureaucratic Power in Lesotho. Minneapolis: University of Minnesota Press.

Foucault, Michel

1991 On Governmentality. In The Foucault Effect: Studies in Governmentality. Graham Burchell, Colin Gordon, and Peter Miller eds. Chicago: University of Chicago Press.

Francis, David

2012 Senate Fight Today over Palestinian "Refugees." Foreignpolicy.com, May 25. http://foreignpolicy.com/2012/05/24/senate-fight-today-over-palestinian-refugees, accessed February 12, 2015.

Francis, Paul

2001 Participatory Development at the World Bank: The Primacy of Process. In Participation: The New Tyranny? Bill Cooke and Uma Kothari, eds. Pp. 72–87. London: Zed Books.

GAPAR

2002 al-hay'a al-ʿāmma lil-lāji'īn al-filasṭīniyyīn al-ʿarab wa al-laji'ūn al filasṭīniyyūn fi al-jumhūriyya al-ʿarabiyya al-sūriyya: qawānīn, marāsīm, qarārāt, khadamāt, bayānāt, iḥṣā'iyyāt. [The General Authority for Palestinian Arab Refugees and for Palestinian Refugees in the Syrian Arab Republic: Laws, Principles, Decisions, Services, Declarations, Statistics].

George, Alan
  2003 Syria: Neither Bread nor Freedom. London: Zed Books.
Grandi, Filippo
  2010 Keynote address. Conference titled "From Relief and Works to Human Develop-
    ment: UNRWA and Palestinian Refugees after Sixty Years." Issam Fares Institute
    for International and Comparative Studies. American University of Beirut. http://
    www.unrwa.org/etemplate.php?id=822, accessed September 28, 2011.
Gupta, Akhil
  2012 Red Tape: Bureaucracy, Structural Violence, and Poverty in India. Durham:
    Duke University Press.
Haddad, Toufic
  2010 Palestinian Forced Displacement from Kuwait: The Overdue Accounting. Al
    Majdal 44 (summer/autumn):35–42.
Hailey, John
  2001 Beyond the Formulaic: Process and Practice in South Asian NGOs. In Participa-
    tion: The New Tyranny? Bill Cooke and Uma Kothari, eds. Pp. 88–101. London: Zed
    Books.
Hanafi, Sari
  2010 Reconstructing and Governing Nahr el Bared Camp: Bridge or Barrier to Inclu-
    sion? ArteEast Quarterly (spring):1–5. http://www.arteeast.org/2012/02/08/recon
    structing-and-governing-nahr-el-bared/3/, accessed October 31, 2015.
  2002 Opening the Debate on the Right of Return. Middle East Report 222:2–7. http://
    www.merip.org/mer/mer222/opening-debate-right-return, accessed October 31, 2015.
  1996 The Palestinians in Syria and the Peace Process. Majallat al-Dirasat al-Filastiniyya
    7(2):85–103 [in Arabic].
Hanafi, Sari, and Taylor Long
  2010 Governance, Governmentalities and the State of Exception in the Palestinian
    Refugee Camps of Lebanon. Journal of Refugee Studies 23(2):134–159.
Hansen, Peter
  2004 UN Relief and Works Agency: A Tour of the Palestinian Refugee Camps. Inter-
    national Herald Tribune, May 19. http://www.miftah.org/display.cfm?DocId=3809
    &CategoryId=5, accessed May 5, 2015.
Hartman, Saidiya
  1997 Scenes of Subjection: Terror, Slavery and Self-Making in Nineteenth Century
    America. Oxford: Oxford University Press.
Harvey, David
  2008 The Right to the City. New Left Review 53 (September/October):23–40.
Hassan, Budour
  2012 The Myth of Palestinian Neutrality in Syria. Maan News Agency. http://www
    .thejerusalemfund.org/ht/display/ContentDetails/i/35244/pid/895, accessed Sep-
    tember 15 2012.
Hassan, Ismael Sheik, and Sari Hanafi
  2010 (In)security and Reconstruction in Post Conflict Nahr el Barid. Journal of Pales-
    tine Studies 40(1):27–48.

Hazboun, Norma Masriyeh
   1996 Israeli Resettlement Schemes for Palestinian Refugees in the Gaza Strip since
      1967. The Palestinian Diaspora and Refugee Center (Shaml). Monograph 4.
Henkel, Heiko, and Roderick Stirrat
   2001 Participation as Spiritual Duty; Empowerment as Secular Subjection. In Partici-
      pation: The New Tyranny? Bill Cook and Uma Kothari, eds. Pp. 168–184. London:
      Zed Books.
Hinnebusch, Raymond
   2001 Syria: Revolution from Above. New York: Routledge.
Hinnebusch, Raymond, Marwan J. Kabalan, Bassma Kodmani, and David Lesch
   2009 Syrian Foreign Policy and the United States: From Bush to Obama. St. Andrews
      Papers on Contemporary Syria.
Holston, James
   2008 Insurgent Citizenship: Disjunctions of Democracy and Modernity in Brazil.
      Princeton: Princeton University Press.
Human Rights Watch
   2014 Jordan: Palestinians Escaping Syria Turned Away. August 7. https://www.hrw
      .org/news/2014/08/07/jordan-palestinians-escaping-syria-turned-away, accessed
      August 7, 2015.
   2012 Bias at the Border: Palestinians Face Detention, Threat of Forced Return. July 4.
      http://www.hrw.org/news/2012/07/04/jordan-bias-syrian-border, accessed April 14,
      2015.
   2010 Stateless Again: Palestinian-Origin Jordanians Deprived of Their Nationality.
      February 1. http://www.hrw.org/reports/2010/02/01/stateless-again-0, accessed
      May 5, 2015.
   2003 Flight from Iraq: Attacks on Refugees and other Foreigners and Their Treatment
      in Jordan. 15 (4E). http://www.hrw.org/en/reports/2003/05/09/flight-iraq, accessed
      May 5, 2015.
Hyndman, Jennifer
   2000 Managing Displacement: Refugees and the Politics of Humanitarianism.
      Minneapolis: University of Minnesota Press.
ICRC (International Committee of the Red Cross)
   2014 Syria: Urgently Needed Aid for People in Yalda, Babilla, and Beit Sahem. https://
      www.icrc.org/en/document/syria-urgently-needed-aid-people-babila-yalda-and
      -beit-sahem, accessed October 31, 2015.
Isin, Engin F., and Kim Rygiel
   2007 Of Other Global Cities: Frontiers, Zones, and Camps. In Cities of the South:
      Citizenship and Exclusion in the 21st Century. Barbara Drieskens, Franck Mermier,
      and Heiko Wimmen, eds. Pp. 170–209. Beirut: Saqi Books.
Jayyusi, Lena
   2007 Iterability, Cumulativity, and Presence: The Relational Figures of Palestinian
      Memory. In Nakba: Palestine, 1948, and the Claims of Memory. Ahmad H. Sa'di
      and Lila Abu-Lughod, eds. Pp. 107–135. New York: Columbia University Press.
Kagan, Michael
   2010 Is There Really a Protection Gap? UNRWA's Role vis-à-vis Palestinian Refugees.
      Theme issue, "UNRWA and the Palestinian Refugees 60 Years Later," Refugee Survey
      Quarterly 28(2–3):511–530.

Keinon, Herb

2011 Ayalon Blasts UNRWA Saying It Perpetuates Conflict. Jerusalem Post. http://www
.jpost.com/Diplomacy-and-Politics/Ayalon-blasts-UNRWA-saying-it-perpet
uates-conflict, accessed January 11, 2014.

Kennedy, David

2004 The Dark Side of Virtue: Reassessing International Humanitarianism. Princeton: Princeton University Press.

Kershner, Isabel

2011 Fighters Shoot Protesters at Palestinian Camp in Syria. New York Times. http://
www.nytimes.com/2011/06/08/world/middleeast/08damascus.html, accessed September 15, 2012.

Khalidi, Rashid

1992 Observations on the Right of Return. Journal of Palestine Studies 21(2):2
9–40.

Khalili, Laleh

2007 Heroes and Martyrs of Palestine: The Politics of National Commemoration.
Cambridge: Cambridge University Press.

2005 Places of Commemoration and Mourning: Palestinian Refugee Camps in Lebanon. Theme issue, "Mourning and Memory," Comparative Studies of South Asia,
Africa, and the Middle East 25(1):30–44.

Kimmelman, Michael

2014 Refugees Reshape Their Camp, at the Risk of Feeling at Home. New York Times,
September 6. http://www.nytimes.com/2014/09/07/world/middleeast/refugees
-reshape-their-camp-at-the-risk-of-feeling-at-home.html?_r=0.

Kleinman, Arthur, Veena Das, and Margaret Lock, eds.

1997 Introduction. In Social Suffering. Arthur Kleinman, Veena Das and Margaret
Lock, eds. Pp. ix–xxvii. Berkeley: University of California Press.

Kodmani-Darwish, Bassma

1997 La Diaspora Palestinienne [The Palestinian Diaspora]. Paris: Presse Universitaire
de France.

Kothari, Uma

2001 Power, Knowledge and Social Control in Participatory Development. In Participation: The New Tyranny? Bill Cooke and Uma Kothari, eds. Pp. 139–152. London:
Zed Books.

Levy, Gideon

2014 Israel, Save the Palestinians in Syria. Haaretz. http://www.haaretz.com/opinion
/.premium-1.570006, accessed February 6, 2014.

Li, Tania Murray

2007 The Will to Improve: Governmentality, Development and the Practice of Politics. Durham: Duke University Press.

Lindholm Schulz, Helena

2003 The Palestinian Diaspora: Formations of Identity and the Politics of Homeland.
London: Routledge.

Lindsay, James G.

2009 Fixing UNRWA: Repairing the UN's Troubled System of Aid to Palestinian Refugees. Policy Focus #91, January. http://www.washingtoninstitute.org/policy

-analysis/view/fixing-unrwa-repairing-the-uns-troubled-system-of-aid-to-pales
tinian-refuge, accessed October 30, 2015.

Malkki, Liisa

1996 Speechless Emissaries: Refugees, Humanitarianism, and Dehistoricization. Cultural Anthropology 11(3):377–404.

1995 Purity and Exile: Violence, Memory, and National Cosmology among Hutu Refugees in Tanzania. Chicago: University of Chicago Press.

Meyer, Sarah

2006 The Refugee "Aid and Development Approach" in Uganda: Empowerment and Self-Reliance of Refugees in Practice. New Issues in Refugee Research. Research Paper 131. University of Oxford. http://www.unhcr.org/4538eb172.html, accessed November 30, 2010.

Misselwitz, Philipp

2009 Rehabilitating Camp Cities: Community-Driven Planning for Urbanized Refugee Camps. Ph.D. dissertation. University of Stuttgart, Germany.

Misselwitz, Philipp, and Sari Hanafi

2010 Testing a New Paradigm: UNRWA's Camp Improvement Programme. Theme issue, "UNRWA and the Palestinian Refugees 60 Years Later," Refugee Survey Quarterly 28(2–3):360–388.

Moore, Donald

2005 Suffering for Territory: Race, Place, and Power in Zimbabwe. Durham: Duke University Press.

Morris, Benny

2004 [1987] The Birth of the Palestinian Refugee Problem, 1947–1949. Cambridge: Cambridge University Press.

Morris, Nicholas

2008 What Protection Means for UNRWA in Concept and Practice. UN Relief and Works Agency for Palestine Refugees in the Near East (UNRWA). Consultant's Report, March 31. http://www.unrwa.org/search.php?siteurl=www.unrwa.org%2 F&cx=003175056264303192970%3Asuqyorxnhuu& cof=FORID%3A9&ie=windows -1256&q=nicholas+ morris&sa=Search#307, accessed September 28, 2011.

Mosse, David

2005 Cultivating Development: An Ethnography of Aid Policy and Practice. London: Pluto Press.

Nabulsi, Karma

2006 Palestinians Register: Laying Foundations and Setting Directions. Report of the CI VI T AS Project. Oxford, UK: Nuffield College, University of Oxford. http:// www.forcedmigration.org/research-resources/thematic/palestinians-register-laying -foundations-and-setting-directions, accessed October 30, 2015.

National Public Radio (NPR)

2015 UN Official Calls Situation in Yarmouk "Beyond Inhumane." April 7. http:// www.npr.org/2015/04/07/398123404/u-n-official-calls-situation-at-yarmouk-refugee -camp-beyond-inhumane, accessed April 13, 2015.

Nora, Pierre

1989 Between Memory and History: Les Lieux de Memoire. Marc Roudebush, trans. Representations 26 (Spring):7–24.

OCHA (United Nations Office for the Coordination of Humanitarian Affairs)
2016 "About the Crisis." http://www.unocha.org/syrian-arab-republic/syria-country
-profile/about-crisis, accessed February 20, 2016.

Oesch, Lucas
2014 The Urban Planning Strategy in Al-Hussein Palestinian Refugee Camp in Amman: Heterogeneous Practices, Homogeneous Landscape. In UNRWA and Palestinian Refugees: From Relief and Works to Human Development. London:
Routledge.

Omi, Michael, and Howard Winant
1993 On the Theoretical Status of the Concept of Race. In Race, Identity and Representation in Education. Cameron McCarthy and Warren Crichlow, eds. New York:
Routledge.

Orr, David W.
2003 Four Challenges of Sustainability. Spring Seminar Series, School of Natural
Resources, University of Vermont.

Palumbo-Liu, David
2015 Black Activists Send Clear Message to Palestinians: "Now Is the Time for Palestinian Liberation, Just as Now Is the Time for Our Own in the United States."
Salon, August, 18. http://www.salon.com/2015/08/18/black_activists_send_clear
_message_to_palestinians_now_is_the_time_for_palestinian_liberation_just_as
_now_is_the_time_for_our_own_in_the_united_states/, accessed October 28, 2015.

Panayiotopoulos, Prodomos
2002 Anthropology Consultancy in the UK and Community Development in the
Third World: A Difficult Dialogue. Development in Practice 12(1):45–58.

Parmenter, Barbara Mckean
1994 Giving Voice to Stones: Place and Identity in Palestinian Literature. Austin:
University of Texas Press.

Peteet, Julie
2005 Landscape of Hope and Despair: Palestinian Refugee Camps. Philadelphia:
University of Pennsylvania Press.
1996 From Refugees to Minority: Palestinians in Post-War Lebanon. Middle East Report 200:27–30. http://www.merip.org/mer/mer200/palestinians-post-war-lebanon,
accessed October 31, 2015.
1991 Gender in Crisis: Women and the Palestinian Liberation Movement. New York:
Columbia University Press.

Quilliam, Neil
1999 Syria and the New World Order. Reading, UK: Ithaca Press.

Ramadan, Adam
2013 Spatializing the Refugee Camp: Transactions of the Institute of British Geogra-
phers 38(1):65–77.
2010 In the Ruins of Nahr al-Barid: Understanding the Meaning of the Camp. Journal
of Palestine Studies, 40(1):49–62.
2009 Destroying Nahr el-Bared: Sovereignty and Urbicide in the Space of Exception.
Political Geography, 28(3):153–163.

Redfield, Peter
2005 Doctors, Borders, and Life in Crisis. Cultural Anthropology 20(3):328–361.

Reliefweb
  2015 Gaza Situation Report 89, April 23. http://reliefweb.int/report/occupied-palestin
    ian-territory/gaza-situation-report-89-23-april-2015, accessed May 13, 2015.
Rieff, David
  2002 A Bed for the Night: Humanitarianism in Crisis. New York: Simon and Schuster.
Robins, Steven
  2009 Humanitarian Aid beyond "Bare Survival": Social Movement Responses to
    Xenophobic Violence in South Africa. American Ethnologist 36(4):637–650.
Rueff, Henri, and Alain Viaro
  2010 Palestinian Refugee Camps: From Shelter to Habitat. Theme issue, "UNRWA and
    the Palestinian Refugees 60 Years Later," Refugee Survey Quarterly 28(2–3):339–359.
Sa'di, Ahmad H., and Lila Abu-Lughod
  2007 Introduction. In Nakba: Palestine, 1948, and the Claims of Memory. Ahmad H.
    Sa'di and Lila Abu-Lughod, eds. Pp. 1–24. New York: Columbia University Press.
Salloum, Jakie Reem
  2008 Slingshot Hip Hop. Documentary. Jakie Reem Salloum director/producer/editor.
Sayigh, Rosemary
  2013 The Price of Statelessness: Palestinian Refugees in Syria. Al Shabaka. http://
    al-shabaka.org/price-statelessness-palestinian-refugees-syria?page=4.
  2007 Women's Nakba Stories: Between Being and Knowing. In Nakba: Palestine,
    1948, and the Claims of Memory. Ahmad H. Sa'di and Lila Abu-Lughod, eds.
    Pp. 135–160. New York: Columbia University Press.
  1979 Palestinians: From Peasants to Revolutionaries. London: Zed Books.
Schanzer, Jonathan
  2012 With the Stroke of a Pen a New Bill in Congress Could Slash the Number of
    Palestinian Refugees–and Open a World of Controversy. Foreign Policy. May 21.
    http://foreignpolicy.com/2012/05/21/status-update/, accessed October 30, 2015.
Schiff, Benjamin
  1995 Refugees unto the Third Generation: UN Aid to Palestinians. Syracuse: Syracuse
    University Press.
Schiocchet, Leonardo
  2013 Palestinian Sumud: Steadfastness, Ritual, and Time among Palestinian Refugees.
    In Palestinian Refugees: Different Generations but One Identity. Sunaina Miari, ed.
    Pp. 67–89. Palestine: Ibrahim Abu-Lughod Center for International Studies, Birzeit
    University.
Scott, James C.
  1985 Weapons of the Weak: Everyday Forms of Peasant Resistance. New Haven: Yale
    University Press.
Seale, Patrick
  1988 Asad of Syria: The Struggle for the Middle East. London: I. B. Taurus.
Sen, Amartya
  1999 Development as Freedom. Oxford: Oxford University Press.
Shiblak, Abas
  2005 Reflections on the Palestinian Diaspora in Europe. In The Palestinian Diaspora
    in Europe: Challenges of Dual Identity and Adaptation. Abas Shiblak, ed.
    Jerusalem: Institute of Palestine Studies; Ramallah: Institute of Palestinian
    Refugees and Diaspora Centre.

Simpson, Audra
  2014 Mohawk Interruptus: Political Life across the Borders of the Settler State. Durham: Duke University Press.
Slackman, Michael
  2010 Stripped of Citizenship, Jordanians of Palestinian Origin Are Set Adrift. New York Times. http://query.nytimes.com/gst/fullpage.html?res=9F02E7DC113DF937A 25750C0A9669D8B63, accessed February 6, 2014.
Sly, Liz, and Ahmad Ramadan
  2014 Starvation Reported at Palestinian Camp in Syria. Washington Post. January 15. http://www.washingtonpost.com/world/middle_east/starvation-reported-at-pales tinian-camp-in-syria/2014/01/14/9ff8105c-7d66-11e3-97d3-b9925c, accessed January 18, 2014.
Slyomovics, Susan
  1999 The Object of Memory: Arab and Jew Narrate the Palestinian Village. Philadelphia: University of Pennsylvania Press.
Smith, Anthony D.
  2010 Nationalism. Cambridge: Polity Press.
Smith Daniel J., and Jennifer Johnson-Hanks
  2015 Introduction. Theme issue, "Population and Development: Comparative Anthropological Perspectives." Studies in Comparative International Development 50(4):433–454.
Smith, James Howard
  2008 Bewitching Development: Witchcraft and the Reinvention of Development in Neoliberal Kenya. Chicago: University of Chicago Press.
Stewart, Kathleen
  1996 A Space on the Side of the Road: Cultural Poetics in an "Other" America. Princeton: Princeton University Press.
Suleiman, Jaber
  2010 Trapped Refugees: The Case of Palestinians in Lebanon. In No Refuge: Palestinians in Lebanon. Working Paper Series No 64. Refugee Studies Center, Oxford University. 7–18.
Syria Research and Evaluation Organization (SREO)
  2015 Yarmouk–A Needs Assessment. http://sreo.org/portfolio/yarmouk-a-needs -assessment, accessed July 2, 2015.
Tabar, Linda
  2012 The "Urban Redesign" of Jenin Refugee Camp: Humanitarian Intervention and Rational Violence. Journal of Palestine Studies 41(2):44–61.
Takkenberg, Lex
  2010 UNRWA and the Palestinian Refugees after Sixty Years: Some Reflections. Theme issue, "UNRWA and Palestinian Refugees 60 Years Later," Refugee Survey Quarterly 28(2–3):253–259.
  1998 The Status of Palestinian Refugees in International Law. Oxford: Clarendon Press.
Talhami, Ghada Hashem
  2001 Syria and the Palestinians: The Clash of Nationalisms. Gainesville: University Press of Florida.
Telegraph
  2015 Islamic State-Controlled Yarmouk Refugee Camp: Conditions beyond "Inhumane." April 7. http://www.telegraph.co.uk/news/worldnews/islamic-state/11519106

/Islamic-State-controlled-Yarmouk-refugee-camp-conditions-beyond-inhumane
.html, accessed July 2, 2015.

Terry, Fiona

2002 Condemned to Repeat? The Paradox of Humanitarian Action. Ithaca: Cornell
University Press.

Ticktin, Miriam

2012 Casualties of Care: Humanitarianism and the Politics of Humanitarianism in
France. Berkeley: University of California Press.

2006 Where Ethics and Politics Meet: The Violence of Humanitarianism in France.
American Ethnologist 33(1):33–49.

Tiltnes, Age A.

2007 Keeping Up: A Brief on the Living Conditions of Palestinian Refugees in Syria.
Fafo Research Foundation, Oslo. http://almashriq.hiof.no/general/300/320/327/fafo
/reports/20013.pdf, accessed July 27, 2010.

2006 Palestinian Refugees in Syria: Human Capital, Economic Resources and Living
Conditions. Fafo Research Foundation, Oslo. http://almashriq.hiof.no/general
/300/320/327/fafo/reports/514.pdf, accessed May 20, 2015.

Tugal, Cihan

2007 Memories of Violence, Memoirs of Nation: The 1915 Massacres and the Construction of Armenian Identity. In The Politics of Public Memory in Turkey. Esra
Özyürek, ed. Syracuse: Syracuse University Press.

UNCCP (United Nations Conciliation Commission for Palestine)

1949 Final Report of the United Nations Economic Survey Mission for the Middle
East. http://domino.un.org/pdfs/AAC256Part1.pdf, accessed February 11, 2015.

UNCTAD (United Nations Conference on Trade and Development)

2015 Occupied Palestinian Territory Slides into Recession: Gaza Becoming Uninhabitable. September 1. http://unctad.org/en/pages/newsdetails.aspx?OriginalVersion
ID=1068, accessed November 1, 2015.

UNDP (United Nations Development Programme)

2015 What Is Human Development? http://hdr.undp.org/en/content/what-human
-development, accessed February 20, 2015.

UNGA (United Nations General Assembly)

1948 194 (III) Progress Report of the United Nations Mediator. http://unispal.un.org
/UNISPAL.NSF/0/C758572B78D1CD0085256BCF0077E51A, accessed February 11, 2015.

UN-HABITAT

2003 The Challenge of Slums: Global Report on Human Settlements. http://www
.unhabitat.org/pmss/listItemDetails.aspx?publicationID=1156, accessed October 6,
2012.

UNHCR (United Nations High Commissioner for Refugees)

2015 Commissioner for Refugees António Guterres' Statement on Questions Relating
to Refugees. http://www.unhcr.org/563a17566.html, accessed February 13, 2016.

2005 Handbook for Planning and Implementing Development Assistance for Refugee
(DAR) Programmes. http://www.refworld.org/docid/428076704.html, accessed
November 28, 2014.

2004 Protracted Refugee Situations. http://www.unhcr.org/40c982172.html, accessed
November 13, 2015.

2003 Framework on Durable Solutions for Refugees and Persons of Concern. UNHCR Core Group on Durable Solutions, Geneva. www.unhcr.org, accessed August 30, 2010.

UNHCR and UNDP

2015 Regional Refugee and Resilience Plan. http://www.3rpsyriacrisis.org/the-3rp /strategic-overview, accessed May 4 2015.

UNRWA (United Nations Relief and Works Agency for Palestine Refugees)

n.d. Infrastructure and Camp Improvement Program: Partnering with Refugees: Toward a Better Living Environment until Their Rights Are Fulfilled. Internal document.

2016a Syria Regional Crisis: Emergency Appeal 2016. http://www.unrwa.org/sites /default/files/2016_syria_emergency_appeal.pdf, accessed February 13, 2016.

2016b Yarmouk Situation Report 52. http://www.unrwa.org/newsroom/emergency -reports/yarmouk-situation-report-52, accessed February 18, 2016.

2015a What We Do: Relief and Social Services. http://www.unrwa.org/what-we-do /community-based-organizations?program=40, accessed May 3, 2015.

2015b Palestine Refugees. http://www.unrwa.org/palestine-refugees, accessed January 20, 2015.

2015c Syria Crisis. http://www.unrwa.org/syria-crisis#Syria-Crisis-and-Palestine -refugees, accessed November 7, 2015.

2015d Syria Crisis Response Progress. http://www.unrwa.org/sites/default/files/2015 _syria_crisis_response_progress_report.pdf, accessed November 7, 2015.

2015e Syria Regional Crisis Update 87 (May). http://www.unrwa.org/newsroom/emer gency-reports/syria-regional-crisis-response-update-87, accessed November 7, 2015.

2015f Where We Work: Camp Profiles. http://www.unrwa.org/where-we-work/syria /camp-profiles?field=16, accessed May 5, 2015.

2015g The Crisis in Yarmouk. http://www.unrwa.org/crisis-in-yarmouk, accessed May 5, 2015.

2015h Syria Crisis: Update# 45. http://www.unrwa.org/newsroom/emergency-reports /syria-crisis-situation-update-issue-45, accessed May 5, 2015.

2015i Yarmouk Situation Update 48. http://www.unrwa.org/newsroom/emergency -reports/yarmouk-situation-update-48, accessed October 31, 2015.

2015j Gaza Emergency. http://www.unrwa.org/gaza-emergency, accessed November 13, 2015.

2013a Statement by the Commissioner General on Palestinians Trapped inside Yarmouk. http://www.unrwa.org/newsroom/official-statements/statement -commissioner-general-palestine-refugees-trapped-inside, accessed May, 2015.

2013b Top 20 Donors to UNRWA. http://www.unrwa.org/sites/default/files/top_20 _donors_overall.pdf, accessed February 12, 2015.

2012 Camp Improvement Manual. Internal document.

2009 UNRWA Medium Term Strategy: 2010–2015. http://www.unrwa.org/sites /default/files/201003317746.pdf, accessed March 9, 2015.

2008 Infrastructure and Camp Improvement. http://www.unic.or.jp/files/ee/files /pdfs/UNRWA_Infra_and_Camp_Improvement_Fact.pdf, accessed May 13, 2015.

2007 Neirab Rehabilitation Project: Phase II, the Development of Neirab Camp. Project Document. Aleppo, Syria. 2006 A Socioeconomic Analysis of Special Hardship Case Families in the Five Fields of UNRWA Operations. http://www.unrwa.org

/resources/reports/socio-economic-analysis-special-hardship-case-families-five
-fields-unrwa, accessed October 31, 2015.

2005a Medium Term Plan: A Better Future for Palestine Refugees, 2005–2009. http://
www.unrwa.org/userfiles/2010011812234.pdf, accessed June 24, 2010.

2005b Neirab Rehabilitation Project: Phase I: Development of Ein el Tal Camp. Communication: Neirab Rehabilitation Project Newsletter.

2004 Meeting the Humanitarian Needs of the Palestine Refugees in the Near East,
Conference, Geneva, June 7–8. www.unrwa.org/userfiles/con_report_april05(1)
.pdf, accessed March 17, 2011.

2003 Project Document: Neirab Rehabilitation Project: Rehabilitation of Neirab
Camp & Development of Ein el Tal Camp. UNRWA Field Office, Aleppo.

1951 "Assistance to Palestine Refugees." Report of the Director of the UN Relief and
Works Agency for Palestine Refugee in the Near East. UN A/1905 28 September 1951.

UNRWA and TANGO (Technical Assistance to NGOs)

2006 Neirab Sustainable Livelihoods Survey and Asset-Mapping Exercise. Damascus.

2005 Asset-Mapping: Neirab Rehabilitation Project: Phase I, Development of Ein el
Tal (April/May). Damascus.

Vora, Neha

2013 Impossible Citizens: Dubai's Indian Diaspora. Durham: Duke University Press.

Wacquant, Loic

2008a Urban Outcasts: A Comparative Sociology of Advanced Marginality. Cambridge: Polity Press.

2008b Ghettos and Anti-Ghettos: An Anatomy of the New Urban Poverty. Thesis
Eleven 94:113–118.

2007 Territorial Stigmatization in the Age of Advanced Marginality. Thesis Eleven
91:66–77.

Washington Institute

2015 Official website. http://www.washingtoninstitute.org, accessed May 20 2015.

Watts, Michael

1995 A New Deal in Emotions: Theory and Practice and the Crisis of Development. In
Power of Development. Jonathan Crush, ed. Pp. 44–62. New York: Routledge.

Weber, Max

1946 Politics as a Vocation. In From Max Weber: Essays in Sociology. Oxford: Oxford
University Press.

Wedeen, Lisa

1999 Ambiguities of Domination: Politics, Rituals, and Symbols in Contemporary
Syria. Chicago: University of Chicago Press.

Weizman, Eyal

2007 Hollow Land: Israel's Architecture of Occupation. London: Verso.

WHS (World Humanitarian Summit)

2015 About the WHS. https://www.worldhumanitariansummit.org/whs_about,
accessed November 1, 2015.

Wood, Paul

2013 Syrians Must Allow Aid Convoys to Starving Civilians Says US. BBC News.
October, 19. http://www.bbc.co.uk/news/world-middle-east-24590085, accessed
December 29, 2013.

Index

Page numbers in *italics* indicate photographs.

NELL GABIAM is Assistant Professor of anthropology and political science at Iowa State University.